STATISTICS FOR INTERNATIONAL SOCIAL WORK AND OTHER BEHAVIORAL SCIENCES

Statistics for International Social Work And Other Behavioral Sciences

Serge C. Lee

Maria C. Silveira Nunes Dinis

Lois Lowe

and

Kelly Louise Anders

OXFORD

UNIVERSITY PRESS

OXFORD

UNIVERSITY PRESS

Oxford University Press is a department of the University of Oxford. It furthers
the University's objective of excellence in research, scholarship, and education
by publishing worldwide. Oxford is a registered trade mark of Oxford University
Press in the UK and certain other countries.

Published in the United States of America by Oxford University Press
198 Madison Avenue, New York, NY 10016, United States of America.

Library of Congress Cataloging-in-Publication Data
Lee, Serge C., author.
Statistics for international social work and other behavioral sciences / Serge C. Lee,
Maria C. Silveira Nunes Dinis, Lois Lowe, Kelly Louise Anders.
pages cm
Includes bibliographical references and index.
ISBN 978-0-19-937955-2 (alk. paper)
1. Social service—Statistical methods. 2. Social sciences—Statistical methods. I. Title.
HV29.L44 2016
519.5—dc23
2015025939

1 3 5 7 9 8 6 4 2

Printed by Sheridan, USA

This book is dedicated to my beautiful wife, Kia, and to our four wonderful children: Pheng, Tou, Maly, and Chong Dylan—Serge Lee.

I dedicate this book to my family, friends, and colleagues—with thanks to Dr. Serge Lee for the opportunity to work with him—Maria C. Silveira Nunes Dinis.

Thank you, Dr. Lee, for the privilege of working with you and the other authors. It has been a very rewarding experience for me—Lois Lowe.

Thank you to Dr. Lee and the other authors for the opportunity to collaborate on this book. The experience was very fulfilling and intellectually stimulating—Kelly Anders.

CONTENTS IN BRIEF

List of Figures   xvii
List of Tables   xxi
Preface   xxiii

1. Brief Introduction to Research and Statistics   1

2. Variables, Levels of Measurement, and Ethical Responsibilities   7

3. Descriptive Statistics: Frequency Distributions   17

4. Descriptive Statistics: Measures of Central Tendency and Variability   25

5. Normal Distribution and *Z* Score   35

6. Probability and Hypothesis Testing   47

7. Inferential Statistics: Cross Tabulation and Chi-square   61

8. Inferential Statistics: Correlation   73

9. Inferential Statistics: The *T* Tests   87

10. Inferential Statistics: Simple Linear Regression   105

11. Inferential Statistics: One-Way Analysis of Variance   115

12. A Snapshot of Qualitative Research   125

Appendix A: Introduction to Spss   135

Appendix B: Nonparametric Statistics and Post Hoc Tests   157
Appendix C: How to Use Microsoft Excel Analysis ToolPak   167
Appendix D: Critical Values of F   187
Glossary   197
References   203
Index   205

CONTENTS IN DETAIL

List of Figures   xvii
List of Tables   xxi
Preface   xxiii

1. Brief Introduction to Research and Statistics   1

Overview   1
Statistical Concepts   1
You as the Researcher   2
Types of Statistics   2
Descriptive Statistics   2
Inferential Statistics   2
Evidence-Based Practice and Statistics   3
Relationship Between Research Methods and Statistics   3
The Research Cycle   4
Problem Identification   5
Operationalization   5
Methodology   5
Statistical Analysis   5
Summary   6
General Class Discussions   6

2. Variables, Levels of Measurement, and Ethical Responsibilities   7

Overview   7
Variables   7
What is a Variable?   7
Variable Value and Value Category   8
Variable Classification   9

Types of Variables   9
Two Types of Data   10
Quantitative Data   11
Qualitative Data   11
Levels of Measurement   11
Nominal Variable (Nominal Data)   12
Ordinal-Level Variable (Ordinal Data)   12
Interval-Level Variable (Interval Data)   13
Ratio-Level Variable (Ratio Data)   14
Ethical Issues in Social Science Research and Statistics   15
Informed Consent   15
Anonymity   15
Confidentiality   15
Sensitive Information   16
Reliability and Validity   16
Summary   16

3. Descriptive Statistics: Frequency Distributions   17

Overview   17
Frequency Distributions   17
Frequencies   17
Percentage and Valid Percentage   18
Cumulative Frequency and Cumulative Percentage   19
Graphs   19
Bar Graphs (Bar Charts)   20
Pie Graphs (Pie Charts)   20
Histograms   21
Frequency Polygon (Line Graph)   21
Summary   22
Study Questions   23
Answers to Study Questions   23

4. Descriptive Statistics: Measures of Central Tendency and Variability   25

Overview   25
Measures of Central Tendency   25
The Mean   26
Trimmed Mean   27
The Median   27
The Mode   28
Important Note About Outliers   28
Measures of Variation   29
The Range   29
Properties of Mean and Mean Deviation   29

The Variance   30
The Standard Deviation   31
Coefficient of Variation   32
Summary   33
Study Questions   33
Answers to Study Questions   34

5. **Normal Distribution and *Z* Score**   35

Overview   35
Background of the Normal Distribution   36
Properties of the Normal Curve   37
Areas Under the Normal Curve   38
Understanding the *Z* Score   39
Calculate the *Z* Score and Convert to Percentile Rank   41
Additional Note About the *Z* Score   43
Summary   45
Study Questions   45
Answers to Study Questions   45

6. **Probability and Hypothesis Testing**   47

Overview   47
Population and Sample   47
Population   47
Sample   48
Probability and Sampling Distribution of Mean   48
Probability   48
Sampling Distribution of the Mean   49
Hypothesis and Hypothesis Testing   50
Types of Hypotheses   51
Research Hypothesis   51
The Null Hypothesis   52
Direction of the Hypothesis   52
Directional (One-Tailed) Hypothesis   52
Nondirectional (Two-Tailed) Hypothesis   53
Constructing the Confidence Interval   54
What Is the Confidence Interval?   54
Decision-Making Using the Confidence Interval   55
Interpreting Results of Tests of Statistics   56
Constructing the Confidence Interval Using the Z Score   57
Statistics Rules in Converting Proportion into a Z Score   57
Errors in Hypothesis Testing and Alternative Explanations   58
Type I and Type II Errors   59
Alternative Explanations   60

Summary   60

7. Inferential Statistics: Cross Tabulation and Chi-square   61

The Meaning of Bivariate Analysis   61
Overview of Cross Tabulation and the Chi-square   61
Constructing a Contingency Table   62
Understanding the Chi-square Statistic   63
Organizing the Cross-Tabulation Table Into Its Respected
Columns and Rows   64
Formula for Chi-Square   65
Calculating Chi-Square   67
Interpreting Chi-Square   68
Chi-Square for a 2 × 2 Study   70
Calculating Chi-Square for a 2 × 2 Study   70
Summary   71
Study Questions   71
Answers to Study Questions   72

8. Inferential Statistics: Correlation   73

Overview   73
Introduction to Correlation   73
What Is a Correlation?   73
Graphical Display of Different Types of Correlation   74
Direction of the Pearson Correlation Coefficient   74
Is a Positive or Negative Correlation a Better Coefficient?   75
Correlation Is Not Causation   77
Use of Correlation by Health and Human Services Workers   77
The Correlation Coefficient   77
Calculating the Pearson Correlation Coefficient   78
Formula for the Pearson r 78
Practical Example 8.1   79
Practical Example 8.2   82
The Correlation Coefficient Range   84
What is the Coefficient of Determination?   84
Summary   85
Study Questions   86
Answers to Study Questions   86

9. Inferential Statistics: the T Tests   87

Overview   87
The Meaning of T Statistics or T Tests   88
Three Types of T Tests   89
Various Statistical Assumptions About the t Tests   89

The One-Sample *T* Test or *T* Statistic   89
Practical Situation Using the One-Sample *t* Test   91
The Independent Samples *t* Test   92
Independent Samples *t* Test and Its Relation to Health
and Human Services   92
Hypothesizing the Difference Between Two Independent
(Unrelated) Samples   92
Calculating the Child Recidivism Treatment Helpfulness
for Independent Samples   96
The Dependent Samples *t* Test   97
The Dependent Samples *t* Test and Its Relation to
Health and Human Services   98
Effect Size   100
Summary   101
Study Questions   102
Answers to Study Questions   102

10. Inferential Statistics: Simple Linear Regression   105

Overview   105
The Meaning of Linear Regression   106
The Meaning of Prediction in Health and Human Services   107
Statistical Requirements/Conditions for Linear Regression   107
Computational Formula for Linear Regression   108
Practical Example Using Linear Regression   109
Other Statistical Symbols (Notations)   111
Summary   112
Study Questions   112
Answers to Study Questions   114

11. Inferential Statistics: One-way Analysis of Variance   115

Overview   115
The *T* Test and *F* Ratio   115
Statistical Assumptions   116
Overall Meaning of the *F* Ratio   116
Two Sources of Variability for Anova   117
Variability Between Group Means   117
Variability Within Group Means   117
Practical Situation   117
Steps in Calculating the *F* Ratio   118
Computing the Practical Situation   119
Interpreting Results From ANOVA   123
Summary   123
Study Questions   123

Answers to Study Questions   124

12. A Snapshot of Qualitative Research   125

Overview   125
What is Qualitative Research?   125
Qualitative Data Collection Procedures   126
Qualitative Data Recording   127
Narrative Data   129
Qualitative Data Analysis   129
Discovering Patterns   130
Content Analysis   132
Semiotics   132
Conversational Analysis   133
Computer Applications and Online Resources   133
Summary   134
Study Questions   134

Appendix A: Introduction to SPSS   135

Overview   135
Why Computerized Programs?   135
Introduction to IBM SPSS/PASW   136
Data Entry Using SPSS   136
Creating Variable Names   136
Constructing Variable Value for Any Variable   139
Research Questionnaire   140
Saving Data   144
Frequency Distributions Using SPSS   144
Preparing the Data for Analyses   145
Suggested Steps in Preparing the Obtained Scores for Analyses   145
Using SPSS to Compute Descriptive Statistics   148
Using SPSS to Compute Inferential Statistics   150
The Pearson Correlation   151
The Chi-Square Test of Independence   151
Linear Regression   153
The One-Sample T Test   154
Summary   156

Appendix B: Nonparametric Statistics and Post Hoc Tests   157

Overview   157
The Logic of Rank Order   157
Types of Alternative Nonparametric Statistics   158
SPSS for Inferential Nonparametric Statistics
    and Post Hoc Tests   159
One-way Anova Post Hoc Tests   162

Appendix C: How to Use Microsoft Excel Analysis ToolPak   167

Overview   167
Getting Started with Excel   168
Data Entry   168
Difference Between Excel and SPSS in Data Entry   169
Data Analysis Using Excel 2007–2015   177
Frequency Distributions: The Histogram Graph   178
Measures of Central Tendency and Variability:
Descriptive Statistics   181
Correlation   183
Linear Regression   184
t Test   186
Summary   186

Appendix D: Critical Values of F   187

Glossary   197
References   203
Index   205

LIST OF FIGURES

1.1 The research cycle   4

3.1 Simple bar graph   20

3.2 Simple pie graph   21

3.3 Overall GPA of the students   22

3.4 Frequency polygon with a single variable   22

5.1 (a) Symmetrical bell-shaped curve. (b) Positively skewed distributions.
(c) Negatively skewed distributions   36

5.2 Normal distribution curve   37

5.3 Standard deviation on proportion of the normal curve   38

5.4 Calculate the z score and convert to a percentile   40

5.5 Chances that the couple in this situation can reunite with their children   43

6.1 Example of a directional hypothesis   53

6.2 Predicting nondirectional hypothesis for treatment compliance   54

6.3 (a) Confidence interval for nondirectional hypothesis (both sides).
(b) Confidence interval for directional hypothesis (right side)   59

7.1 The Chi-Square Statistic Computation Procedures   65

8.1 Positive correlation   75

8.2 Scatterplot depicting a positive correlation between skills
of children and their family size   76

8.3 Inverse correlation between domestic violence knowledge
and spousal abuse   76

8.4 Scatterplot depicting negative correlation   76

8.5 Scatterplot depicting no (zero) correlation   76

11.1 Visualizing total variability for the F ratio   119

11.2 Computation formula for SS terms   120

A.1   SPSS blank screen   137
A.2   Appearance after **Variable View** is clicked   137
A.3   **Values** column   141
A.4   Miniwindows for **Values** column   142
A.5   **Variable View** for table   142
A.6   **Data View** for the completed variable   143
A.7   **Data View** for the name of the variable   143
A.8   **Dislike statistics** or **Like statistics**   146
A.9   **Recode into Different Variables**   147
A.10   **Recode into Different Variables: Recode Old Value and New Value**   147
A.11   Descriptive statistics computations   149
A.12   Selecting measures of central tendency and variability   150
A.13   Computing the chi-square test of association   152
A.14   Screen for **Linear Regression**   154
A.15   **One-Sample T Test** screen   156
B.1   Nonparametric statistics   159
B.2   The Mann–Whitney U test.   160
B.3   The Wilcoxon test   161
B.4   **One-Way ANOVA** screen   164
B.5   The post hoc test screen   165
C.1   Excel screen at startup   169
C.2   Screen with data entry   170
C.3   Using the formula, Step 1: choose the cell   171
C.4   Using the formula, Step 2: enter the equals sign   171
C.5   Using the formula, Step 3: type the formula   171
C.6   Using the formula, Step 3: type the formula using the cell addresses   172
C.7   Using the formula, Step 4: results   172
C.8   Using the formula: complicated formula with actual values   173
C.9   Using the formula: complicated formula with cell addresses   174
C.10   Manually inserting the function   175
C.11   **Statistical** function in Excel 2013   175
C.12   Use the **Insert Function**   176
C.13   (a) Excel with the Analysis ToolPak. (b) Highlighted area shows **Data Analysis**   177
C.14   Defining the bins   179
C.15   Results of the **Frequency Function**   179
C.16   Analysis ToolPak **Statistical Function**   180
C.17   **Histogram** dialog box   180
C.18   **Histogram** result   181
C.19   **Descriptive Statistics** dialog box   182
C.20   **Descriptive Statistics** result   182

C.21 **Correlation** dialog   183
C.22 **Correlation** result   184
C.23 **Regression** dialog box   185
C.24 **Regression** results   185

LIST OF TABLES

2.1 Race and Steps One Walks Per Day   9

3.1 Research Data   18

3.2 Formula for Percentage and Valid Percentage Calculations   19

4.1 The Sample Mean Computation   26

4.2 Data Illustrating the Properties of the Mean   30

4.3 Mean Deviation Computational Formula   31

4.4 Properties of the Mean Deviation and the Variance   32

5.1 Distance Between the Sample Mean ($\overline{\mathrm{X}}$)and the Standard Deviation (*SD*)   39

5.2 Percentage Area Under the Normal Curve Between the Mean and z 42

6.1a Sample p Value for the Chi-Square Produced by SPSS   56

6.1b Significant Finding Result   57

6.2 The Four Possible Outcomes Associated With Hypothesis Testing   60

7.1 Cross-Tabulation Table for the Variables Gender and Race of Social Worker   62

7.2 Preference of Social Worker Ethnicity by Client Gender   63

7.3 Understand Rows and Columns in a Cross-Tabulation Table   64

7.4 The Chi-Square Statistic   66

7.5 Cross-Tabulation Display of Observed and Expected Data   67

7.6 Critical Values of Chi-Square. Reprinted from Welkowitz, Cohen, and Lea (2012)   69

7.7 Observed and Expected Frequencies Between Gender and Voting Opinion   71

8.1 Pearson's Product Moment Correlation Coefficient r 78

8.2 Data Set for Children Socialization Skills and Family Size   80

8.3 Expanding the Data Set Into Segments for the Pearson r Calculation   80

8.4 Critical Values of Pearson r. Reprinted from Welkowitz, Cohen, and Lea (2012)   81

8.5   Domestic Violence Educational Training   83

9.1   Critical Values of *t*. Reprinted from Welkowitz, Cohen, and Lea (2012)   93

9.2   Behavior Modification for Asian and Caucasian Youth   96

9.3   GAF Score of Clients Before and After Treatment   99

9.4   Self-Assertiveness Training Evaluation   102

10.1   Socialization Skills (*Y*) and Family Size (*X*) of Children   110

10.2   Ideal Family Size That Female and Male High School Would Like to Have   113

11.1   Numbers of Combined Tardiness and Unexcused Absences   118

11.2   Numbers of Combined Tardiness and Unexcused Absences   121

11.3   Display Table for ANOVA   123

11.4   Reaction Time (Seconds)   124

12.1   Example of Magnitude   130

12.2   Semiotics Example   133

A.1.   Research Data   140

A.2   How Students Felt About Statistics   144

A.3   Frequency Distribution for the Recode Variable "Like"   148

A.4   Age of the Students   150

A.5   Computing the Pearson Correlation Coefficient (Pearson *r*)   151

A.6a   Dislike or Like Statistics * Gender of the Students Cross Tabulation   153

A.6b   Chi-Square Tests   153

A.7   Linear Regression Between Self-Esteem and Family Relationship   155

B.1   Alternative Rank-Order Statistics Tests for Nonparametric Statistics   158

B.2   Result of the Mann–Whitney *U* Test   161

B.3   The Wilcoxon test.   162

C.1   Demographic Characteristics of Students in a Statistics Class   168

C.2   Excel Operators, Symbols, and Formula Examples   173

C.3   Grouped Frequencies for Age Category   178

PREFACE

T his book presents statistics using conversational English and universally understandable concepts. Thus, students are enabled to readily understand statistics in social services and health settings as well as in behavioral sciences such as psychology and sociology. This book's course contents, organization, as well as statistical techniques, tools, and procedures are presented as we have been teaching our students over the years. Our goal is to provide students and practitioners a user-friendly, practical, quality textbook to enable them to make sense of, organize, analyze, and interpret data. In addition, it incorporates two powerful statistical software programs, Statistical Package for the Social Sciences (SPSS) and Microsoft Excel ToolPak, into statistical computations.

A distinct feature of this book is the use of illustrative diagrams throughout, mostly systematic illustrations regarding how to conceptualize the statistical concept, prepare data for the calculations, and interpret findings. The course contents have been organized pedagogically so students can see the progression of concepts and hand calculations in conjunction with computerized statistical analysis tools.

Overall, the book is organized as follows: Chapters 1 through 3 focus on methodological concepts. There is a discussion of the correlation between research and statistics, and information pertaining to frequency distributions is provided. Chapters 4–6 address the measures of central tendency, measures of dispersion, normal distribution, and hypothesis-testing procedures. Chapters 7–11 cover basic inferential statistics. The last chapter, Chapter 12, highlights the meaning of qualitative research and provides guidelines to assist with qualitative data analysis.

Four important appendices follow the chapters. Appendix A gives instructions on preparing data for data entry, constructing variable names, and data analysis using SPSS (a statistics program available worldwide). Appendix B provides guidelines to *nonparametric* statistics and post hoc comparisons, which this book does not cover. Appendix C focuses on Microsoft Excel ToolPak, which is available for most personally owned computers and handheld devices such as tablets and smartphones. Appendix D provides a table for critical values of F.

Finally, the book includes high-quality PowerPoint slides. This is certainly the importance of the book. The PowerPoint slides are detailed, and one could easily understand the chapters' contents without reading them.

STATISTICS FOR INTERNATIONAL SOCIAL WORK AND OTHER BEHAVIORAL SCIENCES

BRIEF INTRODUCTION TO RESEARCH AND STATISTICS

OVERVIEW

In this chapter, statistical concepts are introduced, along with the types of statistics and their relationship to research methodology. Statistical terminology is introduced in the description of the research cycle.

STATISTICAL CONCEPTS

A concept is an abstraction formed by generalizing from particulars. A concept becomes operational by identifying variables that can be used to measure a social issue. Essentially, social science concepts are the mental images that symbolize perceptions, categories, personality traits, ideas and thought processes, objects, and events.

In research, statisticians (researchers) may wonder which statistical concepts will likely prove useful in finding a solution to a project. The researcher will likely begin thinking about words having both numerical and nonnumerical meanings, especially those of possible use in presenting the results of a study. Example questions might be "How was your summer?" "On a scale from 1 to 5, how happy are you with your current job?" or "How long have you been working with the county?" Possible responses are "I had a wonderful summer."; "My level of happiness with my current job is a 5."; and "I have been a county employee for 20 years." The responses "wonderful," "5," and "20" are statistical concepts. In simple terms, statistical concepts comprise *statistical data*. In this book, the terms *statistical concepts* and *statistical data* are used interchangeably.

YOU AS THE RESEARCHER

Students often ask one of the following questions in our classes: "Why do I have to study statistics?" or "Why do I need to know statistics in my field of practice?" A quick response is that statistical concepts are already used in everyday life. When thinking about research and statistics, consider that social scientists are constantly experiencing private matters as well as interacting with others in public. Private matters include such things as the relationships that we have with others, our investments in education, years spent with a job, and decisions about family size. Public matters include the effectiveness of working relationships with clients, the degree of collegiality felt toward others with whom we come in contact, the new knowledge produced, the affiliations formed with local health and human services agencies, or the number of volunteer hours spent per week in community activities. With both private and public matters, our performance is sometimes excellent, good, average, or poor. While we can never casually predict the results of our performance or evaluate our degree of effectiveness, we can offer explanations or predictions based on statistical outcomes by applying the concepts and tools of research methodology and general statistics.

TYPES OF STATISTICS

The two types of statistics useful in data analysis are *descriptive* and *inferential*, such as the numerical scores obtained from a research project on factors attributed to child abuse. The two types are not mutually exclusive. For example, information from descriptive statistics, such as the mean and standard deviation, is needed to conduct the inferential *t* tests.

DESCRIPTIVE STATISTICS

Descriptive statistics are used to organize and summarize typical numerical values within a data set. The principle of descriptive analysis is to describe the data by reducing the amount of information in the data set through a process called *data summary* or *data reduction*. Descriptive analyses commonly consist of compiling *frequency distributions* (i.e., percentage tables, graphs, and figures); computing *measures of central tendency* (i.e., mean, median, and mode); and calculating *measures of dispersion or variability* (i.e., range, quartile, mean deviation, variance, and standard deviation). For example, when conducting research, information is compiled from questions such as the following: What is the typical age of the sampled group? What are the typical risk factors for spousal abuse? What is the typical hourly or monthly wage for a master's degree recipient in a specific field? To report findings from the research project, descriptive statistics may be used to summarize the data in a meaningful way. Researchers may then reduce a large amount of data into tables, graphs, or figures that are more understandable to both laypersons and educators. In Chapters 3 and 4, descriptive statistics are discussed in greater detail.

INFERENTIAL STATISTICS

Inferential statistics, through hypothesis testing, utilize more complex procedures and calculations to generalize and draw conclusions about a population based on a sample from that population. Tools used in inferential statistics are commonly referred to as *statistical tests*.

These tools enable researchers and practitioners to use a relatively small number of observations to obtain generalized information about the entire population (Montcalm & Royse, 2002). In other words, is the sample representative of the population? Is there a significant difference between or among the variables? How related are the values of one variable to another? How is one category associated with another category? What variable caused another variable to change? Detailed illustrations of different types of inferential statistics are presented in Chapter 7.

EVIDENCE-BASED PRACTICE AND STATISTICS

In the past, professions such as social work were largely based on humanitarian gestures of personal ideology and values (including common sense and a sense of communal responsibility), as well as programming logic and needs. Scientific knowledge was not as relevant to the professions as personal ideology, values, and agency needs. However, today most employees, whether social workers, nurses, or clinical psychologists, need diversified knowledge and evidence to describe and explain problems faced by their clients and to understand factors related to the difficulties of their clients. These employees more often need new knowledge to guide them in the development of intervention models that best fit unique practice situations and client conditions across diverse settings such as health and human services. The relevance of using knowledge to develop and improve programs reflects what is called *evidence-based practice*. Rubin and Babbie (2014) stated that evidence-based practice "is a process in which practitioners make decisions in light of the best research evidence available" (p. 27).

In this book, various ways for researchers and practitioners to incorporate statistics into their evidence-based practice models—to show the effectiveness of their interventions and therapeutic approaches —are discussed. The relationship between research methods and statistics is detailed next.

RELATIONSHIP BETWEEN RESEARCH METHODS AND STATISTICS

The relationship between research methods and statistics is as complex as the chicken-and-egg phenomenon. Does *research methodology* come before *statistics*, or is it the other way around? What knowledge or evidence enables practitioners to make good decisions? Precise answers to these two questions are unknown. Throughout the research cycle, an understanding of research methodology is required to properly use statistics. Even if the data already exist, an understanding of research methodology is essential to appropriately perform statistical analyses. *Data* are the raw scores, numbers, words, or even the tables or figures collected for a research project.

The process of building a house exemplifies the relationship between research methodology and statistics. Research methods are the procedures used to sketch the house, the techniques used to examine the strength of the foundation, the materials needed to build the house and create ground stability, the tools required for building, and the calculations to determine a price. On the other hand, statistics are numerical and nonnumerical values the builder uses to measure weight, height, length, and conditions of the house. Together, research methodology and statistics form a scientific foundation and design for the builder.

THE RESEARCH CYCLE

Scientific research is a cyclic and continuous process. In the field of social sciences, researchers often focus on a particular issue that is interesting to an agency, to them personally, or to the population at large. In contrast, most social science research projects use a research design similar to that in Figure 1.1. Normally, the researcher develops explanations for the factors observed and then makes predictions regarding how those factors will change if certain treatment modalities are provided or if behaviors are not altered. Most important, confirming facts or factors must be based on a scientific approach and replicable evidence (Rubin & Babbie, 2014). This means that, in many research studies, the findings may lead to additional questions or perhaps to the refinement of the researcher's thoughts about the issue—especially in the event that the researcher is not able to confirm facts. As a result, the steps illustrated in Figure 1.1 can be repeated. For example, after finding that the major antecedents of physical child abuse are family history, chemical dependency, and poor parenting skills, the researcher may ask another question, such as "Beyond those variables (or factors) that have already been identified, what other variables (or factors) are currently unknown to researchers and practitioners?"

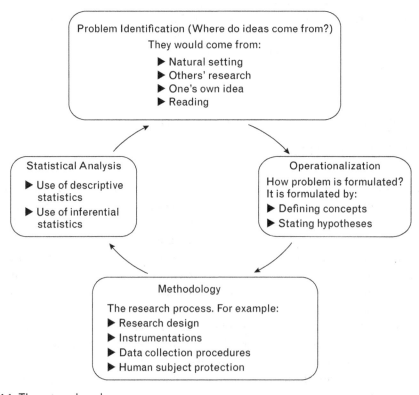

FIGURE 1.1: The research cycle.

PROBLEM IDENTIFICATION

Problem Identification is the first part in the process of diagramming the research project: the idea or problem that the researcher is interested in investigating. In human societies and human conditions, there are an endless number of research topics. One topic may be interwoven with several other topics. For example, factors that contribute to a stressful life could be related to separation and divorce, employment, terminal illness of a loved one, or delinquency of a child. The first part of the diagram in Figure 1.1 illustrates the thinking processes of those who identify research topics. Some people identify a topic from personal experience, such as being a social service worker at a county agency, hospital, community-based agency, or privately owned facility, while others identify their research topic from what they have read, heard, seen, or been told about the issue.

OPERATIONALIZATION

Operationalization is the abstract thinking process whereby vague concepts are organized into clear and precise statements around which specific research procedures can be developed for empirical observation of the target issue in the environment. Translation of abstract thinking is often based on two defining criteria: (a) nominal definition and (b) operational definition. *Nominal definition* is based on the definition of other concepts, such as in a dictionary, online sources, books, and journal articles. In the *operational definition*, a specific set of indicators is used to determine the quantity or quality of an attribute of a particular variable. Some researchers use social science theories to help formulate their operational definitions.

METHODOLOGY

Methods are steps researchers use to complete a study and safeguard the study from errors commonly made in casual human inquiries. Typical elements include research design (e.g., exploratory, descriptive, explanatory); data collection procedures; research instruments (i.e., the questionnaire); human subjects' protection; statistical analysis plan; and research limitations.

STATISTICAL ANALYSIS

Statistical analysis refers to the use of the two types of statistics, descriptive and inferential, to analyze data for a research study. This chapter states that the term *data* (e.g., numbers, scores, images, or words) refers to information collected from a measuring instrument within a research study before analysis. After data from one or more variables have been analyzed and interpretations have been given, it is known as *information*. For example, a score of 5 on a child self-esteem scale from 1 to 5 (higher score indicates a higher level of self-esteem) is the data. The interpretation of the value 5 is information representing a "very high level of self-esteem."

SUMMARY

This chapter discussed types of statistics, highlighted the principle of evidence-based practice, and introduced methodological concepts that commonly appear in research studies during the data analysis phase. Chapter 2 discusses the terms *variable, levels of measurement,* and *ethical responsibilities.*

GENERAL CLASS DISCUSSION

Find a recently published peer-reviewed journal article in psychology, social work, or medical research. Carefully read the article and find methodological and statistical concepts used by the author. Write down the major vocabulary used in this chapter. Then, go through your journal article. Count the number of times that the same words were used by the author. For example, count the number of times the word *statistics* was used in that article. Discuss discrepancies observed between this chapter and the article.

VARIABLES, LEVELS OF MEASUREMENT, AND ETHICAL RESPONSIBILITIES

OVERVIEW

The basic terminology of statistics is discussed in this chapter. These are the terms used by statistics students and professionals, including those involved in health and human services, in developing research questionnaires, organizing data, and conducting statistical analyses. Because computer applications are now in general use, it is crucial that students and professionals recognize that computers will do what is asked whether the data are correctly entered or not. Whether a result is obtained manually or by machine, the calculator must know how to recognize whether a result is reasonable. The prospective researcher must make sense and be able to explain in a meaningful way any and all calculations and results—as well as the reasons for each step in the process.

VARIABLES

WHAT IS A VARIABLE?

A *variable* (commonly using symbols such as X, Y, and Z) is anything the researcher can *quantify, measure,* or *categorize* about the objectives of research subjects; it may contain numerical or nonnumerical meanings. For example, a social science researcher might want to examine the relationship between factors attributed to high school dropouts Y and the school environment X. In this case, "high school dropout" is a key variable (further in the chapter referred to as the dependent variable).

When summing the results of a variable, the Greek capital letter $\sum$ (pronounced sigma) is used for the word *summation*. Therefore, looking at $\sum X$, the two symbols read *the sum of all the numbers in the X set*. For example, assume that data were collected from five high school students on the variable "peer pressures" X_1, on a scale from 1 to 5; a higher score indicates more pressures, and the data look like this:

$$\underline{X}\text{ (peer pressures)}$$
$$5$$
$$2$$
$$4$$
$$1$$
$$5$$
$$\sum X = 17$$

The total scores for the data set can be added together $(5 + 2 + 4 + 1 + 5 = 17)$. In statistical format, $\sum X = 17$. Here, 17 is the total score of the five high school respondents. In contrast, if the respondents were asked about their race $(1 = \text{Asian}, 2 = \text{Latino})$, one would not add Asian to Latino $(1 + 2 \neq 3$ or $\sum X \neq 3)$.

VARIABLE VALUE AND VALUE CATEGORY

Variables, as defined previously, are ideas/speculations that represent what researchers are targeting. Some examples may be gender, family size, educational background, annual income, self-esteem, life satisfaction, cultural competency, stressful life events that affect personal well-being, the volume of alcoholic beverage consumption in a particular period, or the magnitude of child abuse and neglect for a particular period or region. In quantitative research, a variable is always accompanied by one or more *values* or one or more *value categories*. Simply put, *values* are the possible responses to a measurement that may or may not be precoded. *Precoded* means that some type of numerical value was assigned to represent a word or category (see the detailed discussion of variable names in Appendix A). For example, "1" might represent the word *Happy* and "2" *Very happy*. *Value categories* are similar to values, except that the possible responses to a question are not scaled but categorical. For example, *hourly wage* is a value, whereas the *gender of a person* is a value category. Similarly, the *number of steps* a person walks per day is the value, whereas the *race of the person* is the value category.

The first column of Table 2.1 refers to respondents 1, 2, 3, and so on. The second column represents racial background of the respondents. Race of respondent has no numerical meaning because adding a Latino to an African American has no numerical meaning. The third column refers to the steps each respondent walks per day (numerical meaning). The variable "Steps walked per day" is a variable with numerical meaning (see Table 2.1) because the total steps a respondent walked per day can be added to another respondent's total steps, and then meaningful calculations are possible from the additions. Table 2.1 illustrates what was described previously as having numerical and nonnumerical meanings.

Table 2.1: Race and Steps One Walks Per Day

Participant No.	Race of Respondent	Steps Walked per Day
1	Latino	5,000
2	African American	10,000
3	Asian	8,000
4	Caucasian	3,500
5	American Indian	8,600

The next topic, variable classification, should make it easier to understand the numerical and nonnumerical concepts.

VARIABLE CLASSIFICATION

More specifically, variables can be *classified* as discrete or continuous based on their values. *Discrete variables* take only finite responses, such as nominal or ordinal scale values. The meaning of the nominal or ordinal scale is discussed further in this chapter. Here, be aware that *categorical variables with finite numbers are considered discrete*. Racial identification, type of employment, and marital status are examples of discrete variables. In descriptive and inferential statistics, discrete variables require special attention to their statistical applications. *Continuous variables* are those whose values are interval or ratio (see the discussion of interval- or ratio-level data in this chapter). Continuous variables can be arranged on a number line (scale) without breaking or being omitted (infinite numbers). The following are examples of continuous variables: annual income, household size, the volume of beverages consumed in a week, steps walked per day, or a score obtained from an examination.

TYPES OF VARIABLES

Two *types* of variables, dependent and independent, are commonly used by researchers. Types of variables include subjects of interest to investigators, for example, the effects of school truancy on family well-being. In this case, an attempt is made to operationalize the research concept as much as possible. The types of variables used to measure school truancy—the *dependent variable* and the *independent variable*—must be clearly indicated.

The Dependent Variable

The *dependent variable,* also called the outcome or criterion variable, is the variable that can be affected by other variables. If school truancy is affected by stress levels in the families of students, then higher stress levels will result in higher rates of school truancy. The variable "school truancy" is the dependent variable because the number of days of truancy is affected by, or depends on, the level of family stress. A dependent variable is sometimes called the outcome or "variable of interest" because in most cases the interest is in the variable affected as a result of other factors. In social sciences, examples of dependent variables are those that occur often in society, such as mental health/mental illness and domestic violence. In addition, societal issues such as homelessness, poverty, delinquent behavior, youth crime, racism, and sexism are commonly conceptualized as dependent variables because they are variables that are affected by other variables.

The Independent Variable

Independent variables, also called predictor variables, are those that researchers believe may cause or have an effect on the dependent variable. Depending on the issue, independent variables are the variables that can be systematically manipulated by investigators and practitioners. An important distinction of the independent variable is the time order of the variable. To qualify as an independent variable, the factor must have happened before the outcome of the dependent variable. If school truancy (dependent variable) is found to be dependent on or a result of factors contributing to family stress (independent variable), then researchers can be more confident of social policy recommendations to schools concerning future school truancy. When the time order is unknown, then it is more difficult to know which of the variables had the impact on a particular outcome. In social sciences such as social work and clinical psychology, types of intervention such as behavior modification, medication, and narrative therapy are often conceptualized as independent variables because these interventions are intended to alter outcomes (dependent variables). However, an independent variable can become a dependent variable in a different research context. For example, spirituality, types of churches, other religious faiths, and ancestral beliefs could become the dependent variables.

Dependent and independent variables are used to explain relationships and make predictions for research hypotheses. The findings indicate whether the independent variable influences or contributes to the dependent variable. Knowledge of whether and how the independent variables affect the dependent variable may facilitate the ability to change the dependent variable by intentionally manipulating the independent variables. For example, if social workers find evidence that foster children do better after emancipation if linked to support systems in the community prior to emancipation, policy recommendations to lawmakers may be made using specific predictive factors. To obtain data for the dependent and independent variables, understanding of types of data is necessary. *Data are numbers and words collected from a research project* (as discussed next). Client logs, memos, diaries, and published documents are all considered data.

TWO TYPES OF DATA

When collecting data, researchers hope to collect data that represent the population from which the sample was drawn. Knowledge of the research population allows researchers to construct questionnaires that provide relevant responses in numerical and nonnumerical form. Essentially, better research data allow researchers to understand more clearly the population from which the sample was drawn. Either quantitative or qualitative methods may be used to collect data. The *method* is the form or design used for data collection.

QUANTITATIVE DATA

Quantitative data, or *numeric variables* (Aron, Coups, & Aron, 2011), are things, objects, characteristics, attitudes, behaviors, or personality traits collected from an observation that can be counted or represented as an amount. Quantitative data analysis usually involves responses from a set of individuals who participate in a study or scores from a program evaluation. Such data may also be used to do content analysis, such as examining the frequency of medical noncompliance for a mental health facility. Essentially, quantitative researchers use numbers to represent characteristics, events, attitudes, personality traits, and so on. Examples of quantitative data are the ages of the participants, the amount of money given to charities the previous year, and the level of social support currently received (if coded low, medium, and high). Often, the questionnaires for a research study are precoded prior to data collection. For example, in the case of determining the gender of the respondent, the researcher may precode the questionnaire with 1 = female and 2 = male. Note that the equal sign (=) (see Glossary) is used in statistics to represent the words *equals to, stands for,* or *represents*. In this example, "1" stands for the word *female* and "2" for the word *male*.

Sometimes, the question is asked using an open-ended format. If the respondents answer the question using a number base, the question is still quantitative. For example, even though the question "How old are you?" is open ended, the respondent will give a numeric value for age.

QUALITATIVE DATA

Qualitative data are words or codes representing a category or a class of the sample. Qualitative research is another branch of statistics (see Chapter 12). In short, qualitative researchers often conduct in-depth interviews of small samples to obtain quality information rather than counting or quantifying the numerical data. In addition, qualitative analysis (in scientific application) normally cannot be generalized to the population parameters. For example, social science researchers want to understand how teen mothers nurture their newborns. In this scenario, the researchers may conduct interviews, observe a sample of teen and older mothers from a variety of perspectives, and then provide narratives about best practices with these mothers. If the research study includes both teen and older mothers, then the researchers can also quantify qualitatively the differences between the two groups. However, findings from this observation cannot be applied to teen and older mothers in general.

For quantitative data, the way that the dependent or independent variables are structured automatically determines whether they fall into one of four levels of measurement, discussed next. The term *automatic* is used because the values of the variables do not take shapes and forms beyond these four scales.

LEVELS OF MEASUREMENT

When constructing research questionnaires, particularly quantitative research questions, it is imperative that the researcher think not only about the questions to be asked but also about the expected nature of responses to the questions. *The measurement is the responses (see values or value categories discussed previously) to each individual question.* *Measurement* is the process of assigning numerical values (e.g., 1 = female and 2 = male) and nonnumerical values (e.g., a = American Indian and b = Asian American) to the attributes of the categories of the variable. Clearly, not all measurements are the same. Some measurements are more precise and make it easier to assign numerical and nonnumerical values, while others are not so precise and make it more difficult to assign numbers or letters. To create better measuring instruments, the following four levels of measurement must be taken into consideration: nominal, ordinal, interval, and ratio. Terms such as *nominal data, nominal level of measurement*, and *nominal variable* are used interchangeably throughout this book.

NOMINAL VARIABLE (NOMINAL DATA)

The *nominal-level variable* (commonly known as nominal data) is the simplest measurement. A nominal variable classifies the values of the variable into discrete and separate categories based on some defined characteristic or "names" the variable. These are essentially name tags of each value of the variable. The categories are not numerically rank ordered. In some situations, categories can be divided into subcategories. For example, to make a nominal measurement of ethnic background among students, classification as members of various racial groups may be helpful, followed by counting the number of students in each racial category. Asian Americans, African Americans, Native Americans, Mexican Americans, and Caucasians are examples of nominally measured categories. Asian Americans can then be broken down into additional subgroups, such as Chinese, Hmong, Japanese, Korean, and Vietnamese, but each subgroup remains a category. *Yes and No types of values are all nominal-level data.* Samples of nominal-level data include the following:

1. What is your gender? _____ Female _____ Male
2. Have you ever attended a conference on human relations organized by social scientists?
   a. Yes, I have
   b. No, I have not
   c. Decline to state

In the first question, the terms *Female* and *Male* are name tags of two values of the variable "gender." Unless female and male categories are compared/contrasted with some other features, such as physical appearance (femininity or masculinity), there is no possible way to rank order the values of the categories. The second question, measuring the variable of conference attendance, has three values, which are nominally measured (yes/no/decline to state). Note that "yes" is neither numerically higher nor lower than "no" or "decline to state." Rather, yes is simply different from the other two categories.

ORDINAL-LEVEL VARIABLE (ORDINAL DATA)

When the researchers go beyond categorizing the variable using nominal-level data and seek to rank order cases or values of the variable in terms of the degree given to any characteristic, the researchers are working at the *ordinal level* of measurement. The measurement process is slightly different for ordinal measurement than it is for nominal measurement. When a variable is measured on an ordinal level, differences in the amount of the measured characteristic are rank ordered, and numbers are assigned according to that amount or quality. A *rank-ordered* level of measurement means that one value is more or less important, but this rank ordering does not indicate the magnitude of differences, especially the distance between numbers or letters. The ordinal variable is used by researchers to examine the relative rankings of the values of the attributes. Samples of ordinal-level data include the following:

1. How satisfied are you in your current job with the county?
   a. Not satisfied
   b. Somewhat satisfied
   c. Satisfied
   d. Very satisfied
2. How likely is it that someday you might consider applying for a health and human services position with the Office of the United Nations High Commissioner for Refugees?
   a. Not likely at all
   b. Somewhat likely
   c. Likely
   d. Very likely

Again, the values revealed by the first question, "Not satisfied," "Somewhat satisfied," "Satisfied," and "Very satisfied" indicate the rank order from smallest (not satisfied) to highest (very satisfied), which nominal-level variables do not have. However, notice that the distance between the attributes (or unit of the variable) cannot be measured. There is no way to tell how far the distance is between Not satisfied and Very satisfied. Also, note that the wording of the responses can come in any order, for example, possibly beginning with the highest order (very satisfied) and ending with the lowest order (not satisfied) or vice versa.

INTERVAL-LEVEL VARIABLE (INTERVAL DATA)

The difference between two continuous values such as temperature at 8 a.m. and 11 a.m. or age of person A and person B at any specific time of the year is called an *interval*. The *interval level* of measurement reveals the ordering of values, does not have a zero point, and indicates the exact distance between them (equal interval or "unit"). This indicates that the distance between the first and second values is the same as the distance between the second and the third values and so on. For example, when time is measured, the distance between 11:00 a.m. and 11:01 a.m. is the same as the distance between 11:02 a.m. and 11:03 a.m. There is an equal interval of 1 minute, the unit of time. Similarly, when household size is measured, a response may be "My family size is 3" or "My family size is 7." The difference between the two families is 4. Three sample questions related to interval variable follow:

1. What is the monthly salary for a newly hired nurse for hospital X? _____ amount/month
2. On average, how long (in months and years) does it takes a person to complete a 4-year college degree? _____ /months or years
3. What are the typical sleeping times for newborn babies per week? _____/hours

In the first question, the variable to be measured is the current monthly wage for someone with a nursing degree. Imagine that hospital X's current monthly salary for a newly graduated individual with a nursing degree is $5,000. Presumably, the wage increases for all nurses in hospital X will be the same over a continuum timeline. For example, the increases could be something like $1.38 per hour per year for the next 5 years. Overall, all individuals with a nursing pay rate will fall under some type of scale instead of getting no pay at all (no zero dollar/hour). In the second example, the amount of time it takes any college student to complete the baccalaureate degree could be any length of months or years but cannot be zero months. For the third question, typically (common sense or scientifically measured), newborn babies sleep so many hours per week. An argument may be that when the child is sick, the child will not sleep. Well, in a 1-week period, it is improbable that a newborn will not sleep for at least an hour (again, no zero hours).

RATIO-LEVEL VARIABLE (RATIO DATA)

The highest and most precise measurement scale is the ratio-level variable. This level of measurement has all the properties of nominal ("names/categories"), ordinal ("rank order"), and interval levels ("equal distance") plus a property other scales do not have: the zero point that reflects a possible absence of the characteristics measured. Thus, when variables are measured on a ratio scale, statements can be made not only about the equality of the differences between any two points (i.e., number of siblings, number of family interactions per month, number of times a person has been hospitalized) on the scale but also about the proportional amounts of the characteristics that two objects possess (i.e., amount of liquor consumption per week, money spent on college textbooks per term). Sample questions that can be used with ratio-level scale include the following:

1. How many siblings do you have? _____ /# of brothers/sisters
2. What was your annual household income last calendar year? _____
3. How many times have you been a consumer of mental health services? _____

In the first question, the responses can vary from one to two, three, four, or even five or more; at the same time, zero is another possible response. While one, two, three, four, or five represent the different numeric levels of "some siblings," zero has a specific meaning of "no siblings." Likewise, the zero dollar amount in the second question means that the respondent did not earn any money or did not report any income in the previous year. Similarly, the third question focuses on individuals who perhaps have never been a consumer of mental health or a consumer of mental health one or more times.

When collecting data, it is advisable to use interval- or ratio-level variables wherever possible because statistical results are more powerful when common statistical applications are used. For example, if the annual income of a family is examined as a ratio-level measure (dollar amount), the economic status of the family can be computed based on the amount of money the family reported and the government's economic classifications. Essentially, the government's poverty classifications can be used to determine whether a family is at, above, or below the poverty line. Before discussing types of statistical calculations, some of the ethical responsibilities of which researchers must be aware are highlighted next.

ETHICAL ISSUES IN SOCIAL SCIENCE RESEARCH AND STATISTICS

Preparation to become a future employee or new researcher must emphasize that the work is not only a job but also a professional activity. Students, faculty, and professional researchers may unknowingly violate research ethics in pursuit of their goals. To help student researchers avoid ethical mistakes and to protect research participants, a brief discussion about the required content with regard to the protection of human subjects is provided. Statisticians must concern themselves with the possibility that the reliability and validity of results may be affected whenever researchers are not careful.

Most college campuses and universities now have an institutional review board (IRB), a committee to protect human subjects and to review and approve research protocols. In their duties, the committee for the protection of human subjects concentrates on potential harm that a research project may unnecessarily place on respondents, particularly physical, social, and psychological risks. To ensure that the research project is ethically carried out and does not burden respondents, the reviewers may examine one or more of the following content areas: informed consent, anonymity, confidentiality, sensitive information, reliability, and validity. Each of these content areas is briefly highlighted next.

INFORMED CONSENT

Informed consent is used to ensure that prospective participants understand the nature of the research and can knowledgably and voluntarily decide whether to participate in the study. It protects both the participant and the investigator, who otherwise may face legal risks. The prospective participants or their representatives must be provided with sufficient opportunity to consider whether to participate in a way that minimizes the possibility of real or perceived coercion or undue influence.

ANONYMITY

Anonymity means that participants cannot be identified by the researcher or by anyone else assisting with the data collection. Typically, this requires that no personally identifiable information be collected (e.g., no names, telephone numbers, home addresses, Social Security numbers, or driver's license numbers). One way to protect anonymity is to create a coding or numerical scheme to represent each research subject.

CONFIDENTIALITY

Maintaining and protecting the information collected is of the utmost importance in research. Researchers must keep the collected information secure so that it is not easily visible or obtainable by another person. Safekeeping procedures may include such things as locking the collected information in a file cabinet, numbering the questionnaires instead of using identifiers such as names and addresses, separating names and Social Security numbers as soon as data are collected (if name and Social Security numbers are required by the project), destroying hard copies of the questionnaires as soon as raw scores are entered into a statistical program, destroying/erasing a recording device or CD, making sure that the Internet provider (IP) address of the respondent is not identifiable (if SurveyMonkey is used), and taking cultural competency issues into consideration. Survey Monkey (Finley, 1999) is an online survey development cloud-based company that provides free, customizable surveys, as well as a suite of paid back-end programs that include data analysis, sample selection, bias elimination, and data representation tools (Finley, 1999).

SENSITIVE INFORMATION

It is good practice never to collect more information than called for by the research purposes. Most often, collecting sensitive information, such as name, age, sexual practices, phone numbers, history of arrests, drug and alcohol habits, and socially unacceptable behavior, should be avoided. Asking these questions, if irrelevant, may turn research subjects off and cause second thoughts about participating in the research project. Collecting unnecessary sensitive information also may bring harm to research subjects if the collected information is not properly protected and subsequently leaked to outsiders.

RELIABILITY AND VALIDITY

When constructing the questionnaires and collecting data, researchers must take into consideration the reliability and validity of the measurement. In quantitative research, the questionnaires as well as the statistical analyses are parts of ethical responsibilities due to the fact that even in a perfectly designed research project, the reliability coefficient (the result of the computation) does not ensure that the measurement tool (questionnaire) is valid. Will the questionnaire capture the intended information? How well will the information obtained represent the population from which the sample was drawn? Can the information be trusted by social workers or other health and human services professionals at large? These questions can be explained by reliability and validity. In brief, *reliability* is the consistency of the measuring instrument and *validity* means it describes what it is intended to measure and the findings accurately reflect the concept being measured. For example, the significant difference between self-esteem and level of school truancy for high school students could be considered a reliable factor that commonly contributes to delinquent behavior. There are several types of reliability and validity, both internal and external.

SUMMARY

This chapter discussed the term *variable*, especially variable classification and types of variables. Types of data were introduced. Levels of measurement and ethical responsibilities were introduced. Common ethical issues, including informed consent, anonymity, confidentiality, sensitive information, and reliability and validity were discussed briefly. Chapter 3 introduces frequency distributions as a branch of descriptive statistics.

DESCRIPTIVE STATISTICS

Frequency Distributions

OVERVIEW

This chapter discusses frequency distributions, one of the main tools of descriptive statistics. The purpose of any statistical analysis is to organize the collected data clearly and precisely so that readers can easily understand data summaries. In today's technological age, data are rarely organized by hand. Software programs, such as the Statistical Package for the Social Sciences (SPSS; see Appendices A and B) and Excel (see Appendix C), do the job more efficiently and accurately if data are entered correctly. The processes involved in research design, question-naire construction, data collection procedures, and preparing data for analyses are complex and should be taken in a research methods course. As stated in Chapter 2, after the variables are operationally structured, the first order of business is to organize and summarize the variables. There are two relatively simple tools that researchers use to organize and summarize the find-ings: frequency distributions and graphs.

FREQUENCY DISTRIBUTIONS

FREQUENCIES

The term *frequency distributions* (frequencies in computer applications such as SPSS) refers to raw scores, percentage, valid percentage, cumulative percentage, and graphs or charts. Graphs and charts are included within frequency distributions because these figures are always accom-panied with numerical scores, percentages, or both.

Table 3.1 depicts a hypothetical situation involving 15 students enrolled in an introductory statistics class and their anxiety during the first week of the term. Note that Table 3.1 presents

Table 3.1: Sample Research Data

ID	Gender	Age	Statistic	Esteem	Family	Exercise
01	2	23	4	9	10	60
02	1	19	3	7	8	40
03	2	22	1	8	9	120
04	2	20	2	5	6	0
05	1	28	4	7	4	15
06	2	31	4	5	6	30
07	1	29	3	6	7	60
08	2	26	4	4	6	30
09	2	21	1	5	7	20
10	1	24	3	6	8	0
11	2	20	4	9	8	45
12	2	34	3	8	8	100
13	2	23	4	9	7	30
14	1	26	4	7	8	15
15	2	23	4	8	9	0

four variables: age (interval level), class standing (nominal level), anxiety level (ordinal level), and overall grade point average (GPA; interval level). The anxiety-level variable has the following values: 1 = no anxiety at all, 2 = little anxiety, 3 = some anxiety, 4 = high anxiety, and 5 = extremely high anxiety. First, notice that the table is helpful only when the sample size n is small. Table 3.1 is long even though only 15 hypothetical students are displayed. If 1,500 or 150,000 college students were represented instead of just 15, the table would consist of several pages. This table lists individual records. A listing is different from data grouped in a table. Some tables group the data by category showing the frequencies and provide averages for each of the rows. For this table, one could group by gender and then average the responses for each of the other columns.

Showing four variables with 150,000 student participants to an audience in a meaningful way would be impossible if not for the functions of statistics. *Frequencies* representing the raw counts of participants/respondents in research studies drawn from the population usually appear in the literature as absolute frequency, or frequency count designated with the lowercase f (*f*). The American Psychological Association (APA) requires that not only is it to be designated with the lowercase f but also it is to be *italicized*.

PERCENTAGE AND VALID PERCENTAGE

Table 3.2 shows the typical formula used to calculate *percentage* and *valid percentage*. The first part of the formula shows percentile calculation without any missing scores. *Percentile* calculation is how people typically calculate percentage. Suppose that in a research project there are 50 research subjects ($n = 50$), 20 females and 30 males, and 35 questions. In this case, when doing percentage calculation, divide the total frequency counts f of gender by 50. What this means is that when calculating a percentage, the denominator will be the same throughout, even if no questions were answered.

Table 3.2: Formula for Percentage and Valid Percentage Calculations

Percentage Formula	Valid Percentage Formula
Percentage (%) = $\dfrac{\sum f}{\text{n total}}$(100%)	Valid percentage (Valid %) = $\dfrac{\sum f}{\text{Valid n}}$(100%)

$\sum$ = Greek sigma, used to represent the sum
    of a particular value or category
f = Actual frequency count
n = Number of all cases, including the cases
    with missing scores
Valid n = Number of the cases with valid scores
      only (no missing scores)

When it comes to valid percentage, the second part of the formula in Table 3.2 takes into consideration that, from time to time, research participants do not answer every question in the research questionnaire; therefore, when calculating valid percentage, the denominator may differ from question to question. Using the same scenario as described previously, suppose that for one of the questions, only 12 females and 15 males responded. Then, total scores of that variable would be divided by 27 ($n = 27$) instead of 50 ($n \neq 50$).

CUMULATIVE FREQUENCY AND CUMULATIVE PERCENTAGE

Cumulative frequency and *cumulative percentage* are used to indicate the position of a particular value/value category. Researchers use the term *cumulative frequency* to indicate the number of cases that have been accounted for in a value/category and *cumulative percentage* to represent the proportion of the sample or population of that value/category. For example, in a nonprofit organization employing 200 workers, 10 of them have been with the agency for 5 years or less. If the agency wants to discuss how the 10 workers represent the overall population in the agency, then cumulative frequency and cumulative percentage will be helpful. The 10 workers are represented by the cumulative frequencies of individuals hired within the past 5 years or less. By dividing 10 by 200 and then multiplying the difference by 100% ($10/200 \times 100\% = 5\%$), the finding is that the 10 workers who have been with the agency for 5 years or less represent 5% of the total employees in that particular agency. The 5% of the total workers is the cumulative percentage of total social workers in this particular agency. Simply put, cumulative frequency and cumulative percentage are used by researchers to add the results of rows. Similarly, if the data are arrayed by years of service (see the discussion of *array* in Chapter 4), by adding frequencies and percentages for each of the rows, the result will be a cumulative percentage at 5 years or less.

GRAPHS

Beyond absolute frequency, percentage, valid percentage, and cumulative percentage, graphs are helpful in summarizing data, especially in visualizing the values of the variables, and in

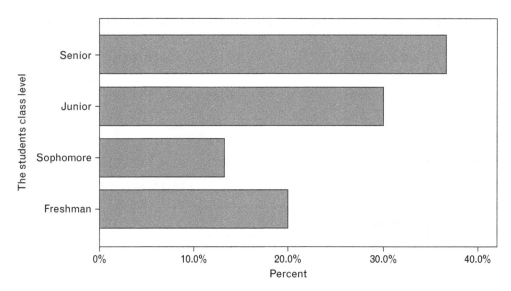

FIGURE 3.1: Simple bar graph.

making a large group of scores easy to understand. The APA refers to *graphs, charts,* and *diagrams* in a manuscript as *figures.* In contrast to tables, figures simply illustrate condensed data, conveying only essential facts. This reduction in the amount and type of data presented tends to make the information easier to read and understand; however, the risk is that if used excessively, valuable written information may be overlooked. Four of the commonly used graphs are discussed next.

The four figures often used by researchers are *bar charts, pie charts, histograms,* and *frequency polygons* (better known as line graphs or line charts). Even though there are suggestions regarding which type of graph is the best fit to illustrate a particular measurement, the fact is that there is no single correct way to graph data.

BAR GRAPHS (BAR CHARTS)

Bar charts or *bar graphs* are best used to depict frequency data associated with a *nominal-level variable.* It makes sense to use an individual bar to represent an individual category. As discussed in Chapter 2, nominal variables have finite values; therefore, variables that use bar graphs reflect the fact that there is no continuity among the categories on the scale. For purposes of illustration only, the bars in Figure 3.1 are displayed vertically. In practical applications, the bars can be displayed vertically or horizontally, depending on one's preferences.

PIE GRAPHS (PIE CHARTS)

Pie graphs are better known as the *crossover* type of graph (Rubin, 2013). This means that they can be used with all four levels of measurement. However, be cautioned that variables that have several values, such as race, age, and the number of clients served by an agency in the past months, may not be suitable for a pie graph. When the figure of a pie is broken into many pieces,

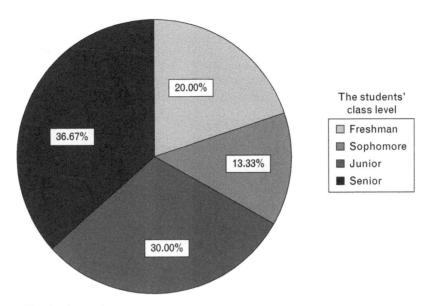

FIGURE 3.2: Simple pie graph.

it is difficult to see how the pieces represent the situation. An example is the racial background of students at a college campus. At any college campus, the racial background could have as many as 20 or more categories. By graphing the 20 categories on a pie graph, they will become too small to read. When there are more than five categories or values, consider other forms of graphs such as bar graphs, instead of pie graphs. Figure 3.2 illustrates current student class levels; because there are just four, a pie chart is appropriate.

HISTOGRAMS

Histograms (see Figure 3.3) are best suited for use with interval-/ratio-level data. A histogram depicts the frequencies of individuals or scores gathered on an ordinal, interval, or ratio level of measurement. Like the bar graph, the histogram uses bars of different heights to convey how frequently the values associated with a variable occurred. The difference between a bar graph and a histogram is that the bars of a histogram touch one another and the bars in a bar graph do not. Histograms are more appropriate for use with variables whose values are continuous instead of discrete. Figure 3.3 illustrates the histogram. The numbers inside each bar represent the correspondence of students who have a GPA within that range. Please note that in some situation, not all bars on the histogram touch. This is because when the values between two bars are absent, the bars will not touch each other.

FREQUENCY POLYGON (LINE GRAPH)

Similar to the histogram, a *frequency polygon* (Figure 3.4) assumes that the distribution of interval- or ratio-level scores can be represented by the midpoint of the bar in the histogram created with those measures. The frequency polygon is also known as the *line graph* or *line*

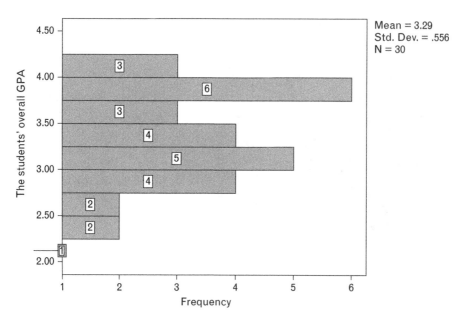

FIGURE 3.3: Histogram showing the overall GPA of the students. Std. Dev. = standard deviation.

chart. Frequency polygons are particularly useful when two or more frequency distributions are to be included in the same graph. Figure 3.4 displays a frequency polygon for a single variable (Age). The numbers inside each bar represent the number of students that fall within that age range.

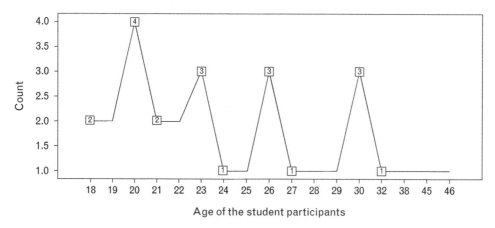

FIGURE 3.4: Frequency polygon with a single variable.

SUMMARY

This chapter introduces frequency distributions, particularly percentages and graphs. It also discusses the levels of measurement researchers should take into consideration when consider specific type of graph. For example, it is inappropriate to use histogram for racial background of the research subjects. Instead, the appropriate type of graphs are bar and pie.

STUDY QUESTIONS

1. Distinguish the differences between the following terms:
   - Frequency distributions and graphs
   - Bar graphs and histograms
2. Suppose that 250 college students are surveyed regarding whether they have traveled abroad. Overall, the total number of persons who had traveled abroad was 106. However, after inputting every student's response on a spreadsheet, you noticed that 78 students did not response to your question. What is the valid percentage for this group of students who had traveled abroad?

ANSWERS TO STUDY QUESTIONS

1.
   - Frequency distributions represent the summation or count of numerical scores after calculation or conversion to percentiles, such as valid percentage and cumulative percentage. Graphs are used to visually display the values or categories of the variables.
   - Bar graphs are different from histograms in the sense that they are used to represent categorical values, whereas histograms are used to display interval- and ratio-level data. Also, the bars of bar graphs never touch each other, while the bars of histograms always touch each other unless one or more scores are missing.
2. Valid percentage = 61.63%.

DESCRIPTIVE STATISTICS

Measures of Central Tendency and Variability

OVERVIEW

This is one of two chapters in which descriptive statistics are discussed. Chapter 3 presented statistical tools useful for summarizing data using simple frequencies and graphs. In this chapter, some ways to organize and summarize data using procedures that are more complex are introduced, thus providing you with the core foundation necessary for understanding this statistical complexity. As discussed in Chapter 2, the kinds of *data* and their corresponding *levels of measurement* are of utmost importance in helping you select correct statistical procedures. Statistical tools discussed in this chapter are key to understanding the scattering of values in the data set, especially the *central tendency* or *central locations* and *variability* for the distribution set.

The term *central tendency* has different meanings across professions; however, statisticians generally use it to refer to the *mean, median,* and *mode* of the distribution set, which is the research data (e.g., numerical and nonnumerical scores) obtained from a research project. When analyzing data beyond the simplest forms of statistics, such as counting the absolute frequencies, calculating percentage and valid percentage, and building charts/graphs, the next step is usually examining the *measures of central tendency*.

MEASURES OF CENTRAL TENDENCY

Generally, after data have been examined for frequency distributions, *measures of central tendency* determine how values in a given distribution of scores are clustered and identify the key central locations in the set. When reporting data beyond frequency distributions (i.e., percentage and figure), statisticians use terms such as "typical," "average," "middle," and "most frequently" to describe findings in preference to terms such as "relationship," "association," and "cause or effect." For example, researchers may speak about the "typical" salary earned by college graduates at a particular level of college education and the "average" time it takes someone to complete a task. A typical wage could be $15 per hour for those with a BA/BS and $25 for those with an MA/MS. Average time could be 30 minutes per client/task.

When dealing with statistics, especially when the data are at the interval and ratio levels of measurement, the words "average," "middle," and "most frequently/most often" can be explained by the terms *mean, median,* and *mode.* Please note that unless one is knowledgeable in statistics, measures of central tendency do not have much meaning in nominal or ordinal data. For example, it would be incorrect to report the average gender of the employees at a nonprofit organization.

THE MEAN

The mean (often denoted by $\overline{X}$; pronounced x bar), better known as the *sample mean* or *simple statistic,* is the arithmetic average or the numerical center of the scores in the distribution set. Within descriptive statistics, *if scores are measured at the interval and ratio levels and evenly distributed, the mean is most often used and reported along with the standard deviation.* This reporting condition is required by the American Psychological Association (APA). In Chapter 5, the discussion is expanded regarding the informative attributes of the mean when reported with the standard deviation and another statistical configuration, the *confidence interval.*

To compute the mean $(\overline{X})$, all the scores in the distribution set $\left(\sum X\right)$ for that particular variable are normally added or summed and then divided by the total number of subjects (n) $[\overline{X} = \sum X / n]$ who participated in the research study (Table 4.1). For example, when using scores that range from 1 to 5 on a self-estecm (X) variable, the following data may appear: 5, 1, 4, 5, 3, 2, and 5 (higher scores indicate better self-esteem).

Based on the values of the self-esteem variable, Table 4.1 shows that the average self-esteem for this set of data is 3.57. Calculating the mean is simple, yet it contributes to data interpretation in many different ways, particularly when the data set is drawn from the total population.

Table 4.1: The Sample Mean Computation

$$\overline{X} = \frac{\sum X}{n}$$

where

$\overline{X}$ = Sample mean

$\sum$ = Sum of the variable: add all the items to the right of the symbol

X = Individual score obtained from the research study

n = Total number of research subjects

Based on the information from the self-esteem variable, the average self-esteem is computed by

$$\overline{X} = \frac{5+1+4+5+3+2+5}{7}$$

$\overline{X} = 25 / 7$

$\overline{X} = 3.57$

TRIMMED MEAN

The trimmed mean is an averaging method that eliminates a partial percentage (X%) of the largest and smallest values (often in a large data set) before computing the sample mean. The trimmed mean is helpful if the data set is extremely skewed and unstable. For example, in a self-esteem scale, the scores include 1, 4, 5, 3, 5, 8, 4, 5, and 9. Typically, 20% is trimmed from the data set. To compute the trimmed mean from this hypothetical data set, follow these steps:

1. Multiply the self-selected proportion (change percentage to a decimal value) by the sample size ($0.20 \times 9 = 1.80$). Round off the multiplication to 2. The result indicates that the two lowest and highest numbers will be removed before the mean is computed.
2. Arrange the scores into an array: 1, 3, 4, 4, 5, 5, 5, 8, 9. Remove first two (1, 3) and last two (8, 9) numbers from the distribution set.
3. Compute the trimmed mean the same way as computing the sample mean ($\overline{X}$) $(4+4+5+5+5+5)/5 = 4.6$. Without the trimmed mean, the sample mean would have been $(1+3+4+4+5+5+5+8+9)/9 = 4.89$.
4. As shown by this example, trimming the mean can reduce the effects of outlier bias in a sample by 0.29 ($4.89 - 4.6 = 0.29$).

THE MEDIAN

The *median* is another measure of central tendency for data gathered using an interval or ratio scale that can be formed into an array. An *array* is an ordering of every raw score value that occurred from the lowest or smallest to the highest or largest. The *median* is also the second quartile, or the 50th percentile, which divides the scores into two equal proportions or halves (Aron et al., 2011; King, Rosopa, & Minium, 2011). A *quartile* (also called an *interquartile range*) represents the 25th, 50th, and 75th percentile of an array. Practitioners, especially in school districts, often use the quartile range to identify students who are at risk of certain behaviors or to identify students who may need additional remedial education. The median can be identified by following these two statistics rules:

- *Arrange the scores in descending or ascending order (from highest to lowest or lowest to highest)*
- *If the number of scores (n) is odd, the median is the middle score. If the number of scores is even, then average the two middle scores.*

Viewing the self-esteem example from a different perspective, a hypothetical seven individuals who recently participated in a self-esteem (X) study is depicted: $X = 5, 1, 4, 5, 3, 2,$ and 5 ($n = 7$). By arranging the scores into an array, $X = 1, 2, 3, 4, 5, 5, 5$, notice that the seven scores cannot be divided into two equal halves. No matter what is tried, three scores (1, 2, 3) or four scores (1, 2, 3, 4) will be on one side and four scores (4, 5, 5, 5) or three scores (5, 5, 5) will be on the other side. By following the statistics rules provided, notice that the data set is an *odd array*. Because it is an odd array, select the middle score of 4 as the median (three scores to the left and three scores to the right of it).

Similarly, suppose that the same self-esteem test was administered to six different individuals and that their scores were 5, 2, 1, 4, 4, and 3 ($n = 6$). The new self-esteem scores are labeled as X_2 = 5, 2, 1, 4, 4, and 3. The sub-X_2 is designated as the new group of participants. Arrange them into an array, X_2 = 1, 2, 3, 4, 4, and 5, with scores 1, 2, and 3 on one side and 4, 4, and 5 on the other side. Because it is an even array ($n = 6$), average the two middle scores to obtain the median, which is 3.5 (3 + 4/2 = 3.5).

Again, please note that the median has a percentile rank of 50. When there are many scores, researchers tend to use the 50th percentile as cutoff to identify the range of the data set. For example, the income of a group that ranges from $0 (no income) to say $2,000,000 per year, the median is the percentile closest to the 50th percentile below or above it. The simplest computation is to use SPSS (Statistical Package for the Social Sciences) to compute the quartile (i.e., 25th, 50th, and 75th percentile). Similarly, there are many situations that use the Likert Scale, such as "strongly disagree" to "strongly agree" and the data set is large. Because the median is the middle score, the best possible scenario is using SPSS to find the 50th quartile. There are many suggestions, but the wiser idea is finding the cumulative percentage that is closest to the 50th percentile of the data set. Be mindful that some statisticians suggest selecting the percentage closest to the 50th percentile of the distribution set.

THE MODE

The term associated with the simplest type of central tendency is the *mode*. The mode is the value category that appears most frequently within a data set. Because it does not lend itself to mathematical manipulation, it has limited value as a statistics tool (Aron et al., 2011; King et al., 2011). The mode is the best measure of central tendency for nominal variables.

In the first example about self-esteem, the mode can be calculated by displaying the values of the variable again, this time as

$$X = 1, \; 2, \; 3, \; 4, \; 5, \; 5, \; 5$$

Because the number 5 occurs three times (more than any other score in the data set), the mode is 5. In the second set (X_2 = 1, 2, 3, 4, 4, 5), the mode is 4 because it occurs twice.

In a data set where frequency counts are evenly distributed among the categories, there is *no mode*. In contrast, in data sets where the frequency is identical in several categories, there are *multiple modes*.

IMPORTANT NOTE ABOUT OUTLIERS

A *statistical outlier* is a value that, when plotted as Y for a given X, lies far beyond the average for the scores. The outlier can be a recording error or an actual value. If the value is so extreme that it affects the arithmetic mean or another statistic, then special steps must be taken to account for the unusual value. An example is the annual income of individuals in a research study. Some may have no earnings at a given time whereas others might have earnings in the millions, thereby causing the mean to be of limited or no use to the researcher. If the value is simply an error, it can be corrected or handled as a missing value. If an actual value is like that described in the next example, then the median would be a better indicator of the average for the study group.

Suppose that a team of social science researchers is interested in the financial status of a sparsely populated geographic area. A door-to-door survey taker collects annual household income from seven persons. The array values are 0, 0, $40,000, $50,000, $60,000, $100,000, and $1,000,000. The arithmetic mean is $1,250,000/7 = $178,571. The median is $50,000, and the mode is 0. In this outlier situation, the median provides a better description of the area than the mean, which is severely affected by one data point, the $1,000,000.

MEASURES OF VARIATION

Although measures of central tendency are helpful when summarizing research findings, it may be desirable to know how the data are spread out. *Data spread* essentially refers to how a normally distributed score deviates from the sample mean $(\overline{X})$. Data spread is called *variability* or *dispersion* (King et al., 2011). According to King and colleagues, *variability* is a measure of the variation or difference among observations in a distribution. Most statistics books use the term *dispersion* to describe the spread of a data set for a research variable. Use of the term *variability* or *dispersion* is your personal preference. Common measures of variation are the *range, quartile or interquartile range, mean deviation, variance,* and *standard deviation.*

THE RANGE

The range is the simplest measure of variation. It is simply a measure of the difference between the highest and the lowest values in the distribution, and it is calculated as follows:

$$Range = Maximum\ value\ (score) - minimum\ value\ (score)$$

Suppose that 10 employees are randomly selected from a community-based agency and their ages recorded as 23, 24, 20, 24, 21, 26, 28, 27, 25, and 28 (10 values). In computing the range, take 28 (the highest age) minus 20 (the lowest age), which equals 8. This result simply indicates that there are eight intervals for the values of the variable. The first interval is between ages 20 and 21. The second interval is between 21 and 22. The last interval is between ages 27 and 28.

Range is helpful in understanding the sample drawn from the population. For example, in a research study that examines income, age, years of employment, family size, or minutes and hours one exercises per week, the range enables researchers to estimate the probability of the least (smallest) and most (highest) values the population may encompass.

PROPERTIES OF MEAN AND MEAN DEVIATION

To find how a data set clusters about the mean, especially when a particular score falls above or below the mean, the interest is in the difference between the score and the mean and how far the score deviates from the mean. The result is called the *properties of the mean* and *mean deviation.* Some statistics books do not distinguish the slight difference between the two terms. Essentially, they are used to measure distance between each score (X) from the sample mean $(\overline{X})$.

Generally, the formula for mean deviation (*MD*) is $(MD = (X - \overline{X})/n)$. Properties of mean and mean deviation indicate almost the same thing. *The minor difference between them is that, in the mean deviation, the sum of the absolute value is divided by the sample size* (n), *whereas in the properties of the mean, the goal is to find the difference between the pluses and minuses.* Properties of mean and mean deviation are discussed and illustrated in this chapter.

Table 4.2 illustrates the scores clustered between 1 and 5, and the reported mean for the sample is 3.57. If the mean is subtracted from every score in the distribution, the total of all values with the negative sign is –4.71. Similarly, by adding all the positive values together, the total is +4.72. This finding shows that the sum of the properties of the mean is almost zero. This illustration confirms what Witte (1993) stated: "The sum of the deviations of all observation scores from the mean is balanced at the center point on the number line, which is equal to or very near to zero" (p. 63).

Beyond the properties of the mean, the mean deviation enables the researcher to clearly understand the average distance between the mean and the overall scores in the distribution set. The *mean deviation* is a measure of dispersion, which is equal to the mean of the absolute values of the deviation scores. An *absolute value* is one in which the algebraic sign of the variable is disregarded (Witte, 1993). In Table 4.3, by ignoring the positive or negative sign for the differ-ence between X and $\overline{X}$, by adding the two values together and dividing the result by the sample size, the precise variation among the scores is indicated. The result of the mean deviation shows that *on average*, every score across the batch has a 1.35-unit difference either above or below the mean—assuming that the mean is centered on the zero point.

Students often have difficulty understanding the slight difference between properties of mean and mean deviation. To make it simpler, look at two other characteristics of the measures of variability: the *variance* and *standard deviation*.

THE VARIANCE

The *variance*, also known as the *sum of the squared deviations from the mean (SS²)*, provides an understanding of the spread of scores about the mean $(\overline{X})$. This provides a more precise measure than the range and the mean deviation. A function of the variance is to help eliminate all the

Table 4.2: Data Illustrating the Properties of the Mean

ID	Variable (*X* = Self-Esteem)	Properties of the Mean
1	5	5 – 3.57 = +1.43
2	1	1 – 3.57 = –2.57
3	4	4 – 3.57 = +0.43
4	5	5 – 3.57 = +1.43
5	3	3 – 3.57 = –0.57
6	2	2 – 3.57 = –1.57
7	5	5 – 3.57 = +1.43
$n = 7$	$\sum X = 25$ $\overline{X} = 25/7 = 3.57$	Sum of positive (+) = +4.72 Sum of negative (–) = –4.71 Difference = +0.01

Table 4.3: Mean Deviation Computational Formula

$MD = \dfrac{(X - \overline{X})}{n}$ ← This is the computational formula.

$MD = \sum \dfrac{|(X - \overline{X})|}{n}$ ← Treat the result as an absolute value.

MD = Mean deviation

n = Sample size

$\sum |(X - \overline{X})|$ = Sum of mean square from all scores in the distribution set

$MD = \dfrac{4.72 + 4.71}{7}$ (by ignoring ± sign)

The summation of MD = 9.43.

Property of $MD = \dfrac{9.43}{7}$ = 1.35

pluses and minuses so that the data set can be used to make a more accurate estimation about the population from which the sample was drawn. Variance is also helpful in many other statistical functions, such as correlating variables and comparing means.

Variance (SS^2) is obtained by first squaring the difference between the deviation scores $(X - \overline{X})$ for each score (X) and the sample mean $(\overline{X})$ and then dividing the total summation by the sample size minus 1 (see the formula for variance at the end of this paragraph). One of the main goals in research is to obtain an unbiased estimate of the population from which the sample was drawn. For this reason, statisticians suggest that the sum of squares be divided by $n - 1$ (unbiased sample) instead of just n (biased sample). This is often referred to as *definition variance*. Notice that the formulas in Table 4.4 for the mean deviation and the variance are nearly identical. The difference between the formulas is that in the variance, the difference is squared between the score and the sample mean, and then the values are summed and divided by the sample size minus 1.

Formula for variance (SS²):

$$\text{Variance} \left(SS^2 \right) = \frac{\sum (X - \overline{X})^2}{n - 1}$$

THE STANDARD DEVIATION

In descriptive statistics, the standard deviation is the most used and useful measure of variability, especially when used along with the mean $(\overline{X})$. *Just as the mean is the most informative measure of central tendency, the standard deviation is the most informative measure of variability.* The standard deviation is integral to two other statistical analyses: (a) It is related to the normal distribution (see Chapter 5), which is the most important distribution in statistics; and (b) it plays a vital role in many common applications of inferential statistics (Aron et al., 2011; King et al., 2011). For a simple explanation, if the data are collected from a randomized sample, then once the standard deviation is computed, it becomes the standardized unit of measurement that is representative of the population from which the sample was drawn.

Table 4.4: Properties of the Mean Deviation and the Variance

ID	X = Self-Esteem	Mean Deviation (MD)	Variance
1	5	$5 - 3.57 = +1.43$	$(+1.43)^2 = 2.04$
2	1	$1 - 3.57 = -2.57$	$(-2.57)^2 = 6.60$
3	4	$4 - 3.57 = +0.43$	$(+0.43)^2 = 0.18$
4	5	$5 - 3.57 = +1.43$	$(+1.43)^2 = 2.04$
5	3	$3 - 3.57 = -0.57$	$(-0.57)^2 = 0.32$
6	2	$2 - 3.57 = -1.57$	$(-1.57)^2 = 2.46$
7	5	$5 - 3.57 = +1.43$	$(+1.43)^2 = 2.04$
$n = 7$	$\sum X$ 25 $\overline{X} = 25/7 = 3.57$	Notice that it is easier to square MD to get the variance	Summation of total variances = 15.68 $SS^2 = \dfrac{15.68}{7-1} = 2.61$

The formula for the *sample standard deviation* (*SD*) is simple: Insert the formula for the sample variance SS^2 inside the square root or take the square root of the variance. The formula for the sample standard deviation is as follows:

Standard deviation formula (SD):

$$SD = \sqrt{\frac{\sum\left(X - \overline{X}\right)^2}{n-1}} \text{ or } SD = \sqrt{SS^2}$$

To compute the standard deviation for the hypothetical self-esteem scale discussed previously in this chapter, take the square root of the sample variance computed in Table 4.4:

$$SD = \sqrt{2.61} = 1.62$$

Assuming that the data set is drawn from a randomized sample, the computed 1.62 becomes the standardized unit of measurement for the self-esteem variable. This means that unless something new is done to the self-esteem scale (i.e., adding/subtracting scores), the difference among the values of the variable is set at 1.62. This result essentially says that if the seven hypothetical self-esteem scores actually come from a randomized sample, then the average self-esteem score for the population from which the sample was drawn will cluster around 1.62 above or below the mean of 3.57.

COEFFICIENT OF VARIATION

In reading research reports, the authors typically do not display the data set other than reporting the mean and standard deviation as required by the APA. One way to interpret the relative magnitude of the standard deviation is to divide it by the mean. This is called the *coefficient of variation* (*CV*). For example, if the mean for income is $47,280 and the standard deviation is $6,987, the coefficient of variation is computed by dividing $SD/\overline{X}$ $[6,987 / 47,280 = 0.1478 \text{ or } 15\%]$.

The result indicates that variability for the variable is approximately 15%. Even knowing nothing about the data set, the coefficient of variation helps us see that even a lower standard deviation does not mean less variability. The coefficient of variation plays three important roles:

1. The coefficient of variation is derived from the ratio of the standard deviation to the nonzero mean, and the absolute value is taken for the mean to ensure it is always positive. Recall that to obtain the standard deviation, the variance is squared inside the square root. The sum of squares essentially eliminates negatives.
2. It helps researchers understand the relative variability of a variable when only the sample mean and its corresponding standard deviation are present.
3. It helps researchers to compare variability between or among variables in the data set. For example, the relative variability among college students on college stress, hours of study per week, and energy level.

Coefficient of variation formula (CV):

$$CV = \frac{SD}{X}\,(100\%)$$

Note that some people call it the *coefficient of the variance*.

SUMMARY

Chapters 3 and 4 discussed descriptive statistics. Statistical procedures from either chapter can be helpful to student learners and practitioners in all types of social sciences and health and human services settings. The focuses of these chapters were on how practitioners as well as student learners can enhance their knowledge about diverse client situations (i.e., self-esteem of college students) based on descriptive statistics (such as measures of central tendency and variability). For example, clinical psychologists, social workers, and nurses can use statistical tools in a variety of ways, such as to identify persons in their caseload who are more or less depressed or to gather information on average treatment compliance of their clients/patients. Overall, descriptive statistics can make an impact on the understanding of client/patient situations and the effectiveness of the types of treatments.

STUDY QUESTIONS

1. List all concepts that fall under measures of central tendency and measures of variability and then discuss the meaning of each concept. Give an example for each concept discussed.
2. Suppose that information is gathered on income data from nine randomly selected individuals in the city where you currently reside. Assume that their reported incomes

for the previous year were $46,900, $35,000, $19,210, $68,800, $23,000, $81,250, $50,000, $55,320, and $65,300. Complete the following tasks:

a. From Chapter 2, indicate the level of measurement applicable to the variable income for the previous year. What is/are the measure(s) of central tendency that may prove useful in reporting income earnings of these nine randomly selected individuals? Discuss a reason for choosing the particular measure(s) of central tendency.

b. Calculate the measure(s) of central tendency and measure(s) of variability for the variable income.

ANSWERS TO STUDY QUESTIONS

1.

Measures of central tendency are

a. Mean, median, mode

b. Measures of variability are quartile, mean deviation, variance, standard deviation

2.

X = income in previous year $\left(\sum X = \$442{,}780 \right)$

a. Interval; no zero income

b. The mean because of normally distributed income (low =$19,210; high = $81,250)

c. Measures of central tendency and variability:

Mean = $49,197.78

Median = $50,000

Mode = 0 or no mode

Range = $62,040

Variance = $430,129,619.40

Standard deviation = $20,739.56

CHAPTER 5

NORMAL DISTRIBUTION AND Z SCORE

OVERVIEW

Frequency distributions and measures of central tendency and variability for the distribution set were discussed in Chapters 3 and 4. Another statistical configuration that is helpful in understanding interval- or ratio-level data is the *shape* of the distribution. When plotting interval-/ratio-level data along the *x* axis (the horizontal line called the *abscissa*) and the *y* axis (the vertical line called the *ordinate*), the data distribution will be scattered, with different shapes based on the scores obtained from the research study.

Each distinctive shape of the distribution enables researchers to better understand the relationship between the *x* and *y*, particularly the sample mean $(\overline{X})$ and the standard deviation (*SD*). Usually, if the data set is normally distributed (not skewed or with a breaking point along the scale), the mean is the most frequently used measure of central tendency as it constitutes the numerical center of a distribution. For the ages of 50 health and human service workers with a range from 24 to 44, the mean age will be around 36 (center between 24 and 44). Most important, the property of the mean states that if all the scores cluster closely to the mean, then

the sum of the deviations of all observation scores from the mean is balanced at the center point on the number line, which is equal to or very near to zero.

(Witte, *1993, p. 62*)

In summary, if all things are equal, then the measures of central tendency (mean, median, and mode) will be equal. The shape of such a distribution is referred to as a *normal distribution* or *normal curve*. However, in most human conditions, the mean will not be equal to the median, and the median will not be equal to the mode. The explanation for this is that participants in a research project are not likely to provide researchers with the same numerical responses. For example, when asked about factors attributed to their personal good health, respondents will likely give different answers. Even a simple question like, "On a scale from 1 to 5, how happy are

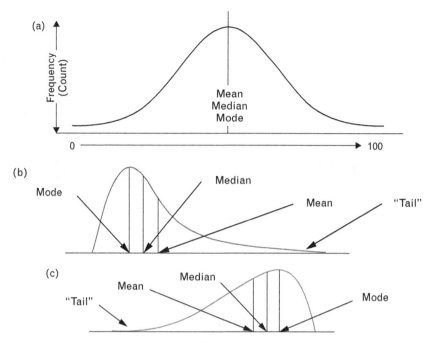

FIGURE 5.1: (a) Symmetrical bell-shaped curve. (b) Positively skewed distributions. (c) Negatively skewed distributions.

you with your current living conditions?" one respondent may state that it is a 1 while another replies with a 5.

Therefore, when viewing the shapes of distributions, some appear perfectly symmetrical as in Figure 5.1a, while others are skewed either negatively or positively as in Figures 5.1b and 5.1c, respectively. Scores distributed heavily to the right-hand side are *positively skewed* (Figure 5.1b) and when clustered heavily to the left side, *negatively skewed* (Figure 5.1c). Notice that in Figure 5.1b, the mode was hypothetically placed at the very left end, the median (middle) in the center, and the mean (average) to the right of the bell-shaped curve.

Suppose that Figure 5.1b and 5.1c show the frequencies of parental visitations to children who were removed from their homes by Child Protective Services (CPS) because of abuse. Even without other statistical computations, and just by glancing at the shape of the distribution curve, one can make an educated guess about the differences in visits that parents made to their children while in protective custody. Essentially, Figure 5.1b shows that more parents visited less frequently, whereas Figure 5.1c shows that more parents visited more frequently.

BACKGROUND OF THE NORMAL DISTRIBUTION

The main distribution statistic is referred to as a *normal curve* or *normal distribution* (Welkowitz, Cohen, & Lea, 2012; Witte, 1993). The normal curve is illustrated by a bell-shaped curve: equal but opposite shape on each side of a curve drawn on a paper folded down the middle.

According to Witte (1993), the concept of normal distribution was developed by a French mathematician, Abraham de Moivre, who based it on his observations of games of chance and then created the equation to determine the probability of certain outcomes. King and colleagues (2011) discussed the concept of probability as the number of possible successes divided by the total number of possible outcomes. Probability can range from 0 (no chance of success) to 1 (certainty of success), and the sum of probabilities for all possible outcomes must be equal to 1 or 100%.

In his observations, de Moivre stated that normally distributed interval-/ratio-level variables must contain relatively few extreme outliers to no outliers. In this situation, most values tend to cluster near the mean, and few values cluster far from the mean. Witte (1993) explained de Moivre's concept of a normal distribution as not an empirical distribution but rather a theoretical or ideal model distribution. This means that a normal distribution does not come from an actual research project but from a mathematical equation.

PROPERTIES OF THE NORMAL CURVE

First, as stated previously here and illustrated in Figure 5.1a, a normal curve is obtained from a mathematical equation based on its symmetrical bell-shaped curve. The degree of *peakness* (the highest peak of the distribution) in the bell-shaped curve of the standard normal distribution is known as *kurtosis*. Any distribution with a high kurtosis has (relative to a normal distribution) a higher proportion of cases in the very center of the distribution. A normal distribution that displays a kurtosis shape is a direct result of the size of the standard deviation.

Freeman, Pisani, and Purves (1978) and Mogull (2004) explained *symmetry* as follows: The single highest point (the peak) of the curve in the data set is also where the ideal measures of central tendency (the median, the mode, and the mean) are all equal to one another. The peak of the curve is what makes the normal curve *unimodal*. The area under the normal curve is divided into two equal halves (50/50); in Figure 5.2 (the same as Figure 5.1a), the left half (below 0) is labeled as negative, and the right half is labeled as positive.

Second, a normal distribution is asymptotic and continuous. *Asymptotic* means that the farther the curve moves from the mean, the closer it gets to the *x* axis, but the curve never touches the *x* axis, no matter how far a particular score is from the mean of the distribution. Continuous means that there is a value of *y* (the vertical line or height) for every value of *x* (the horizontal line) where *x* is assumed continuous rather than discrete.

As discussed in Chapter 2, discrete variables take only finite responses, such as nominal- or ordinal-scale values. The value for *x* is the scale of the measuring instrument used for the study.

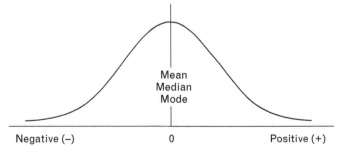

Mean
Median
Mode

Negative (−)   0   Positive (+)

FIGURE 5.2: Normal distribution curve.

This continuous value will enable the normal curve to peak above a point midway along the horizontal axis and then taper off gradually in either direction, but the curve will never touch the horizontal axis. In theory, the tails of a normal curve extend infinitely. The ends of the normal curve extend infinitely because of the probability that, while the curve contains virtually all values of a variable, a very small number of values may exist that represent extremely large or extremely small measurements of the variable, which are commonly referred to as *outliers*. Also, the universe is not static; and as a result, the population is subject to change over time. Because people, including the environment, continuously change, subsequent research on the same concept may produce slightly different outcomes. And, because the lives of people revolve around time, economic conditions, social-cultural factors, and mental challenges, the normal curve does not touch the horizontal line.

Finally, the third important property of the normal curve is the location of the standard deviation from the mean. Approximately 68% (absolute value is 68.26%) of cases in the distribution have values located within 1 *SD* of the mean. As shown in Figure 5.3, 1 *SD* equals 34.13%. By multiplying 34.13 by 2 (1 *SD* to the left and 1 *SD* to the right [±1 *SD*] under the areas of the normal curve), 68.26% of all cases are accounted for within 1 *SD*.

AREAS UNDER THE NORMAL CURVE

Initiated by de Moivre from 1654 to 1705 (as cited by King et al., 2011), the normal curve is divided into six equal units. Montcalm and Royse (2002) stated that this is sometimes known as the "1/6 rule." Early mathematicians, such as de Moivre and other statisticians, used the notion that nearly all scores of a normally distributed variable will fall within 3 *SD* above (right side) or below (left side) the mean. The six units collectively reflect the variation that exists within virtually all values of a normally distributed interval- or ratio-level scale variable. Each unit corresponds to 1 *SD* (±1 *SD*). The more variations among the values in the data set, the flatter the curve, and when variations among the values are less in the data set, the curve will be narrower and the peak of the distribution will be higher.

Figure 5.3 shows the mathematical distribution of the normal curve with 3 units of standard deviation to the left (−3 *SD*) and 3 units of standard deviation to the right (+3 *SD*) of the mean. To the right, the notations for the 3 *SD* are +1 *SD*, +2 *SD*, and +3 *SD*. Similarly, to the left, the notations are −1 *SD*, −2 *SD*, and −3 *SD*. Statisticians, such as Hays (1994) and Nowaczyk (1988), use complex tables to display values of areas under a normal curve. This book uses simple steps as presented by King et al. (2011) and Welkowitz et al. (2012). That is, tracking the *percentile*

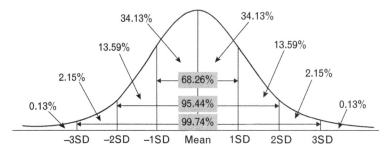

FIGURE 5.3: Standard deviation on proportion of the normal curve.

Table 5.1: Distance Between the Sample Mean ($\overline{X}$) and the Standard Deviation (*SD*)

Distance From the Mean and Standard Deviation	Left Side Only of the Curve Between Mean and SD (−SD)	Right Side Only of the Curve Between Mean and SD (+SD)	Both Sides Under Areas of the Normal Curve
1 *SD*	34.13	34.13	68.26
2 *SD*	13.59	13.59	27.18
3 *SD*	2.15	2.15	4.30
Total areas under the normal curve	49.87	49.87	99.74

This is the confidence interval (CI), the areas that constitute 99.74%.

rank to the left with a minus and *percentile rank to the right with a plus in front of the calculated* z *score*. We discuss the meaning of the *z* score further in this section.

Due to the symmetrical shape (see Figure 5.3 and Table 5.1), the distance between the sample mean and 1 *SD* always corresponds to 34.13% to the left and 34.13% to the right of the mean for a total of 68.26% (34.13% × 2 = 68.26%). The distance between 1 *SD* and 2 *SD* is 13.59% or 27.18 (as shown in Table 5.1) for both sides under the areas of the normal curve (13.59 × 2 = 27.18). Because of this, anything that falls 2 *SD* to the left or right of the mean is equal to 47.72% (34.13 + 13.59 = 47.72). And, the distance between 2 *SD* and 3 *SD* corresponds to 2.15% to the left and 2.15% to the right of the mean for a total of 4.30% (2.15 + 2.15 = 4.30). Therefore, the distance between the mean and 3 *SD* is equal to 49.87% (34.13 + 13.59 + 2.15) to either side of the curve for a total of 99.74% (49.87 × 2 = 99.74). The total summation of ±3 *SD* is called the *confidence interval* (CI). The regions in the remaining areas of 0.26% (100 − 99.74 = 0.26) for one-sided or 0.13% (0.26/2 = 0.13) for two-sided tests are called *rejection* or *extreme regions* and are typically reserved for hypothesis testing. In Chapter 6, the meaning of one-sided and two-sided tests is explained. Note that 99.74% is based on a mathematical equation formulated by de Moivre for games of chance. In actual research studies, a researcher may adjust the confidence interval to accommodate other percentages, such as 97% or 99.997%. Similarly, in Chapter 6, the mechanisms for increasing or decreasing confidence intervals using the normal curve are discussed and illustrated (see Table 5.1 for information on how to construct a personal confidence interval).

Confidence intervals enable researchers to calculate the standard error of a sampling distribution and estimate with a certain degree of confidence the closeness of the true population to the sample mean. Essentially, they enable researchers to examine how closely the sample is representative of the population from which it was drawn. The primary statistical tool used to estimate the population based on the normal curve is called the *z score*. The z score is commonly referred to as the *standard score* because, once computed, the value of the *z* score is comparable to the standard deviation unit.

UNDERSTANDING THE *Z* SCORE

As discussed, mathematicians created a standardized, unimodal, symmetrical, bell-shaped curve with a mean ($\overline{X}$) of 0 and standard deviation of 1. A mathematical equation called the *standard score* or the *z score* is used to convert the original scores to new scores. Every score in a normally distributed population has a corresponding *z* score that reflects how many standard deviations it falls above or below the mean (Hays, 1994). The solution from the *z* score enables researchers to rank the value of any interval or ratio variable and serves two major purposes: (a) Because the mean is zero, a given score is above (right) or below (left) the mean; and (b) because a standard deviation is 1, the numerical size of a standard score indicates the number of standard deviations above or below the mean. Because *the z-score is based on mathematical probability, the solution can be converted to a percentile.* The main question is how a raw score can be transformed to a *z* score and then be converted to a percentile. While the calculation for the *z* score is simple and straightforward (see Figure 5.4), its interpretation is powerful. Figure 5.4 and the *statistics rules* in the figure are the simplest way to calculate the *z* score and then convert the result of the *z* score to a percentile for interpretation.

Suppose that the CPS division states that parents who have lost custody of their children must go through the family reunification (FR) process to regain custody of their children. A part of the rule requires that parents must visit their children who have been placed in foster care under the supervision of a social service worker as often as possible. In addition, the rule specifically states that parents with 90% compliance can get their children back within 3 months; those with 80–89% compliance must wait 4–6 months, and parents with 79% or less compliance must wait 6 months or longer.

Assume further that the CPS division is using measures of central tendency and variability to determine that the average number $(\overline{X})$ of visitations parents made in past years was six times per month with a standard deviation of 1.75. Now, suppose that a couple lost custody of their children to CPS, and in 1 month accumulated only two visits ($X = 2$). Using the cutoff points as indicated by the CPS rule, how likely will it be for this couple to get their children back home within the 3-month period? To calculate the compliance percentage for this couple, use the formula in Figure 5.4.

Formula for calculating the z score and statistics rule for percentile conversion:

$$z = \left(\frac{X - \overline{X}}{SD} \right)$$

z = Standard *z* score. Once calculated, the value of the *z* score is comparable to the value of the standard deviation.

  X = Score of a particular case

  $\overline{X}$ = Sample mean

  SD = Sample standard deviation

Statistics rules for the conversion of the z score into percentile rank:

> ➢ Always round the calculated *z* score to two decimal places.

> ➢ When finding the critical values for the calculated *z* score, move downward on the first column with the letter *z* to locate the first two digits, then move across to locate the third digit.

> ➢ If the calculated *z* score is positive (+), add 50% to the percentile obtained from the standard normal curve table, typically called the critical values ($z_{critical}$).

> ➢ If the calculated *z* score is negative (–), subtract the percentile obtained from the critical values of the standard normal curve table ($z_{critical}$) from 50%.

FIGURE 5.4: Calculate the *z* score and convert to a percentile.

As displayed in Figure 5.4, to compute a *z* score, subtract the score *X* from the mean $(\overline{X})$ of the sample and then divide by the corresponding standard deviation $\left[Z = \frac{(X - \overline{X})}{SD} \right]$. Note that the resulting *z* score depends largely on the score *X* of an individual and the sample mean. If a score *X* is larger than its mean, the deviation will be positive, which in turn will result in a positive z score. If a score *X* is smaller than its mean, then the deviation score will be negative, which in turn will result in a negative *z* score. Divide the deviation score $(X - \overline{X})$ by the standard deviation to determine how many standard deviations a score falls above or below its mean. Statisticians refer to this type of computation as *producing a standard score or standard normal curve* (King et al., 2011; Welkowitz, Cohen, & Ewen, 2006). Also, note that to obtain an accurate reading of the critical values from the standard normal curve table, it is important to round the result of the calculated *z* score to two decimal places (see statistics rule in Figure 5.4).

CALCULATE THE *Z* SCORE AND CONVERT TO PERCENTILE RANK

Figure 5.4 shows the steps for calculating the *z* score and the statistics rule for converting the *z* score into percentile rank. Once the *z* score is calculated, it may apply to situations in social services and many other health and human services settings. Calculating the *z* score for the CPS example is done as follows:

Calculating the z score based on the CPS situation:

X = 2 (number of times per month the couple met obligations ordered by the court)
$\overline{X}$ = 6 (average number of times parents met their court-ordered obligations in past years)
SD = 1.75 (standard deviation unit for the division of CPS)

$$Z = \left(\frac{2 - 6}{1.75} \right)$$
$$= -\frac{4}{1.75}$$

z = –2.29 (notice that the calculation produced a negative *z* score)

How can this calculated *z* score be converted to a percentile so that it can be used to interpret the rule set up by CPS? Notice these three items before converting *z* scores to percentiles:

1. As discussed in the confidence interval section, this calculated *z* score is comparable to a 2.29 *SD*;
2. Not only is it comparable to a 2.29 *SD*, but also it is below the mean (the negative sign); and
3. The last part of the statistics rule in Figure 5.4 reflects this calculated *z* score.

The next step is figuring out how the calculated value (–2.29) corresponds to the area of the standard normal curve (the critical values in Table 5.2).

Table 5.2: Percentage Area Under the Normal Curve Between the Mean and z

z	0.00	0.01	0.02	0.03	0.04	0.05	0.06	0.07	0.08	0.09
0.0	00.00	00.40	00.80	01.20	01.60	01.99	02.39	02.79	03.19	03.59
0.1	03.98	04.38	04.78	05.17	05.57	05.96	06.36	06.75	07.14	07.53
0.2	07.93	08.32	08.71	09.10	09.48	09.87	10.26	10.64	11.03	11.41
0.3	11.79	12.17	12.55	12.93	13.31	13.68	14.06	14.43	14.80	15.17
0.4	15.54	15.91	16.28	16.64	17.00	17.36	17.72	18.08	18.44	18.79
0.5	19.15	19.50	19.85	20.19	20.54	20.88	21.23	21.57	21.90	22.24
0.6	22.57	22.91	23.24	23.57	23.89	24.22	24.54	24.86	25.17	25.49
0.7	25.80	26.11	26.42	26.73	27.04	27.34	27.64	27.94	28.23	28.52
0.8	28.81	29.10	29.39	29.67	29.95	30.23	30.51	30.78	31.06	31.33
0.9	31.59	31.86	32.12	32.38	32.64	32.89	33.15	33.40	33.65	33.89
1.0	34.13	34.38	34.61	34.85	35.08	35.31	35.54	35.77	35.99	36.21
1.1	36.43	36.65	36.86	37.08	37.29	37.49	37.70	37.90	38.10	38.30
1.2	38.49	38.69	38.88	39.07	39.25	39.44	39.62	39.80	39.97	40.15
1.3	40.32	40.49	40.66	40.82	40.99	41.15	41.31	41.47	41.62	41.77
1.4	41.92	42.07	42.22	42.36	42.51	42.65	42.79	42.92	43.06	43.19
1.5	43.32	43.45	43.57	43.70	43.82	43.94	44.06	44.18	44.29	44.41
1.6	44.52	44.63	44.74	44.84	44.95	45.05	45.15	45.25	45.35	45.45
1.7	45.54	45.64	45.73	45.82	45.91	45.99	46.08	46.16	46.25	46.33
1.8	46.41	46.49	46.56	46.64	46.71	46.78	46.86	46.93	46.99	47.06
1.9	47.13	47.19	47.26	47.32	47.38	47.44	47.50	47.56	47.61	47.67
2.0	47.72	47.78	47.83	47.88	47.93	47.98	48.03	48.08	48.12	48.17
2.1	48.21	48.26	48.30	48.34	48.38	48.42	48.46	48.50	48.54	48.57
2.2	48.61	48.64	48.68	48.71	48.75	48.78	48.81	48.84	48.87	48.90
2.3	48.93	48.96	48.98	49.01	49.04	49.06	49.09	49.11	49.13	49.16
2.4	49.18	49.20	49.22	49.25	49.27	49.29	49.31	49.32	49.34	49.36
2.5	49.38	49.40	49.41	49.43	49.45	49.46	49.48	49.49	49.51	49.52
2.6	49.53	49.55	49.56	49.57	49.59	49.60	49.61	49.62	49.63	49.64
2.7	49.65	49.66	49.67	49.68	49.69	49.70	49.71	49.72	49.73	49.74
2.8	49.74	49.75	49.76	49.77	49.77	49.78	49.79	49.79	49.80	49.81
2.9	49.81	49.82	49.82	49.83	49.84	49.84	49.85	49.85	49.86	49.86
3.0	49.87									
3.5	49.98									
4.0	49.997									
5.0	49.99997									

Reprinted from J. Welkowitz, B. H. Cohen, & B. R. Lea. (2012). *Introductory statistics for the behavioral sciences* (7th ed.). Hoboken, NJ: Wiley. With permission from Wiley & Sons.

To find the percentage of parents accumulating just 2 points per month while complying with court-ordered tasks, go to the first column with the letter z, scan down to the row labeled 2.2 (the first two digits in the calculated z score), put a mark on that spot, then move across that row until locating the value 0.09 (with the 9 the third digit in the calculated z score). Move across

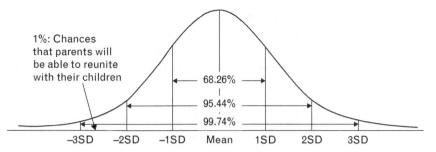

FIGURE 5.5: Chances that the couple in this situation can reunite with their children.

the row labeled 2.2, and while simultaneously moving down from the decimal 0.09, notice that the two values meet at 48.90. As a result, the research study produced critical values of 48.90% inside the areas of the normal curve. This proportion will be used to arrive at the final solution when combined with the statistics rule in Figure 5.4. *Notice that in the calculation a minus sign is placed in front of the calculated z score for the parents that accumulated just 2 points during the previous month.*

Now, use the rules of statistics in Figure 5.4 to explain the final percentile, which will inform the parents regarding whether retrieval of their children from CPS, particularly FR, may occur sooner rather than later. To reiterate the statistics rules in Figure 5.4, when the calculated *z* score is negative (−), subtract the percentile obtained from the normal curve table from 50%. Applying this statistics rule to the couple that accumulated just two visits ($X = 2$) during the previous month, their final percentile is

$$+ 50 - 48.90 = 1.1 \leftarrow \textit{Final percentile for the couple}$$

By comparing this couple's percentile rank to the CPS rule, because of the ranking at the bottom of the bell-shaped curve (1.1%), the wait will be at least 6 months before the court even considers their case. Applying this situation to the population in general, there is little chance that parents in a similar situation will see their children any time soon. Figure 5.5 shows the area under the normal curve indicating when the couple may expect to reunite with their children.

ADDITIONAL NOTE ABOUT THE *Z* SCORE

The algebraic equation for the *z* score can be used for a variety of purposes: discovering whether a health and human services worker may need additional training for such purposes as evaluating the effectiveness of job performance, improving rank performance on an examination, or estimating living conditions of a population parameter. As long as two or three values (scores) in the *z*-score equation are given, the unknown value can be recovered algebraically. Researchers frequently use the *z*-score equation/formula to determine the value of the score (X) when the final percentile and its corresponding standard deviation are known. The *z* score can be helpful in such circumstances.

This next example is based on the same scenario discussed previously, but this time suppose that instead of the CPS staff giving you the parents' compliance score, they provide just the current mean for all parents in the county at 6 ($\overline{X}$ = 6) and the overall compliance standard deviation of 0.95. What compliance score would parents need to rank at the top 95%? Algebraically, we display the z-score formula as follows:

$$Z = \frac{\text{score one must get (X)} - \text{County mean }(\overline{X})}{\text{County standard deviation (SD}_{\text{County}})}$$

To find the compliance score (X = ?) for any parents at the top 95%, algebraically rearrange the z-score formula as

$$X = (Z)(SD) + \overline{X}$$

Applying the algebraic operations to the z-score formula, solve for X by

- *First, multiply SD on both sides of the equation. Notice that SD on the right-hand side is cancelled.*
- *Add the mean* ($\overline{X}$) *to both sides of the equation. Again, notice that the mean* ($\overline{X}$) *on the right side is cancelled as well.*
- *The new formula for* X *is now* X = (Z)(SD) + $\overline{X}$.
- X *is the score needed to be ranked at the top of 95%.*

To solve this equation algebraically, first take note that 95% of the scores fall above the mean. Because of this, subtract 50% from 95%, which is equal to 45%. Now, go to the body of Table 5.2 to find the z score for the equation. The two z scores that are closest to 45% are 44.95% and 45.05%. Choosing the correct z score for the analysis depends on the criteria set forth by the investigator. By reading the statement carefully, notice that the example talks about the *top* 95% of parents complying with court orders to visit their respective social workers and their children. In this case, the area that constitutes 45.05% best fits the criteria and is equivalent to a z score of 1.65. The overall score for this hypothetical situation is

$$X = ?$$
$$z = 1.65$$
$$SD = 0.95$$

Solving X algebraically,

$$X = (1.65)(0.95) + 6$$
$$= 1.57 + 6$$
$$X = 7.57$$

Therefore, parents who want to be ranked by CPS at the top 95% when it comes to compliance with court orders must earn roughly 8 points per month.

SUMMARY

This chapter discusses the meaning of z-score and its usefulness in social work and other health and human services professions. It also discusses the conversion of any numerical raw score into scientific evidence by using the areas under the bell-shape curve.

STUDY QUESTIONS

1. Assume that $\overline{X}_1$ = 5.67 (average depression score for people without healthcare insurance) and $\overline{X}_2$ = 6.68 (depression score for homeless individuals), with an overall SD = 0.59. Based on general observations, indicate the group that is *more* depressed. How do you know?

2. For normally distributed scores, where would the following z scores fall?
   a. $z = +1.25$
   b. $z = -1.25$
   c. $Z = \pm 1.25$

3. For normally distributed scores, where would the following z score fall?
   a. $z = -0.33$ below the mean
   b. Between $z = -2.00$ and $+3.0$

4. Suppose that as a school social worker your duties include helping high school students prepare for college entrance. In past years, one of the main college admission determinants was high school grade point average (GPA). The local unified school districts reported that the average GPA for students to be offered admission to any college in the country is 3.45, with a standard deviation of no less than 0.7. Three students recently presented their GPAs as follows: 3.85, 3.39, and 3.88. The problem at hand is to determine if these scores are enough to secure offers of admission to college.
   a. Carefully rank these students' GPAs so that when you meet again they can be informed of their chances of being offered admission to college. Do not make your decision based solely on the face values of the GPAs; show all your calculations in ranking.
   b. Based on the report by the local unified school districts, which student might not be admitted to college? How do you know? Fully justify your reasons.

ANSWERS TO STUDY QUESTIONS

1. Group 2 $(\overline{X}_2)$ is more depressed than group 1 due to higher sample mean. The scores for the distribution set are
   a. Above the mean at 89.44%
   b. Below the mean at 10.56%
   c. Around the mean

2. The z score would
   a. Fall below the mean at 37.07%
   b. Ball between 2% and 99.87%
3. The three students' scores are
   a.
      - $z_1 = 0.57$, which is comparable to percentile 71.57 among the admission scores
      - $z_2 = -0.09$, which is comparable to percentile 46.41 among the admission scores
      - $z_3 = 0.61$, which is comparable to percentile 72.91 among the admission scores
   b. The second student has almost no chance of being admitted to college because the student's overall GPA ranked below the national average. Among the three students, the third student ranked at 73%, so this student has the best chance of being admitted. The reason is that this student's overall GPA is much closer to the third-quartile range among the top students in the national distribution set.

PROBABILITY AND HYPOTHESIS TESTING

OVERVIEW

Thus far, the meaning of data has been discussed, as well as how to organize and summarize data, display basic research findings, and display rank-ordered values of the variables of a distribution set. Usually, these are all the statistical analyses needed to describe the distribution of the values of variables within a sample or population. However, sometimes researchers also want to know if findings can be generalized to the population from which their sample was drawn. *Generalization suggests findings from a particular research study represent causal effect or relationship and apply to the population beyond the study conditions* (Rubin & Babbie, 2014). The concept of generalization from the sample to the population from which it was drawn is called *inference*. Inference requires researchers to assess their degree of confidence in the data analysis after they have concluded that the real relationship between the dependent variables (DVs) and independent variables (IVs) from a sample is representative of the population from which it was drawn.

To assess their degree of confidence in the relationship between or among variables, researchers must follow several important statistical guidelines. These guidelines, such as probability and sampling distribution, hypothesis and hypothesis testing, and confidence interval (CI) estimation, are discussed in this chapter.

POPULATION AND SAMPLE

POPULATION

The term *population* refers to the real or hypothetical group of people, personal attributes, organisms, or events intended for study. If the goal is to count the number of wild plants that grow near your front porch during the summer months, then plants become your targeted population. Wild plants were selected as an example because it is unlikely that there is any way to make a precise count of all wild plants near anyone's front porch. In short, population is used to describe all potential observations that can be accessed at the time of the study. Because this book does not aim to discuss organisms, the focus is on populations related to health and human services. Examples of populations in health and human services typically include the total number of workers in a particular county, types and quality of patient care at a local hospital, number of homeless individuals in a particular region, number of active child protective cases, and the annual poverty rate. A distribution of all the raw scores or complete group of observations is called a *population distribution*. Descriptive summaries of measurements, such as the proportion of homeless individuals at a location in a particular year, are *parameters*, sometimes referred to as the *population parameters*.

SAMPLE

If a population parameter is large, it may be impractical or impossible to observe behaviors or personal attributes of everyone in the population. Therefore, a subset of the population must be either conveniently or randomly drawn as research respondents. The subset of the population is characterized as a *sample*. The sample population is commonly referred to as a *group* or *condition*. Statisticians suggest that randomized sampling provides the best technique to generalize findings to the population from which it was drawn. The concept that directly links drawing samples from the population is called *probability*.

PROBABILITY AND SAMPLING DISTRIBUTION OF MEAN

PROBABILITY

As briefly discussed in Chapter 5, *probability* is a mathematical equation that shows the proportion or fraction of times that a particular outcome will occur. A probability can range from no chance of the event occurring (0% or 0) to an event that is absolutely occurring (100% or 1.0). The term *probability sample* refers to sampling approaches in which each member of the population has an equal chance of being selected for inclusion in the sample. (Many times the chance is unknown—the reason data are collected.) The most common sampling strategy is the *simple random sample,* for which a name is drawn randomly, or an identification card, or a score from a list that contains the true or an estimated population. The reason that researchers use the simple random sample is to lessen the role of bias, which thereby increases the likelihood that a sample will be representative of the study population. The probability theory is depicted as follows:

$$Probability \ of \ an \ event = \frac{\text{Number of ways the event can occur}}{\text{Total number of outcomes possible}}(100\%)$$

For example, if in a random draw of 1 of 20 names of people attending a community event, the likelihood that a person in this facility will be drawn is 1 of 20 or .05 (1/20 = .05). Thus, multiplying this ratio by 100%, every attendee has a 5% chance of being drawn.

As discussed in Chapter 1, in inferential statistics the goal is to move from a known sample distribution to a potentially observable, yet unknown, population distribution. To help move from the known to the unknown, a theoretical concept known as *sampling distribution of the mean* proves useful. Sampling distribution of the mean is a social construct that takes into consideration the size of a sample as well as the sampling error it theoretically may contain (Freeman et al., 1978; King et al., 2011). The data distribution reveals how closely related the mean, median, mode, quartile, mean deviation, and standard deviation are to each other and the population sample.

SAMPLING DISTRIBUTION OF THE MEAN

The *sampling distribution of the mean* is the advanced version of the z score. It is the probability distribution of means for all possible random samples of a given size from the same population. In simple vocabulary, the distribution of the mean of all possible random samples will form a normal curve.

In inferential statistics, one of the major theoretical principles of probability that helps us understand this distribution of the sample mean is the *central limit theorem*. Essentially, this theorem states that as the size (*n*) of the sample becomes sufficiently large, the sampling distribution of the mean will become normal regardless of how the characteristics are distributed within the population (Engel & Schutt, 2013; Witte, 1993). More specifically, King et al. (2011) stated that "the random sampling distribution of the mean tends to move toward a normal distribution irrespective of the shape of the population of observation sampled; the approximation to the normal distribution improves as sample size increases" (p. 176).

For example, when examining the mental health issues of 1,000 homeless individuals in a metropolitan area, after completing the data collection, 50 people from the pool of 1,000 were randomly sampled to examine the length of time they had been homeless compared to all homeless individuals in the state. The observation, as expected, revealed a normal distribution of the timeline for the 50 sampled participants as well as for the entire homeless population of the state. Thus, the sampling distribution of the mean had the following properties:

- The distribution was normal.
- The mean of the distribution was equal to the population mean.
- The standard deviation (*SD*) of the distribution of the sample means is called the standard error of the mean (SD_E), and is computed using this formula:

$$Standard\ error\ of\ the\ mean\ \left(SD_E\right) - \frac{\text{SD}}{\sqrt{\text{n}}}$$

Note that the means of individual samples vary from the population mean and from each other. Sampling distribution of any sample size is based on an infinite number of samples, and overall, the law of averages eventually prevails. *This means that samples with lower means and those with higher means cancel each other out when they are averaged together; therefore, the mean of means is exactly the same as the true population mean, no matter what sample size produced the sampling distribution.*

Also, note that the standard error of the mean is not simply the standard deviation of the samples. This is because sample size and sampling error must be factored into the standard deviation. Remember that, as sample size increases, the probability of either drawing all small or all large values decreases.

HYPOTHESIS AND HYPOTHESIS TESTING

We defined a *hypothesis* as a statement of an educated hunch or speculation about a presumed relationship in the real world. In most social science and behavioral research, a hypothesis is used as a prediction for testing in a research project. The prediction can be based on formal observation (i.e., experimental study), informal observation (i.e., hospital records), or a theoretical approach (i.e., behavior modification) based on previous research. Essentially, to discover whether there is a significant difference between educated hunches (i.e., relationship between the variables), a *hypothesis test* must be conducted.

One of the key focuses of hypothesis testing is the distinction between population and sample as discussed previously in this chapter. A systematic procedure for deciding whether the results of a research study, which examines the sample, support the *predictions* (plural because most research uses more than one hypothesis) the researcher made about the population.

More specifically, hypothesis testing provides a more precise decision-making framework for determining whether an estimated value for a given population parameter is reasonable. Hypothesis testing is done because of the need to generalize research outcomes beyond the sample group and its face value and to make sure that the significant difference was not produced by chance or sampling error (Aron et al., 2011; Freeman et al., 1978). When the data are not correct, that is, not representative of the population from which the sample was drawn, researchers tend to explain the nonsignificant finding as sampling error. *Sampling error* is the degree of error to be expected for a given research study based on probability theory as discussed in the section on probability.

When conducting hypothesis testing, statisticians suggest attention to the statistical assumptions, summarized as follows:

- The *level of measurement of the variable*. Essentially, researchers must clearly understand the level of measurement for each and every one of the variables in the research project. This way, the researchers are able to tell whether the data are nominal, ordinal, interval, or ratio level.
- The *method of sampling or sampling design*. Researchers must be able to explain whether the data were collected from a probability sampling design like true random sampling or nonrandom (nonprobability) sampling, such as convenience sampling, snowball sampling, or purposive sampling. Note that all statistical tests assume random sampling; therefore, when data are collected from nonrandom sampling, researchers need to consider that during data analysis.
- The *shape of the distribution*. The shape of the distribution influences the outcome of the study project. Researchers must consider whether the shape of the distribution is normally distributed or negatively or positively skewed.
- *Sample size and tests of mean difference*. Statistical significance with fewer subjects may be less meaningful than with a larger sample size.

- *Tests of mean difference* always assume interval and ratio data, particularly for the DV.
- *State the null hypothesis (H$_0$) first and then state the research hypothesis (H$_a$).* Research hypothesis and null hypothesis are discussed in the next section.

Many students find that the most difficult part of mastering inferential statistics is to understand two complimentary, yet mutually exclusive, concepts regarding the predicted value of the targeted population parameter. These two complimentary concepts are types of hypothesis and directions of the hypothesis.

TYPES OF HYPOTHESES

When conducting a research study, there are two types of hypotheses that are related to the project. These two hypotheses are called the research hypothesis and the null hypothesis.

RESEARCH HYPOTHESIS

In research, the major aim of the research question is often stated as a predictive direction or solution about one or more presumed relationships. It is a wishful declarative statement about the outcome of the research study. This type of statement is known as a *research hypothesis* (often designated with either H_1 or H_a). Depending on the researchers' definitions, H_1 and H_a can be used interchangeably. In this book, H_a represents the research hypothesis.

A *research hypothesis* is a declarative sentence that predicts how changes in one variable (usually the IV) are proposed to cause or explain changes in another variable (usually the DV). The following examples illustrate this type of declarative predictive statement:

1. The public assistance programs requiring recipients to participate in volunteer work at least 30 hours or more per week are more likely to have their clients stop receiving welfare benefits than those programs that do not require recipients to work.
2. If administered properly, the Michigan Alcoholism Screening Test will have different scores for men and women.
3. The average healthcare needs for people without health insurance are twice as much as those who have health insurance.

Why are these three statements called research hypotheses H_a? Let us examine the first statement more closely. By using the definitions about the DV and IV from Chapter 3, the DV is public assistance, and the IV is hours required to work per week. If the hypothesis is based on an actual research study, then researchers are examining whether requiring public assistance recipients to volunteer 30 or more hours per week deters them from dependency on public assistance programs.

For the third statement, the researchers are trying to examine the differences in healthcare needs between the populations that have and those that do not have healthcare coverage. The presumption is that the researchers are trying to show that people who have healthcare coverage are healthier because doctors are available whenever there is a need. In contrast, people who do not have health insurance are less able to see their doctors for preventive care and become ill more often. Some people may argue that they do not see their doctors often because of good health; however, all medical problems do not immediately announce themselves: A person may have an illness that has not yet manifested itself.

THE NULL HYPOTHESIS

The opposite of the research hypothesis is called the *null hypothesis,* which is normally designated H_0. Some statistics texts also use H_2, which indicates the *secondary hypothesis.* This type of declarative statement states that, despite what the sample data suggest, after taking into account sampling errors or chance fluctuations, no real relationship or difference exists between the hypothesized statements (Hays, 1994). Examples of statements using the null hypothesis include the following:

1.   There is no significant difference between public assistance programs requiring or not requiring recipients to volunteer to work 30 hours or more per week and then stopping receiving welfare benefits.
2.   Children whose parents are supportive of them at school have the same level of self-esteem scores as children whose parents are not supportive.
3.   Wages earned by college graduates do not correlate with the reputations of the colleges/universities from which they graduated.

The third statement is used as a nonpredictive statement about the wage earning of college graduates. The DV in this case is hourly wage or monthly salary of college graduates, and the IV is "reputation" of the institutions. The statement essentially says that if college graduates are randomly drawn from all college campuses of a particular region or country, we will find that the monthly salaries of graduates are not related to the institutions from which they graduated. For example, a nurse with an RN/BSN from popular Y School of Nursing will receive the same beginning pay as someone with an RN/BSN who graduated from a less prestigious local campus.

DIRECTION OF THE HYPOTHESIS

When testing a hypothesis, one may use a directional or nondirectional hypothesis. The terms are not used interchangeably. The direction of a hypothesis depends on the prediction and speculation about the probability that the relationship may exist along the z score (see Chapter 5).

DIRECTIONAL (ONE-TAILED) HYPOTHESIS

The term *directional (one-tailed or one-sided) hypothesis* is used to test hypotheses that researchers are certain of or able to predict the direction that the relationship of the variable under investigation will fall on the normal curve. When forming a directional (one-tailed) hypothesis, the researchers have predicted significant observation to be on either the left or the right side of

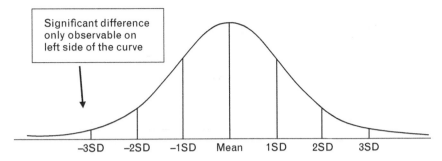

FIGURE 6.1: Example of a directional hypothesis.

Significant difference only observable on left side of the curve.

the normal curve, but not both. The *z* score is divided into two equal halves, the left half (from 0 to –3 *SD* or below the mean) and the right half (from 0 to +3 *SD* or above the mean).

If the researchers know or think that the significant difference will be observed only on the left- or right-hand side under the areas of the mean $(\overline{X})$ of a normal curve, then the hypothesis can be tested using a directional declarative statement. Occasionally, researchers do state their hypotheses using the one-tailed test. Figure 6.1 depicts an example of a directional hypothesis for which significant difference can be observed only at the left side of the curve.

Examples of directional hypothesis include the following:

1. Social workers who carry a higher caseload than the average social worker caseload are more likely to experience burnout than those who do not carry a higher caseload.
2. Mental health clients who do not comply with the recommended medication doses are less likely to get their mental health symptoms under control than those complying with the prescribed doses.

Examining number 2, notice that the phrase "do not comply with the recommended medication doses" (below the mean) refers to an area under the normal curve. Essentially, the researchers are making a prediction that the significant difference will be observed *somewhere below the mean.*

NONDIRECTIONAL (TWO-TAILED) HYPOTHESIS

The term *nondirectional (two-tailed or two-sided) hypothesis* is used to test hypotheses for which researchers believe that significant differences do exist but are unsure or unable to predict the direction of the relationship. Due to the rare use of the directional (one-tailed) hypothesis, *most research studies, including the Statistical Package for the Social Sciences (SPSS) software program, automatically select nondirectional (two-tailed) hypothesis* for all tests of statistical significance. If H_a assumes a positive outcome and the outcome is negative, it is difficult to explain, which is why H_0 is preferred.

Suppose that when working with men and women on mental health treatment compliance, it is unknown which gender complies better than the other with taking medications. One day while working with a noncompliant male, it may seem that too many male clients do not comply

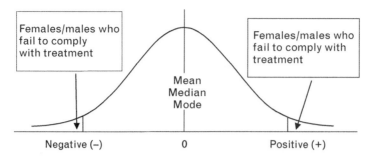

FIGURE 6.2: Predicting nondirectional hypothesis for treatment compliance.

with their treatment plan. Another day, while working with a noncompliant female, it may seem that too many women do not comply with their treatment plan. This doubt may cause staff to wonder, because the situation is difficult to explain, whether the two cases are representative of the mental health population. Essentially, there is a hard time explaining which gender is less compliant with mental health services, and this inconclusive thought, if written into a predictive statement, is an example of a nondirectional hypothesis.

In summary, when examining an issue within a normal curve, a conclusive prediction regarding whether a significant difference will be observed on the left or right side of the curve is not always possible. Figure 6.2 depicts the significant difference that may occur on either side of the standard normal curve. Examples of declarative statements of nondirectional hypothesis include the following:

1. The primary research hypothesis states that, with regard to rates of child maltreatment, there is no statistical significance relating to cultural background or socioeconomic status.
2. There is no significant difference between the charitable donations of men and women in the past 2 years.
3. There is a relationship between lack of healthcare insurance and longevity of men 45 years and older.
4. There is a relationship between treatment compliance and gender (see Figure 6.2).

CONSTRUCTING THE CONFIDENCE INTERVAL

Once a tail (direction) of the hypothesis is determined, another helpful activity is to construct a confidence interval for the research project (Figure 6.3). Due to the advancement of modern technology, researchers generally have no need to construct the confidence interval, but it is important to understand. From political polls to scientific studies, the term *confidence interval* is used throughout the professions.

WHAT IS THE CONFIDENCE INTERVAL?

The *confidence interval*, also called the *interval estimate*, allows the researcher to construct an interval or range of scores around a point estimate (usually around the sample statistic or $\overline{X}$)

and allows the researcher to state a level of confidence in how likely it is that the interval contains the population parameters being estimated (King et al., 2011; Welkowitz et al., 2012). The confidence interval is the range along the 99.74% discussed in Chapter 5. It was discussed in Chapter 5 that the confidence interval is used to calculate the standard error of a sampling distribution and estimate with a certain degree of confidence the closeness of the true population to the sample mean. The value 99.74% is an ideal percentile that researchers can use to understand the relationship between areas under the normal curve and the standard deviation. As a matter of fact, the value 99.74% can be either expanded or contracted depending on one's level of confidence. While constructing a confidence interval, a researcher may be only 80% confident that lack of parental support causes children not to perform well in school. Consequently, the researcher may be mistaken 20% of the time.

Because of the probability of making mistakes in a research study, researchers must select and construct a confidence interval for the research project. *When constructing a confidence interval, the first thing researchers need to do is decide the level of risk of being wrong as well as how much error can be risked.* An estimate is incorrect if the interval developed fails to include the true population parameter. The term *level of significance* or *rejection level* is the probability value used as the criterion in deciding whether an obtained sample statistic (normally the mean $\bar{X}$) has a low probability of occurring by chance alone if the null hypothesis is true (King et al., 2011).

In statistics, probability is designated with the Greek letter *alpha* (α *coefficient*). When it is used to explain the relationship between variables, the lowercase *p (p value)* is used. In social science research, particularly behavioral issues and social services, probability (p value) is used to explain relationships between variables found within a sample where a significant difference may have been produced by a sampling error. Leon-Guerrero and Frankfort-Nachmias (2012) added that the "p-value is the probability associated with the obtained value of z which is where the null hypothesis is rejected" (p. 164). In classical research studies for which computerized software programs were not available, by convention, researchers often set the α level at .01 [which resulted in a confidence interval of 99% (1.0 − .99 = .01)] or .05 (CI = 95%) level of confidence. *Currently, computer applications use the 95% and 99% confidence intervals as the preset values for hypothesis testing.*

DECISION-MAKING USING THE CONFIDENCE INTERVAL

Normally, when the predetermined standardized rejection level or critical value is smaller than the researcher's calculated coefficient, H_0 is retained with the conclusion that there is no significant difference between the variables. In addition, as the p value increases, the likelihood that H_0 will be rejected also increases. For example, a study not significant at the .01 level might be significant at the .05 level. However, note that the error rate will also be increased. When the degree of confidence increases, level of significance (the p value) decreases along with less chance of rejecting the null hypothesis.

In the literature, statement such as the following may appear: "There is a strong correlation between self-care and longevity," $p < .05$. The p (as required by the American Psychological Association [APA]) in this case stands for the rejection level (α coefficient), and the expression itself is a shorthand way of saying that the estimated errors between self-care and longevity would be expected to occur by chance less than 5% of the time. To put it another way, the researcher is confident that the relationship between self-care and longevity is 95% or higher (i.e., people that take better care of themselves are likely to live longer). By convention, researchers can accept a 5% chance of committing a statistical error; or, should there be a 5% chance, that the results from the sample data are due to sampling error (see the discussion of types of error in a further section of the chapter).

INTERPRETING RESULTS OF TESTS OF STATISTICS

With both introductory and advanced statistics courses, findings from *any* inferential statistics follow the same guidelines. When reporting inferential statistics, use the following three guidelines:

1. When manually calculating the result of a test of a statistic, visually compare the calculated values (result of the calculation) with the critical values (values obtained from the chart/table of a statistics book). *If the calculated value is larger than the critical value, state that there is a significant **finding**.* Depending on the type of statistical test being calculated for the research study, replace the word *finding* with the appropriate term being discussed. For example, replace the word *finding* with a term such as *relationship, correlation, association, mean difference, regression*, or *cause or effect*.

2. When computing the result of a statistical test from a computerized program, look for the *p* value computed by that particular software program (see Chapter 5 and Tables 6.1a and 6.1b for samples of the *p* value produced from SPSS). As stated, most software programs, including SPSS (see Appendix A), use 95% or 99% as the preset confidence interval to estimate the strength of the significance of the population. By using these preset confidence intervals, the computer will provide a new and computed confidence interval based on the result of the data set. For this reason, there is no longer need to manually compare the calculated values with the critical values. Use the *p* value given by the computer program and make a decision accordingly. Normally, the *p* value is displayed next to or below the word *Sig.* The abbreviation Sig. stands for significance. *In case Sig. is between .000 and .05, accept that there is a significant finding.* For any *p* value computed by the computer program that is larger than .05, the researcher may have to consider retaining H_0.

3. As an APA condition, when H_0 is retained, use the scientific notation $p > \#$, and when H_0 is rejected, use $p < \#$. The italicized *p* stands for probability. The greater than (>) (not significant) or less than (<) symbols (significant) are the standardized shorthand

Table 6.1a: Sample *p* Value for the Chi-Square Produced by SPSS

	Value	*do*	Sig. (2 Sided)
Pearson chi-square	1.137[a]	4	.888
Likelihood ratio	1.148	4	.887
Linear-by-linear association	0.065	1	.799
N of valid cases	150		

Table 6.1b: Significant Finding Result

		Students' Anxiety Level	Students' Overall GPA
The students' anxiety level	Pearson correlation	1	−.434*
	Sig. (2 tailed)		.017
	N	30	30
The students' overall GPA	Pearson correlation	−.434*	1
	Sig. (2 tailed)	.017	
	N	30	30

This is the p value for correlation produced from SPSS. Note the similar p values because of vicariate analysis (the same variable is analyzed twice). The small p value indicates that there is a significant relationship between GPA and anxiety (see discussion on the meaning of $p < .017$). Additional discussion on the meaning of $p >$ or $p <$ is presented in Chapters 7 to 11. The asterisk (*) denotes significant difference between the variables.

symbols for *significance and no significance. The number symbol (#) indicates where you will insert either the self-selected* p *value or the* p *value given by the computer program.* Keep in mind that in manual calculations, the researcher sets the α level for the research study. Professional researchers understand what the results mean when they see these scientific notations. If a researcher uses $p =$ (and then inserts the p value #), that fact should be revealed.

Table 6.1a shows a nonsignificant finding because the p values produced by SPSS are within the acceptable range of .000 to .05 (see explanations in this section and in Chapter 5).

CONSTRUCTING THE CONFIDENCE INTERVAL USING THE Z SCORE

Once the level of confidence is selected, such as the one discussed about self-care and longevity, the researcher may want to transform the selected proportion (percentile) into a z score. The statistics rule for converting a particular level of confidence into a z score is simple and is presented in the next section. While the rule for converting a proportion to a z score may be stated differently by people who teach statistics, the transformation remains the same.

STATISTICS RULES IN CONVERTING PROPORTION INTO A Z SCORE

For a two-tailed hypothesis, do the following:

1. Subtract the selected proportion from 100% or 1.0. Be consistent. If decimals are preferred, then keep everything in decimals. If percentages are preferred, then keep everything in percentages.
2. Divide the difference from the subtraction by 2 (due to a two-tailed or nondirectional hypothesis).
3. Subtract the result from the second subtraction from 50% or .50 (one half of the standard score).
4. Use the result from the final subtraction to find the z score (see Chapter 5). If you are using a standard normal curve table that is different from Table 5.2, such as the table using decimals, then change everything to *two* decimal places.

For a one-tailed hypothesis, proceed as follows:

1. Subtract the selected proportion from 100% or 1.0.
2. Subtract the difference from the first subtraction from 50% or .50.
3. Use the result from the final subtraction to find the z score (Table 5.2).

Now, what z score is required for a two-tailed hypothesis to build a 95% confidence interval? Follow the statistics rules in Figure 6.2.

- Subtract 95% from 100% (100 – 95 = 5%).
- Divide 5 by 2 (5/2 = 2.50%).
- Subtract the difference from 50% (50 – 2.50 = 47.50).
- Use 47.50 to find the needed z score.

Next, from Table 5.2, and you will notice that the value 47.50 corresponds to a z score of 1.96 (see Figure 6.3a). As a result of the two-tailed hypothesis test at a 95% confidence interval, a z score of ±1.96 (plus and minus for the two-tailed hypothesis) is needed. Proceed to a one-tailed hypothesis with the same level of confidence.

- Subtract 95% from 100% (100 – 95 = 5%).
- Subtract the difference from 50% (50 – 5 = 45.00)
- Use 45.00 to find the z score needed from Table 5.2.

Notice that to construct a 95% confidence interval for a one-tailed hypothesis, a z score of between 1.64 and 1.65 (Figure 6.3b) is required. Depending on the situation specified by the researcher, the correct z score is going to be either 1.64 or 1.65 (because it is at 95% confidence where the researcher is safe to assume that the needed z score is going to be positive [+1.64 or +1.65]).

ERRORS IN HYPOTHESIS TESTING
AND ALTERNATIVE EXPLANATIONS

When conducting a hypothesis test, researchers need to be aware that conclusions about the research study are based only on available data. Compared to the medical sciences, there are no

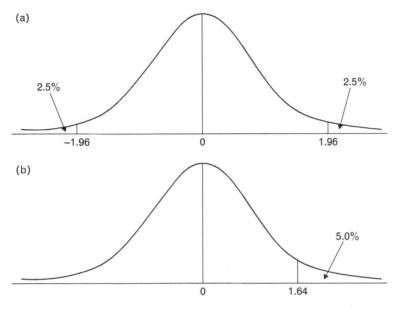

FIGURE 6.3: (a) Confidence interval for nondirectional hypothesis (both sides). (b) Confidence interval for directional hypothesis (right side).

standardized measuring instruments that accurately measure human services issues in the social sciences, particularly in social services. Most often, in social services, the degree or severity of an issue can only be diagnosed based on common symptoms or level of needs. Because social services issues are not like diseases that can accurately be diagnosed using specific diagnostic tools or devices, confidence in retaining or rejecting H_0 cannot be guaranteed. For example, in a hypothesis test, a researcher may claim with 99% confidence that chemical dependency affects personal functioning, but such a conclusion may not come from a true result. In measuring social problems, for example, a conclusion about the null hypothesis on domestic violence and poverty can be both true and false. Due to the plausible true and false conclusions in research findings, researchers must take into consideration the types of errors that can occur in all research projects. *Errors in statistics are called Type I and Type II errors.*

TYPE I AND TYPE II ERRORS

The Type I error occurs when the null hypothesis is true and researchers reject it. *Essentially, researchers rejected the wrong portion of the null hypothesis.* The researchers are supposed to explain that *there is not a significant finding* but conclude that there is and reject the null hypothesis. The problem for a Type II error is the opposite of that for a Type I error. Type II error occurs when the null hypothesis is false and researchers fail to reject it. The researchers are supposed to explain that *there is a significant finding,* but instead they accept (some statisticians called it retain) the null hypothesis and claim that there is no significance. Table 6.2 illustrates the four possible outcomes associated with hypothesis testing (Geber & Hall, 2014).

Table 6.2: The Four Possible Outcomes Associated With Hypothesis Testing

Decision regarding the null hypothesis (H_0)	Truth Regarding the Research Hypothesis (H_a)	
	H_a is true	H_a is false
Reject H_0	Correct decision	Type I error
Fail to reject H_0	Type II error	Correct decision

ALTERNATIVE EXPLANATIONS

In addition to Type I and Type II errors to explain research findings, consider the following alternative explanations:

- *Rival hypotheses* are often referred to as the other variables that were not part of the research. Because of rival hypotheses, variables being observed may cause a relationship to occur, but outcomes may not actually represent the purposes of H_0 and H_a. This occurs when something unknown is not measured or results are positive for something that has no bearing on what is being tested.
- *Design flaws* usually occur when the researchers are not careful with the measuring instruments and sampling bias. For example, when studying depression, the questionnaire may be constructed to focus largely on anxiety syndrome. Even though there are co-occurring anxiety symptoms in depressed persons, there are depressive symptoms very different from people who suffer from anxiety.
- *Sampling error* could happen with any research project. Usually, sampling error occurs because of unequal size, small sample, and changes of data collection procedures.

SUMMARY

This chapter provided information concerning some aspects of hypothesis testing. At this point, the reader has gained more knowledge about hypothesis testing and common concepts in inferential statistics. The following list provides an overall summary for conducting any hypothesis test:

- Clearly understand the level of measurement for the data set.
- Clearly define the DVs and IVs.
- Make assumptions about the research purposes and specify the variables that will be used to answer those purposes.
- Clearly state the null and the research hypotheses. Consider stating one null hypothesis and two or three research alternative hypotheses.
- Select a confidence interval. Based on the selected confidence interval, the α coefficient needed to draw conclusions and to determine the results of the study is derived.
- Calculate the test of statistics. If doing it by hand, pay attention to the selected α level. If the test is made using a computer program, pay attention to the level of significance computed by the statistical program.

Regarding interpreting the findings, *do not elaborate beyond the evidence presented.*

CHAPTER 7

INFERENTIAL STATISTICS

Cross Tabulation and Chi-Square

THE MEANING OF BIVARIATE ANALYSIS

In inferential statistics, *analyzing the relationship between two variables is called bivariate analysis*. The prefix *bi-* here means two variables. These variables can be a combination of two variables of the same type or one level of measurement versus all others.

OVERVIEW OF CROSS TABULATION AND CHI-SQUARE

Cross tabulation (crosstab for short) is one of the bivariate analyses. Crosstab and chi-square (pronounced *ki square*), when used together, are the typical inferential statistics used to organize two *nominal-level variables* into a table called a *contingency table*. In statistics, the terms *crosstab* and *contingency table* are used interchangeably. The purpose is to see whether the two nominal variables are discretely related. The test itself is called the *chi-square statistic* or *test of association* (also known as the *test of independence*).

The *chi-square statistic* is popular in social sciences and behavioral sciences, especially human services. Practitioners often want to know whether there is a relationship between two nominal-level variables, such as the relationship between gender (nominal) and type of popular college degree (nominal) or perhaps intervention types (nominal) and racial origin (nominal) of clients. Therefore, the principle guideline is that any two questions that produce nominal-level data are well suited for the chi-square statistic. *Calculating chi-square and explaining the result of the findings involve four important steps*:

1. Creating a *contingency table*, either manually or using software such as SPSS (see Table 7.1)
2. Calculating the *expected frequencies*

3. Calculating the *chi-square statistic*
4. Interpreting the chi-square *results*

CONSTRUCTING A CONTINGENCY TABLE

Before conducting a statistical test for two nominal-level variables, one way to transform the raw scores meaningfully is to place the values of the two variables into a table. Displaying data this way is called a cross-tabulation or contingency table, the purpose being visualization of the values of the variables individually in each of the cells as well as the total scores for the distribution set. In contingency tables, frequency distributions can be summarized based on *columns* (sum downward), *rows* (sum across), or *total* (*N*) with respective percentages placed immediately next to the scores obtained. Table 7.1 displays the raw scores of a contingency table depicting the gender of 150 hypothetical clients in a social service program and their preferences for particular racial background of the social workers.

In Table 7.1, the values 10, 22, 21, 14, and 6 under the female column and 12, 22, 20, 13, and 10 under the male column are called *cells* (also known as *cell frequencies*). Researchers want to know how the value of each cell is represented for the total number of clients in this hypothetical situation. To make it easier, the letters a, b, c, and so on have been assigned next to each of the numerical values. Certainly, *any symbol can be assigned next to each value or across rows or down the columns*.

The letter assignments make it easier to identify the cells as cell a, cell b, cell c, and so on instead of having to refer to the values as 10, 12, 22, and the like. (This works as long as no more than 26 letters are required. Spreadsheets and some other software programs use representations of rows versus columns, such as R_1C_2). For each cell, there is a need to know proportionally how much is represented of the 150 clients in the agency.

To compute the proportion for the cells (e.g., cell a), divide the frequency count of that cell by the total clients included in this project, then multiply it by 100% [(10/150)(100%) = 6.67%]. This computation indicates that cell a represents 6.67% of the total number of clients depicted in this illustration. Repeat the computations for all 10 cells, and the contingency table looks like Table 7.2.

Table 7.1: Cross-Tabulation Table for the Variables Gender and Race of Social Worker

Racial Origin of Preferred Social Worker	Gender of Client		Total
	Female	Male	
Asian American	10 (a)	12 (b)	22
African American	22 (c)	22 (d)	44
Mexican/Latino	21 (e)	20 (f)	41
Caucasian	14 (g)	13 (h)	27
Others	6 (i)	10 (j)	16
Total	73	77	N= 150

Table 7.2: Preference of Social Worker Ethnicity by Client Gender

Racial Origin of Preferred Social Worker	Gender of Client		
	Female	Male	Total[a]
Asian American	10 (a)	12 (b)	22
	6.67%	8.0%	14.67%
African American	22 (c)	22 (d)	44
	14.67%	14.67%	29.33%
Mexican/Latino	21(e)	20 (f)	41
	14.0%	13.33%	27.33%
Caucasian	14 (g)	13 (h)	27
	9.33%	8.67%	18.00%
Others	6 (i)	10 (j)	16
	4.0%	6.67%	10.67%
Total	73	77	150
	48.67%	51.33%	100%

[a]Due to rounding error, the total percentages do not always add to exactly 100%.

The displays and calculations for each of the cells (Tables 7.1 and 7.2) provide a clear visualization of the total distribution in the data set. For example in Table 7.2, in the female column, 10 (6.67%) female clients of the total clients stated that they preferred Asian American social workers, 22 (14.67%) said African American, followed by 21 (14%) who said Mexican/Latino, 14 (9.33%) who indicated Caucasian, and 6 (4%) who preferred social workers with other racial origins. (These percentages are for the female cells of the total N. If computing percentages of total females [or males], then calculate according to the female [or male] column total.)

UNDERSTANDING THE CHI-SQUARE STATISTIC

The best-known statistical test for two nominal-level data is the *Pearson chi-square*, usually represented by the Greek lowercase letter chi (χ) to eliminate confusion between the terms *discrete variables* and *continuous variables*. Recall that in Chapter 2 discrete variables referred to variables whose values were categorical, such as those of gender, race, and ethnicity, while continuous variables are those whose values are continuous under the number line. Examples include age, college grade point average (GPA), and family size.

There are several types of chi-squares, the two most common being the *chi-square test of association* and *chi-square for goodness of fit* (see discussion of nonparametric statistics in Appendix B). As discussed here, the chi-square test of association is the statistical test used in this book. Even though the chi-square test for goodness of fit is not covered, it is used when the tests of statistics involve dichotomous nominal variables, meaning that just two values for the variables are permitted. Yes and no or gender types of questions are a perfect match for the goodness-of-fit test. The procedures for calculating the chi-square for goodness of fit are the same as for the Pearson chi-square.

ORGANIZING THE CROSS-TABULATION TABLE
INTO ITS RESPECTIVE COLUMNS AND ROWS

Founding statisticians such as Pearson coined a specific term to correspond with a specific component of the cross-tabulation table. As discussed in the preceding section, each component (a, b, c, …) inside the cross-tabulation table is called a cell or cell frequency. Row totals are obtained by adding the values of the cell in row 1 to the values in row 2 and those in successive rows, as designated in Table 7.2. To get the first row total, add the scores in cell a to cell b (10 + 12 = 22). The second row can be obtained by adding cell c to cell d (22 + 22 = 44). The subsequent rows can be added by the same manner. The result of the row additions is called the *row total* or *marginal row total*, designated with the capital letter R. Depending on the number of categories for the rows, a subscript for each row may be designated. For example, in Table 7.3 assign R_1 (Asian American) for the first row, R_2 (African American) for the second row, and R_3 (Mexican/Latino) for the third row. Among the 150 clients participating in the research project, 22 indicated their preference for their social workers as Asian American, 44 for African American, 41 for Mexican/Latino, 27 for Caucasian, and 16 for others.

To calculate column totals, add the values of cells a + c + e + f + i. The result of the column additions is called the *column total* or *marginal column total*, designated with a capital C. Similar to the rows, assign C_1 (female) for the first column and C_2 (male) for the second column. The additions indicate that 73 of the clients were female and 77 of them were male.

When adding the totals of the respondents, either across or downward, the totals should match. The *grand total* of respondents for the research project is always designated with a capital N.

A research project that constitutes two columns and five rows as in Table 7.1 is called a 2 by 5 crosstab (or a 2 × 5 or 5 × 2). The numbers in each cell (cells a, b, c, …) are called the *observed frequencies* (designated with the capital letter O). *These are the numerical scores obtained from the research subjects.* Depending on the number of cells available, assign subscripts to represent the cells: O_a, O_b, O_c, and so on to the last cell. *The subscript a in O_a indicates that the researcher will calculate the chi-square for cell a based on a particular observed frequency (O).*

Table 7.3: Understand Rows and Columns in a Cross-Tabulation Table

Racial Origin of Preferred Social Worker	Gender of Client		Total
	Female	Male	
Asian American	10 (a)	12 (b)	22
African American	22 (c)	22 (d)	44
Mexican/Latino	21 (e)	20 (f)	41
Caucasian	14 (g)	13 (h)	27
Others	6 (i)	10 (j)	16
Total	73	77	$N = 150$

Marginal rows total (R) such as R_1, R_2, and so on.

Observed frequencies (O) such as O_1, O_2, and so on.

Marginal columns total (C), such as C_1, C_2, and so on.

Grand total, N.

The null and research hypotheses for Table 7.1 can be stated as follows:

H_0: There is no association between client gender and preferences for a particular racial background of the social workers.

H_a: There is a significant difference between client gender and preferences for a particular racial background of the social workers.

FORMULA FOR CHI-SQUARE

This is the second step in the preparation for calculating the chi-square statistic whose formula is depicted in the following equation (see Figure 7.1 for detailed instructions):

Purpose	*Null Hypothesis (H_0)*	*Research Hypothesis (H_a)*
Test the association between two nominal variables (i.e., dependent and independent)	There is no significant association between the variables in the population; therefore, the variables are statistically independent	There is a significant association between the variables in the population; therefore, the variables are statistically dependent

Probability Value (p-value): Self-selection at 95% confidence interval or higher

Chi-Square Formula $(\chi^2) = \sum \dfrac{(O-E)^2}{E}$

Where:

χ^2 = The Pearson chi-square coefficient (also called chi-square statistic)

O = Observed frequencies (scores obtained from the subjects)

E = Expected frequencies (also called unknown frequencies)

Since E is unknown, it must be calculated using this formula:

$E = \dfrac{(C)(R)}{N}$

E = Marginal Columns Total

R = Marginal Rows Total

N = Grand sample size

FIGURE 7.1 The Chi-Square Statistic Computation Procedures.

The formula in Figure 7.1 and the statistical symbols presented in Table 7.3 have insufficient information for completing chi-square: The formula states that when E is subtracted from O, the difference is squared and then divided by E, a letter that cannot be found anywhere among all the statistical symbols discussed thus far in this chapter. *The letter E stands for the expected frequencies for each of the cells in a cross-tabulation table. It is also called the unknown frequencies.* The expectation is that to retain the null hypothesis H_0, the numerical scores for each cell must be statistically independent. For example, in the situation discussed, verification of client gender is required, along with proof that their choices of social workers are independent of each other. Because E is unknown, it must be calculated using the second part of the formula in Table 7.4 $\left[E = \dfrac{(C)(R)}{N} \right]$.

Table 7.4 *The Chi-Square Statistic*

Purpose	Null Hypothesis (H_0)	Research Hypothesis (H_a)
Test the association between two nominal variables (i.e., dependent and independent).	There is no significant association between the variables in the population; therefore, the variables are statistically independent.	There is a significant association between the variables in the population; therefore, the variables are statistically dependent.

Probability Value (p value): Self-selection at 95% confidence interval or higher

Chi-square formula: $(\chi^2) = \sum \dfrac{(O-E)^2}{E}$

Where

χ^2 = Pearson chi-square coefficient (also called the chi-square statistic)
O = Observed frequencies (scores obtained from the subjects)
E = Expected frequencies (also called unknown frequencies)
Because E is unknown, it must be calculated using this formula:

$E = \dfrac{(C)(R)}{N}$

E = Marginal columns total
R = Marginal rows total
N = Grand sample size

The researcher must calculate the expected frequencies for every cell in the cross-tabulation table. For example, in cell a, the expected frequency is calculated as

$$E_a = \frac{(C_1)(R_1)}{N} \text{ which is translated to} \rightarrow E_a = \frac{(73)(22)}{150} = 10.71$$

where

E_a = Expected frequency for cell a
C_1 = Marginal column total for the first column
R_1 = Marginal row total for the first row
N = Total respondents for the research project

The marginal column total and marginal row total are used to calculate the expected frequencies. Students may wonder why we use the numbers outside the respective cells to calculate the expected frequencies. Notice that in Table 7.1, neither row total nor column total was assigned symbols (i.e., a, b, c) as individual cells. In cell a, if gender and choice of social workers are independent of each other, then 10.71 clients might be expected; however, in the research project there are 10 ($n = 10$) respondents. The explanation is that if the observed frequencies are equal to the expected frequencies or closely related ($O = E$), then the statistical test will not produce a significant difference between the variables. In this case, H_0 is retained. This is one of the reasons why statisticians state that the chi-square statistic should be avoided when

Table 7.5: Cross-Tabulation Display of Observed and Expected Data

Racial Origin of Preferred Social Worker	Gender of Client		Total
	Female	Male	
Asian American	10 (a) [10.71]	12 (b) [11.29]	22
African American	22 (c) [21.41]	22 (d) [22.59]	44
Mexican/Latino	21 (e) [19.95]	20 (f) [21.05]	41
Caucasian	14 (g) [13.14]	13 (h) [13.86]	27
Others	6 (i) [7.79]	10 (j) [8.21]	16
Total	73	77	$N = 150$

- In a 2 × 2 (four-cell) table, at least one cell has an expected frequency of less than 5 (see the section on calculating chi-square for a 2 × 2 study).
- In a table that is larger than 2 × 2 (more than four cells), more than 20% of the observed cells have an expected frequency of less than 5, or any cell has an expected frequency of 0.

These two rules of statistics simply say that when any of these two situations occur in any cell, even if chi-square is calculated, the result will be so small that nothing of value will be contributed to the finding of statistical significance. In calculating the expected frequencies for cell b, the same formula is followed (cell b is in the second column). Cell b is calculated using slightly different symbols (the formula remains the same):

$$E_b = \frac{(C_2)(R_1)}{N} \text{ which is also translated to} \rightarrow E_b = \frac{(77)(22)}{150} = 11.29$$

Repeat the same process for all cells in the contingency table. When finished with all the calculations, observed frequencies along with their expected frequencies will look exactly as in Table 7.5. *Expected frequencies are put inside brackets for ease in calculating chi-square. Notice that in Table 7.5, none of the cells has an expected frequency count of less than 5; therefore,* based on the statistics rules given, the next step is to proceed with calculating the chi-square statistic.

CALCULATING CHI-SQUARE

The last step in computing the chi-square statistic for the group of 150 clients in a hypothetical social services agency is, using the chi-square formula in Table 7.5, to substitute the corresponding observed O and expected E frequencies into the formula. Notice that, depending on the number of cells used for the two nominal variables, the final calculation can be quite long due to the sigma (Σ = summation) in front of the formula. The chi-square statistic for Table 7.5 is now calculated by the following:

$$\chi^2 = \frac{(10-10.71)^2}{10.71} + \frac{(12-11.29)^2}{11.29} + \frac{(22-21.41)^2}{21.41} + \frac{(22-22.59)^2}{22.59} + \frac{(21-19.95)^2}{19.95}$$

$$+ \frac{(20-21.05)^2}{21.05} + \frac{(14-13.14)^2}{13.14} + \frac{(13-13.86)^2}{13.86} + \frac{(6-7.79)^2}{7.79} + \frac{(10-8.21)^2}{8.21}$$

$$\chi^2 = .047 + .045 + .016 + .015 + .055 + .052 + .056 + .053 + .411 + .390$$

$$\chi^2 = 1.14$$

The result 1.14 is now called the *calculated Pearson chi-square coefficient* (χ^2). The subscript "*cal*" is used as a shorthand symbol for the *calculated value*, and it is used to determine whether there is a significant difference between the variables. Typically, researchers use rows for the dependent variable and columns for the independent variables; however, there is no consensus. The main guideline is that researchers must know the variables well—because it is very likely that the statistics (which variables are dependent and which are independent) will have to be explained to others, perhaps clients. Based on the tables concerning gender and client choice of social workers, the Pearson chi-square still says nothing about the relationship between the variables. To either support or reject the null hypothesis, an *interpretation* step is required.

INTERPRETING CHI-SQUARE

To interpret the result of any chi-square coefficient, its *degrees of freedom* (*df*) must be calculated, and these are slightly different from one statistical test to another. Normally, degrees of freedom are the attributes that are free to vary in a population or sample size. In chi-square, it is used to correct the number of cells in a cross-tabulation table. Essentially, degrees of freedom are used to reduce the number of cells in columns and rows. The formula for degrees of freedom for the chi-square is calculated by

$$Degrees\ of\ freedom\ (df) = (C-1)(R-1)$$

where

C = Marginal columns total (number of actual values/categories for the column)
R = Marginal rows total (number of actual values/categories for the row)

Therefore, the degrees of freedom for our hypothetical situation are calculated by

$$df = (2-1)\ (5-1) \rightarrow 4$$

In Chapter 6, in the section "Interpreting Results of Tests of Statistics," the statistical rules for hand calculations were discussed. To conclude findings from *any* inferential statistics, the calculated value (result of your calculation) must be visually compared with the critical value (value obtained from the chart/table of a statistics book). *If the calculated value is larger than the critical value, state that there is a significant **finding** and then replace the word finding with*

Table 7.6 *Critical Values of Chi-Square*

df	Level of Significance					
	.20	.10	.05	.02	.01	.001
1	1.64	2.71	3.84	5.41	6.63	10.83
2	3.22	4.61	5.99	7.82	9.21	13.82
3	4.64	6.25	7.82	9.84	11.34	16.27
4	5.99	7.78	9.49	11.67	13.28	18.46
5	7.29	9.24	11.07	13.39	15.09	20.52
6	8.56	10.64	12.59	15.03	16.81	22.46
7	9.80	12.02	14.07	16.62	18.48	24.32
8	11.03	13.36	15.51	18.17	20.09	26.12
9	12.24	14.68	16.92	19.68	21.67	27.88
10	13.44	15.99	18.31	21.16	23.21	29.59
11	14.63	17.28	19.68	22.62	24.72	31.26
12	15.81	18.55	21.03	24.05	26.22	32.91
13	16.98	19.81	22.36	25.47	27.69	34.53
14	18.15	21.06	23.68	26.87	29.14	36.12
15	19.31	22.31	25.00	28.26	30.58	37.70
16	20.46	23.54	26.30	29.63	32.00	39.25
17	21.62	24.77	27.59	31.00	33.41	40.79
18	22.76	25.99	28.87	32.35	34.81	42.31
19	23.90	27.20	30.14	33.69	36.19	43.82
20	25.04	28.41	31.41	35.02	37.57	45.32
21	26.17	29.62	32.67	36.34	38.93	46.80
22	27.30	30.81	33.92	37.66	40.29	48.27
23	28.43	32.01	35.17	38.97	41.64	49.73
24	29.55	33.20	36.42	40.27	42.98	51.18
25	30.68	34.38	37.65	41.57	44.31	52.62
26	31.80	35.56	38.89	42.86	45.64	54.05
27	32.91	36.74	40.11	44.14	46.96	55.48
28	34.03	37.92	41.34	45.42	48.28	56.89
29	35.14	39.09	42.56	46.69	49.59	58.30
30	36.25	40.26	43.77	47.96	50.89	59.70

Reprinted from J. Welkowitz, B. H. Cohen, & B. R. Lea. (2012). *Introductory statistics for the behavioral sciences* (7th ed.). Hoboken, NJ: Wiley. With permission from Wiley & Sons.

the appropriate term. If the reverse occurs, the null hypothesis H_0 must be retained. In most research study, the conventional 95% confidence interval (*p* value = .05), two-tailed hypothesis with 4 degrees of freedom (*df* = 4) is used. *In chi-square, the statistical test rarely (almost never) occurs at the one-tailed hypothesis. In this book, a two-tailed table is used.* Now, in concluding the finding of this hypothetical situation, first look at Table 7.6, which presents the critical values of chi-square. The first column of the table shows degrees of freedom (*df*) from 1 to 30. In typical research using chi-square, if it occurs, use 30 as the highest degree of freedom. The decimal numbers (.20 to .001) next to degrees of freedom are the *p* values. To get the critical value for the study at hand, find 4 ($df = 4$), then look across to .05 (the p value for the self-selected 95% confidence interval). The value between 4 and .05 is 9.49.

$$Calculate\ Chi-Square\ (\chi^2) = 1.14$$

Critical value of Chi−Square $(\chi^2_{crit}) = 9.49$ *(The subscript "crit" stands for critical value)*

Based on the rules of statistics summarized in chapter 6 (Interpreting Result of Tests of Statistics), H_0 has been retained; therefore, the conclusion is that there is no significant difference between client gender and choices regarding racial background of social workers: [$(\chi^2)= 1.14$, $df = 4$, $p > .05$]. The notations inside the square brackets parentheses are in the format required by the American Psychological Association (APA) (see Chapter 6 about when to use $p >$ or $p <$ and reasons for inserting the .05 next to it).

CHI-SQUARE FOR A 2 × 2 STUDY

Many nominal practical situations can use 2 × 2 criteria. Suppose that you are interested in studying voting preference for an upcoming election. The goal is to survey females and males whether they will vote in the next election. The survey simply wants people who are currently registered to vote indicate whether they will or will not vote in the upcoming election. Assume that 3,927 registered voters were surveyed, and their scores were tabulated in Table 7.7.

CALCULATING CHI-SQUARE FOR A 2 × 2 STUDY

By substituting observed and expected frequencies into the chi-square formula in Figure 7.1, the vignette about country and source of stigma can be calculated as

$$
\begin{aligned}
\chi^2_{Cal} &= \frac{(1,595-1,499.4)^2}{1,499.4} + \frac{(1,465-1,562.6)^2}{1,562.6} + \frac{(326-423.6)^2}{423.6} + \frac{(539-441.4)^2}{441.4} \\
&= \frac{(95.6)^2}{1,499.4} + \frac{(-97.6)^2}{1,562.6} + \frac{(-97.6)^2}{423.6} + \frac{(97.6)^2}{441.4} \\
&= 6.1 + 6.1 + 22.49 + 21.58 \\
&= 56.27
\end{aligned}
$$

$$\chi^2 = 56.27$$

The degrees of freedom for the research project are computed as

$$Degrees\ of\ freedom\ (df) = (2-1)\ (2-1) \rightarrow 1$$

By using a 99% confidence interval, 1 degree of confidence, the critical value of χ^2 is equal to 6.63. Because the calculated chi-square statistic is greater than the critical value, the conclusion is that there is a significant association between gender and the choice of voting or not voting in the upcoming election ($\chi^2 = 56.27$, $df = 1$, $p < .01$). For this practical example, H_0 is rejected and H_a has been supported. By computing the gender percentages, 83% of the female

Table 7.7: Observed and Expected Frequencies Between Gender and Voting Opinion

Vote * Gender Cross Tabulation			
Count			
Voting Choice	Gender		Total
	Female	Male	
Vote Yes, will vote	1,597 (83%) 1,499.4	1,465 (73.1%) 1,562.6	3,062 (78%)
No, will not vote	326 (17%) 423.6	539 (26.9%) 441.4	865 (22%)
Total	1,923 (100%)	2,004 (100%)	3,927 (100%)

and 73% of the males stated that they would vote in the upcoming election compared to 17% and 26.9%, respectively, who would not vote. Overall, 78% of the registered voters would vote compared to 22% of those that would not vote.

SUMMARY

This chapter shows how to calculate the first inferential statistic, chi-square. Creating the cross-tabulation table with two nominal variables was introduced. The crosstab table can be used to do a hypothesis test. However, to complete the hypothesis test, several steps must be completed: calculate the expected frequencies; complete the chi-square calculation; and, either manually or electronically, find the critical value corresponding to the degrees of freedom for the research project. Finally, the researcher must discuss whether to retain or reject H_0. Chapter 8 introduces correlation analysis.

STUDY QUESTIONS

PART I

1. Suppose that you are given $\chi^2_{cal} = 24.74$, $df = 15$, $p = .001$. Interpret the finding in relation to H_0 and H_a.
2. Discuss why when reporting chi-square it is more appropriate to use the term *association* rather than *relationship*.
3. If it is given $C = 5$ and $R = 7$, what is its degree of freedom?

PART II

An intake mental health clinician at a local mental health center has observed, in past years, that prospective patients who come to the mental health center with their loved ones, mainly spouse and children, who were provided with treatment such as medication or individual or group counseling, tended to comply better with all the treatment program. Now, because of this observation, a new hypothesis, focusing on racial background and treatment type, is to be tested. The goal is to see whether similar results are obtained regarding treatment compliance.

Assume that data were obtained from 3,320 patients who were served by the center. The overall distributions of the reported scores were as follows: Of those identifying themselves as Asian Americans, 50 stated receiving medications only; 250 received both medications and individual counseling; 100 received medications, individual counseling, and group counseling. Of those identifying themselves as Latinos, 80 received only medications; 340 received medications and individual counseling; and 210 received medications, individual counseling, and group counseling. For those identifying themselves as Caucasian, 140 received only medications, 440 received medications and individual counseling, and 180 received all three treatment types. Moreover, of those who identified themselves as either African American or others, 200 received medications, 700 received medications and individual counseling, and 630 received all three treatment types.

Complete the following tasks to conduct your hypothesis test:

- State your null and research hypothesis.
- Use race for columns and treatment types for rows; construct a contingency table for the research data. Once the contingency table is created, calculate the expected frequencies for all of the cells in the research study.
- Calculate the Pearson chi-square coefficient.
- Use a 98% confidence interval; discuss your findings for the research project in relation to H_0 and H_a for the research study. Include in the report all the required APA designations (scientific notations).

ANSWERS TO STUDY QUESTIONS

PART I

1. *Critical value of Chi-Square* (χ^2_{crit}) = 37.70. H_a is rejected; therefore, retain H_0.
2. The term *relationship* is more appropriate when used to describe values of continuous (infinite) variables, whereas *association* is more appropriate when used to describe values of discrete (finite) variables.
3. $df = 24$.

PART II

- H_0: There is no significant difference between race of clients and types of treatment received.
- H_a: There is a significant association between clients' race and types of treatment received.
- Calculated chi-square (χ^2_{cal})= 95.18.
- $df = 6$; p value = .02.
- Critical value of chi-square (χ^2_{crit})= 15.03.
- H_a has been supported.

CHAPTER 8

INFERENTIAL STATISTICS

Correlation

OVERVIEW

Similar to Chapter 7, this chapter involves bivariate analysis, but it is about correlation that focuses on interval or ratio data. Knowledge of advanced data manipulation, the subject of this chapter, is necessary to test hypotheses with nominal and ordinal data.

INTRODUCTION TO CORRELATION

WHAT IS CORRELATION?

In academic arenas such as social and health services, correlation is commonly used to study numerical statements about the relationship between two interval/ratio variables. More specifically, in professional settings such as psychology, social work, and nursing, correlation is applied to two continuous variables. For example, school psychologists may be talking about socialization skills of children and their family size; social workers may be talking about the relationship between knowledge of domestic violence and the probability of spousal abuse; nurses may be talking about the amount of junk food that children consume per week and child obesity.

Correlation is used to examine the strengths and variations of the relationship between two interval- or ratio-level variables. More specifically, correlation is used to examine the statistical significance of randomized interval/ratio variables. When two variables are correlated (from this point in the chapter), the plural *variables* refers to the relationship between a dependent and another dependent, a dependent and an independent, or an independent and an independent variable) and the *Pearson* correlation is used.

The Pearson correlation is commonly represented by the lowercase letter r, and it is called the *Pearson correlation coefficient* or just *Pearson r*. As cited by King et al. (2011), in 1896, Karl

Pearson studied the relationship between the height of parents and their offspring developed the correlation formula.

The Pearson r is also called the *linear* or *product-moment correlation coefficient*. When the values between two interval/ratio variables are accurately displayed on a graph, assuming that there is no variability, the data set will produce a graph with a straight line. Sometimes, however, the general relationship between two variables does not follow a straight line, so it is called *curvilinear correlation*.

GRAPHICAL DISPLAY OF DIFFERENT TYPES OF CORRELATION

In a scatterplot, when there is a dependent and an independent variable, the dependent variable is normally displayed on the ordinate (the vertical or *y* axis), and the independent variable is displayed on the abscissa (the horizontal or *x* axis). This facilitates a visual determination regarding whether a plausible relationship exists between the two variables or whether to make predictions about the possible effect the independent variable has on the dependent variable. *When the two variables are displayed in this way, the dependent variable is better conceptualized as the criterion variable and the independent as the predictor variable.*

DIRECTION OF THE PEARSON CORRELATION COEFFICIENT

When the values of interval/ratio variables move in the same direction (either increase or decrease together), the result is a *positive correlation coefficient* ($r = +$). In the previous example about children's socialization skills (*Y* or criterion), family size was used as the predictor (*x* axis) variable. The prediction was that one of the factors that enable some children to make friends easily is due to interaction with multiple siblings at home. This prediction is illustrated in Figure 8.1. The assumption is that as family size *X* increases, children's socialization skills *Y* will also increase.

Figure 8.2 is a scatterplot showing a positive correlation between socialization skills of children and their family size. In this hypothetical situation, children's socialization skills are dependent on the size of the families. Whether true or not, this is what is speculated. Complete calculations and discussions are shown in Practical Example 8.1.

A negative or inverse correlation coefficient ($r = -$) means that as the values of one variable (i.e., independent) decrease, the values of the other variable (i.e., dependent) increase, or vice versa. In short, the values of the variables under investigation go in opposite directions.

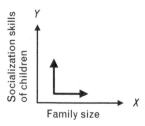

FIGURE 8.1 Positive correlation.

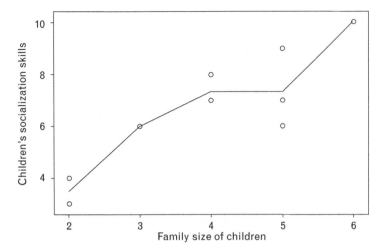

FIGURE 8.2 Scatterplot depicting a positive correlation between socialization skills of children and their family size.

Figure 8.3 illustrates a situation for which if knowledge of domestic violence increases, there is less likelihood of spousal abuse.

Figure 8.4 is a scatterplot depicting a negative correlation for the same scenario (see complete calculations and explanations in Practical Example 8.2).

When the distribution of scores is scattered over the plot, as illustrated in Figure 8.5, there is no (zero) correlation.

IS A POSITIVE OR NEGATIVE CORRELATION A BETTER COEFFICIENT?

Sometimes a researcher may wonder whether a positive, negative, or no (zero) correlation is a better or more desirable coefficient. When critically assessing human behavior in the environment, the answer depends on the situation and the purposes of the researcher's investigation. Sometimes, the purpose may be to obtain a positive correlation; another study may wish a negative or zero correlation. King et al. (2011) stated that a positive or negative correlation is used only to indicate the direction of the correlation, not its degree of severity. *The calculated Pearson correlation coefficient (Pearson r) is never used to explain that a positive correlation is*

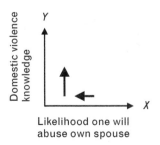

FIGURE 8.3 Inverse correlation between domestic violence knowledge and spousal abuse.

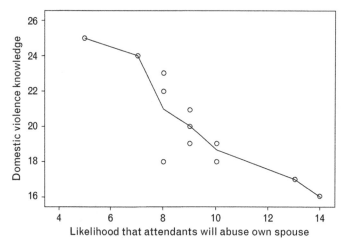

FIGURE 8.4 Scatterplot depicting negative correlation.

stronger than a negative correlation or vice versa. In a situation such as the amount of chemical dependency versus the level of personal functioning, the desirable outcome is a strong negative correlation. For example, when people use fewer illegal drugs or less alcohol (values of the dependent variable decrease), they are more likely to spend quality time with their loved ones (values of the independent variable increase). If this occurs, the values of the independent variable increase and family relationships become stronger. Therefore, a *negative correlation is more desirable to the researchers.*

In some research studies, such as the relationship between age and income and between years of marriage and degree of spousal support, a *no correlation coefficient* is desirable. In other words, the researcher may hope to obtain evidence that, regardless of time, there has been no change in the strength of the spousal relationship.

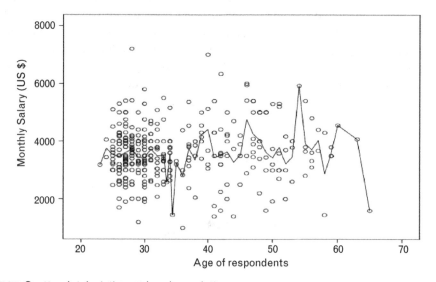

FIGURE 8.5 Scatterplot depicting no (zero) correlation.

CORRELATION IS NOT CAUSATION

Among the statisticians, Weinbach and Grinnell (2015) stated that the correlation coefficient cannot reveal whether the values of the criterion (outcome) variable have been caused by the values of the predictor variable. Pearson r reveals only the pattern of a relationship. Most important, the variations in the predictor variable are beyond the researchers' control. Essentially, researchers observe variations after the fact. Thus, any interpretation of correlation that implies causation is incorrect, so that the result of a correlation coefficient is never acceptable as proof of causality.

Another important note about correlation is that when only two variables are being examined at a time, it is highly likely that other variables may also have an effect. This is often referred to as *spurious association* (Agresti & Finlay, 2009). For instance, excessive drinking tends to lead to depression. Often, long-term alcohol dependency leads to the development of depressive syndromes, but the syndromes can be developed by many other stress-producing factors, such as genetic, financial crisis, and relationship issues.

Last, even though the variations are always observed after the fact, the number of variations observed can be used to make a prediction about the effects they have on the criterion variable. This prediction is discussed in Chapter 10 on regression.

USE OF CORRELATION BY HEALTH
AND HUMAN SERVICES WORKERS

Either consciously or unconsciously, correlations are frequently used by people in social science, such as students, researchers, and practitioners in many different capacities. For example, in social work education, faculty and program administrators may want to know the relationship between the quality of the graduate and undergraduate curriculum content offered and the level of satisfaction that alumni feel toward the knowledge received. Sociologists in the area may want to investigate the relationship between poverty and employment opportunities in a particular region of the country. A correlation study examining these two particular topics may provide sufficient information about (a) the strength of a social work education program and (b) poverty rate and degrees of employment opportunities for residents in the area.

While in school, college students, such as those in social work, nursing, and psychology, can use correlation to examine various issues pertaining to their college education. Possible topics for student research might include one or more of the following:

1. The relationship between study hours and grade point average (GPA)
2. The relationship between enrollment units per term and time spent to obtain a diploma or degree
3. The rigor of an academic program and perceived student appreciation of programs and their respective professors

THE CORRELATION COEFFICIENT

Regardless of the sample size, whether 50 or 50,000, the result of the statistical computation will always produce a correlation coefficient ranging from –1.00 to +1.00. The value of –1.00

represents a perfect negative correlation, while a value of +1.00 represents a perfect positive correlation. Perfect correlation says that there is no variation in the variables (dependent and independent variables) under investigation, particularly the values of the predictor (independent) variable. However, when studying human behavior in the environment, it is unlikely that a perfect correlation coefficient will ever be obtained. A value of 0.00 represents a complete lack of (zero) correlation. A correlation coefficient that gets closer to either end of −1.00 and +1.00 indicates a stronger relationship. For example, when examining the relationship between study hours and GPA of college students, a correlation coefficient of .9501 is observed. Should a researcher conducting a correlation analysis observe a correlation coefficient this large (very close to +1.00), it is safe to conclude that there is a strong relationship between study hours and college GPA.

CALCULATING THE PEARSON CORRELATION COEFFICIENT

FORMULA FOR THE PEARSON R

The computational formula for the Pearson correlation coefficient is found in Table 8.1. Be aware that there are simplified versions of the computational formula, and most of these formulas are carried over from the z score (see Chapter 5). *Whether the computational formula or the simplified version, including computerized software like SPSS (Statistical Package for the Social Sciences) is used, the functions of the formulas are mathematically equivalent and always produce the same result.*

Table 8.1 Pearson's Product Moment Correlation Coefficient *r*

The Computational Formula

$$r = \frac{N\left(\sum XY\right) - \left(\sum X\right)\left(\sum Y\right)}{\sqrt{\left[N\sum X^2 - (X)^2\right]\left[N\sum Y^2 - (Y)^2\right]}}$$

where

r = Correlation coefficient

N = Size of the participant sample

$\sum XY$ = Sum of the cross products of the scores in the X and Y columns

$\sum X$ = Sum of the scores in the X column

$\sum Y$ = Sum of the scores in the Y column

$\sum X^2$ = Sum of the X column squared

$\sum Y^2$ = Sum of the Y column squared

$\left(\sum X\right)^2$ = Squaring the sum of the scores of X

$\left(\sum Y\right)^2$ = Squaring the sum of the scores of Y

PRACTICAL EXAMPLE 8.1

Suppose that you are a school official. Over the years, you have observed that kids who come from large families tend to have an easier time making friends with students on campus. Therefore, you are curious about the contributing factors that led to such capability. As a result, a questionnaire was designed and randomly administered to 10 students at a local school. After data collection was completed and the data preliminarily examined, the socialization skills that kids exhibited with other children on campus, relative to the sizes of their own households, appeared interesting. Therefore, a hypothesis derived from this observation was tested using correlation. *Socialization* (higher score indicates more ease of making friends) was used as the criterion variable and *family size* as the predictor variable. The goal of this research project was to achieve two major objectives: (a) find a relationship between the criterion and predictor variables and (b) discover how much of the variance in the criterion variable could be explained by the predictor variable. Table 8.2 shows the distribution of the 10 students from the hypothetical campus and their respective scores. It was stipulated that the research project be based on a two-tailed hypothesis with a confidence interval (CI) of 95%.

Look at the two sets of scores and compare them to the formula in Table 8.1. To calculate the Pearson correlation coefficient, three additional columns must be created to satisfy the mathematical equation. Table 8.3 shows the columns needed to satisfy these conditions.

Advisement. When calculating the correlation coefficient, remember which variables were selected as the criterion and predictor variables. By doing this, the findings can be clearly explained when reporting the outcome.

The computation for the correlation coefficient (Pearson *r*) can be completed as follows:

$$r = \frac{10(290) - (40)(67)}{\sqrt{[10(176) - (40)^2][10(489) - (67)^2]}}$$

$$r = \frac{2900 - 2680}{\sqrt{[1760 - 1600][4890 - 4489]}}$$

$$r = \frac{220}{\sqrt{(160)(401)}}$$

$$r = \frac{220}{\sqrt{64,160}}$$

$$r = \frac{220}{253.3}$$

$$r = .8685$$

Using Table 8.4, which shows the critical values of the Pearson *r*, with a sample size of 10 ($n = 10$) and a two-tailed hypothesis at 95% confidence interval (*p* value = .05), the critical value is .658. Please note that some statistics book used four decimal places while this book and other used three decimal places. The reason for this is that currently, SPSS only displays three digits for the Pearson *r*.

Table 8.2 *Data Set for Children Socialization Skills and Family Size*

ID	Family Size (X = Predictor)	Socialization Skill (Y = Criterion)
01	4	8
02	2	4
03	5	9
04	6	10
05	5	6
06	4	7
07	3	6
08	4	7
09	5	7
10	2	3

First, notice that the calculated value of .8685 (r_{cal} = .8685) [rounded off to .869] is larger than the critical values of .658 (r_{crit} = .658). Next, use the statistics rule discussed in Chapter 6 (see the section "Decision-Making Using the Confidence Interval"), which stated that when calculating quantitative data by hand, the calculated value must be compared with the critical value based on the self-selected tail of the hypothesis and confidence interval; otherwise, there is no possible way to tell whether to retain or reject H_0. Therefore, in the case of socialization skills and family size, it is safe to conclude that, based on a 95% confidence interval and two-tailed hypothesis, there was a strong correlation between the variables (r = .869, p < .05). The symbols inside the parenthesis are the statistical notations required by the American Psychological Association (APA) and other publication outlets.

In summary, the conclusion is that the socialization skills of children were strongly correlated with family size. In fact, due to the positive correlation coefficient, it is safe to say that the larger the child's family, the better socialization skills the child will have. For this reason, H_0 is rejected and H_a is supported. A finding like this is helpful to school administrators who seek to improve the socialization skills of children.

Table 8.3 *Expanding the Data Set Into Segments for the Pearson r Calculation*

ID	X	X^2	Y	Y^2	XY
01	4	16	8	64	32
02	2	4	4	16	8
03	5	25	9	81	45
04	6	36	10	100	60
05	5	25	6	36	30
06	4	16	7	49	28
07	3	9	6	36	18
08	4	16	7	49	28
09	5	25	7	49	35
10	2	4	3	9	6
	$\sum X = 40$	$\sum X^2 = 176$	$\sum Y = 67$	$\sum Y^2 = 489$	$\sum XY = 290$

Table 8.4 Critical Values of the Pearson *r*

df (= N − 2; N = number of pairs)	Level of Significance for One-Tailed Test			
	.05	.025	.01	.005
	Level of Significance for Two-Tailed Test			
	.10	.05	.02	.01
1	.988	.997	.9995	.9999
2	.900	.950	.980	.990
3	.805	.878	.934	.959
4	.729	.811	.882	.917
5	.669	.754	.833	.874
6	.622	.707	.789	.834
7	.582	.666	.750	.798
8	.549	.632	.716	.765
9	.521	.602	.685	.735
10	.497	.576	.658	.708
11	.476	.553	.634	.684
12	.458	.532	.612	.661
13	.441	.514	.592	.641
14	.426	.497	.574	.623
15	.412	.482	.558	.606
16	.400	.468	.542	.590
17	.389	.456	.528	.575
18	.378	.444	.516	.561
19	.369	.433	.503	.549
20	.360	.423	.492	.537
21	.352	.413	.482	.526
22	344	.404	.472	.515
23	.337	.396	.462	.505
24	.330	.388	.453	.496
25	.323	.381	.445	.487
26	.317	.374	.437	.479
27	.311	.367	.430	.471
28	.306	.361	.423	.463
29	.301	.355	.416	.456
30	.296	.349	.409	.449
35	.275	.325	.381	.418
40	.257	.304	.358	.393
45	.243	.288	.338	.372
50	.231	.273	.322	.354
60	.211	.250	.295	.325
70	.195	.132	.274	.302
80	.183	.217	.256	.283
90	.173	.205	.242	.267
100	.164	.195	.230	.254

Reprinted from J. Welkowitz, B. H. Cohen, & B. R. Lea. (2012). *Introductory statistics for the behavioral sciences* (7th ed.). Hoboken, NJ: Wiley. With permission from Wiley & Sons.

PRACTICAL EXAMPLE 8.2

For another hypothetical example, a community activist is interested in investigating the inverse relationship between awareness of a community educational program on causes of domestic violence and the social and psychological effects on its victims. This activist believes that, possibly, if people in the community are more educated about the effects of domestic violence on people, then the incidence of spousal abuse will decline. To pursue this interest, the activist promotes a program via the school administration to randomly select 15 married persons to participate in an educational program. Assume that after the training, two instruments are used to measure the effectiveness of the training. One of these is designed to measure participant level of knowledge gained concerning social and psychological effects commonly encountered by victims of domestic violence. The other instrument is a self-rated scale used to measure the likelihood that participants will abuse a spouse at least once in their lifetime. Both measuring instruments are based on five items (five statements), with scores ranging from 1 to 5 (higher score indicates higher risk). Using community knowledge gained from their training, the independent (X or predictor) variable and the likelihood of domestic violence as the dependent (Y or criterion) variable, maximum scores for the measuring instruments are summarized as follows:

$$Knowledge \ (X) = \ 5 \ items \times 5(scale \ from \ 1-5) = 25$$
$$Likelihood \ (Y) = \ 5 \ items \times 5 = 25$$

The hypotheses may be stated as follows, based on a two-tailed hypothesis at the 95% confidence interval:

- H_0: *Educational training does not increase community knowledge about domestic violence.*
- H_a: *Educational training significantly increases community knowledge about the social and psychological effects encountered by victims of domestic violence.*

Goals at the end of the educational training period were as follows:

1. To examine the relationship between the degrees to which knowledge is gained about social and psychological effects encountered by victims of domestic violence and the self-rated scale speculating that a spousal partner may be abused at least once in a lifetime
2. How data collected from the randomized 15 individuals can be generalized to all residents in the area
3. To determine the extent of variations in community knowledge about domestic violence

Table 8.5 displays the dummy scores obtained from the randomized 15 adult married individuals as well as the necessary columns that must be completed for this hypothetical study. As presented in Practical Example 8.1, the X and Y columns represent the original data obtained from the research participants. Columns X^2, Y^2, and XY are the new values that must be calculated to satisfy the Pearson r formula. When displaying data, because there are no set rules, either X or Y may be displayed first. Researchers often display X first just because of the alphabetical order. *Whichever way the data are displayed, the result of the Pearson calculation will always be the same.*

Table 8.5 *Domestic Violence Educational Training*

ID	Y	Y^2	X	X^2	XY
01	9	81	21	441	189
02	10	100	19	361	190
03	9	81	20	400	180
04	13	169	17	289	221
05	7	49	24	576	168
06	8	64	23	529	184
07	9	81	20	400	180
08	5	25	25	625	125
09	10	100	18	324	180
10	14	196	16	256	224
11	8	64	22	484	176
12	5	25	25	625	125
13	9	81	19	361	171
14	8	64	18	324	144
15	10	100	19	361	190
$n = 15$	$\sum Y = 134$	$\sum Y^2 = 1,280$	$\sum X = 306$	$\sum X^2 = 6,356$	$\sum XY = 2,647$

It is difficult to see the patterns of the data set, but a careful examination of the interrelatedness of the values between X and Y shows that they are reversed. For example, when the value of knowledge (ID number 8 on X) is 25, the value for Y (likelihood of abusing a spouse) is 5, and when the value for X (ID number 5) is 24, the value for Y is 7. The incremental decreases of the dependent and independent variables flow sequentially until the value for X is 16 and the value for Y is 14 (ID number 10). Because of these inverse patterns, the result of the Pearson r calculation produces a negative correlation coefficient.

The Pearson correlation coefficient can now be calculated as follows:

$$r = \frac{15(2,647) - (134)(306)}{\sqrt{[15(1,280) - (134)^2][15(6,356) - (306)^2]}}$$

$$r = \frac{39,705 - 41,004}{\sqrt{[19,200 - 17,956][95,340 - 93,636]}}$$

$$r = \frac{-1,299}{\sqrt{(1,244)(1,704)}}$$

$$r = \frac{-1,299}{\sqrt{2,119,776}}$$

$$r = \frac{-1,299}{1,455.95}$$

$$r = -.8922$$

The computation results in a correlation coefficient of −.892 (r_{cal} = −.892). Based on the specified confidence interval of 95% (p = .05) as stated previously, a two-tailed hypothesis, and a sample size of 15, the critical value is .558 (see Table 8.4). *Because of the very strong negative correlation coefficient, it is safe to conclude that there is a significant relationship between educational training on domestic violence learned by the participants and the likelihood that the participants will abuse their spouses in the future (r = −.892, p < .05).* Essentially, H_0 was rejected and H_a has been supported. The negative correlation indicates that as spouses become more knowledgeable about the social and psychological effects encountered by victims of domestic violence, they are less likely to abuse their own spouses. Assume that instead of the study being based on a sample of 15, the research questionnaire was in fact randomly administered to 150 married persons in the general public; then, the finding is generalizable to the population in which the sample was drawn.

When H_0 is retained, then there is no relationship between the variables. However, when H_a is supported, terms such as weak, moderate, strong, and very strong describe the correlation under investigation. Next, two other statistical concepts are introduced: first, the range of the correlation coefficient and then the coefficient of determination.

THE CORRELATION COEFFICIENT RANGE

When can terms such as weak, moderate, strong, and very (extremely) strong be used with regard to relationship or correlation? What range of the calculated correlation coefficient (r_{cal}) must exist to support the use of such terminology? Because there is no consensus among statisticians, the result is up to you. The following are some suggested guidelines:

1. Base your conclusion on either the self-selected p value from the table or the p value given by the computer software. Keep in mind that as the p value decreases (confidence interval increases), the chance of random error decreases; for example, a p value of .001 (CI = 99.9%) is stronger than .01 (CI = 99%). As a result, when the p value becomes larger, then chances of rejecting H_0 become stronger.
2. Factor the sample size into findings. When the sample size n is small, as in Practical Examples 8.1 and 8.2, a larger coefficient is needed to reject H_0. Table 8.4 shows that as the sample size n increases, the correlation coefficient becomes smaller. Therefore, for a research project that has 100 or more participants, a much smaller correlation coefficient is needed to reject the null hypothesis.

Now, associate the calculated correlation coefficient with an understanding of the dependent variable. More specifically, how is the correlation coefficient related to variability? That relationship is called the *coefficient of determination*.

WHAT IS THE COEFFICIENT OF DETERMINATION?

The correlation coefficient r represents the strength and variation of the relationship between two continuous variables. In Chapter 4, the concept of variability was introduced, especially the variance. *For single variables, the variance or the sum of squares is used to calculate the standardized unit of measurement, which is called the standard deviation.*

However, when two variables are correlated together, what is the role of the variance in this situation? Essentially, what is the role of the *sum of squares* in this situation? *When the correlation coefficient is squared (r^2) [in SPSS, see R Square] and then multiplied by 100%, the product becomes known as the coefficient of determination.* This transformation to the coefficient of determination represents *the proportion of variance in the dependent variable that is explained by the independent variable.* The coefficient of determination is also called the "strength" or "magnitude" of the research project. When reporting results from correlation analysis, it is important that the coefficient of determination be taken into consideration.

In Practical Example 8.1, the coefficient of determination is calculated by squaring the correlation coefficient and then multiplying by 100%, such as $(.8685)^2(100\%) = 75.43$. The coefficient of determination obtained is 75.43%. Based on this transformation, it is concluded that *children's socialization skills can be explained by family size 75.43% of the time.* Also, 75.43% of the criterion variable (Y = socialization skills) can be explained by the values of the predictor variable (X = family size). *However, the other 24.57% (100 – 75.43 = 24.57) of the factors affecting children's socialization skills cannot be explained.* The remaining factors may be due to cultural background, being shy, being new to the school, or other family or school environmental circumstances.

In Practical Example 8.2, the coefficient of determination can be calculated by

$$Coefficient\ of\ determination = (.8922)^2 (100\%)$$
$$= 79.60\%$$

In this particular situation, when people in the community become more knowledgeable about the social and psychological effects encountered by victims of domestic violence, the chance that one will not abuse a spouse is 79.60%. However, domestic violence is still possible due to some other factors (100 – 79.60 = 20.40) at 20.40%. What is noted here is that *knowledge is not a sole predictor in ending domestic violence.* As a society, other things must happen to decrease the remaining 20.4% of harm to spouses.

SUMMARY

This chapter introduced the basic function of correlation analysis, the Pearson *r*. The Pearson *r* is widely used in examining the interrelatedness of two interval-/ratio-level data in a linear relationship. This relationship indicates the strengths and variations between the criterion and predictor variables ranging between ±1.0 and, when there is no linear relationship, 0. The reason for this is that as the calculated correlation coefficient gets closer to the ±1.0, the relationship between the variables becomes stronger.

When the correlation coefficient *r* is squared (r^2), the cross product is called the coefficient of determination. The coefficient of determination is used to discuss the amount of variation in the dependent (criterion) variable that can be explained by the independent (predictor) variable. In Chapter 9, measures of central tendency, mainly the sample mean ($\overline{X}$), are discussed.

STUDY QUESTIONS

1. Suppose that Y = poverty rate and X = rate of full-time employment. Assume that the report was based on $n = 500$, $r = .8125$ with two-tailed hypothesis, and p value = .05. What conclusions can be drawn about the living conditions of the people in this particular region? What can be said about the null hypothesis?

2. If given $r = .3221$, compute the coefficient of determination. What can be said about the relationship between the criterion and predictor variables?

3. If given $r = -.9415$, compute the coefficient of determination. What can be said about the relationship between the criterion and predictor variables?

4. A data set with two variables is given:
   X = Number of client cases per month; Y = Burnout rates for the staff
   X = 24, 30, 23, 32, 28, 31, 25, 30
   Y = 5, 10, 4, 10, 7, 9, 6, 8

Tasks to be completed:

   a. Indicate level of measurement for the variables.
   b. Create a contingency table, including all the necessary columns for the data set.
   c. Calculate the Pearson r for the data set.
   d. Discuss your finding for the research study. Make sure to state whether H_0 is retained or rejected. In your explanation, make sure to include the statistical notations required by APA.

ANSWERS TO STUDY QUESTIONS

1. There is an extremely strong correlation between poverty and employment rate $(r = .8125, p < .05)$. H_0 is rejected.

2. The criterion is explained by 10.57% of this particular predictor variable.

3. The criterion is explained by 88.64% of this particular predictor variable.

4. For question 4c, the Pearson $r = .9610$.

INFERENTIAL STATISTICS

The T Tests

OVERVIEW

Chapters 7 and 8 introduced procedures for conducting basic hypothesis tests. These procedures normally involve comparing two nominal scores (Chapter 7) or two interval-/ratio-level scores (Chapter 8) with each other. Now, supposing one nominal variable and one interval/ratio variable, what would be a good statistical tool for finding any significant differences between the variables?

1. The goal is to test a hypothesis on weight (interval data) of persons in minority and nonminority groups (two nominal categories) in a particular region of the country. When the term *weight* is brought up, which group's (nominal) weight (interval) is being referenced?
2. The goal is to see whether there is a significant difference between income (ratio) and race (nominal). In this situation, whose (nominal) income (interval/ratio) is being questioned?
3. The goal is to test the hypothesis on degrees of self-care (interval or ratio) among people in a particular region (location is nominal). Is the researcher referring to gender (nominal) or race (nominal)? (Another possibility is total subjects.)
4. The goal is to examine the statistical significance of the effectiveness of a diabetes management (interval/ratio) program involving experimental and control groups (groups are nominal) run by a local hospital (name of place is nominal). Is diabetes management as conducted by the local hospital effective or not effective? "Yes" and "No" types of responses are nominal.

All four statements show only one interval/ratio variable but indicate there may be one or more nominal variables. The statistical tests for situations like these are called *t statistics* or simply *t tests*. In the rest of this chapter, the terms *t test, t statistic,* and *calculated t* are used interchangeably.

THE MEANING OF *T* STATISTICS OR *T* TESTS

Like chi-square and correlation, *t* tests are tools for bivariate analyses and are used to test for statistical differences between the means ($\overline{\text{X}}$) of two groups. *When there are two or more dependent variables and three or more independent variables, the application changes to analysis of variance (Chapter 12) or multiple analyses of variance (beyond the scope of this book).* The groups could be the sample versus the population or one sample with another sample. Essentially, *t* tests are tests of statistical significance that can be used to compare the differences between two means while factoring in sampling error (Witte, 1993). Witte explained that, theoretically, sampling is based on the null hypothesis that there is no difference between the two means in the two populations from which the samples were drawn. Conceptually, the means from any two groups must be thought of as drawn from the distribution of all possible samples. This is so because the theoretical sampling distribution of the null hypothesis assumes no difference between the group means in the population. Therefore, the mean of that population should equal 0, or the difference between the sampling distribution and the population parameter is 0 (King et al., 2011; Witte, 1993). In summary, *t* tests include these two computational conditions:

1. The level of measurement for the *dependent variable must be interval or ratio.* Therefore, weight, income, degrees of self-care, and level of treatment effect as presented in the overview can be used as dependent variables.
2. The level of measurement for the *independent variable must be nominal.* Therefore, the possible concepts are "minority and nonminority groups" for the first statement, "race" for the second statement, "gender or race" for the third statement, and "experimental and control groups" for the fourth statement.

Just as in computing the standard deviation (*SD*), data analyses using the *t* tests *can be complex and time consuming if one is making calculations by hand.* There are two major reasons for this complexity:

1. There are several methods for calculating each of the *t* tests; however, there is no universally agreed-on computational formula. Therefore, researchers must have a clear understanding of the meaning and statistical assumptions regarding each of the *t* tests.
2. Because the computational formula for each of the *t* tests can be expanded to fit the research objectives, the competence of the researcher is critical.

For these two reasons, some of the simple ways to calculate the *t* statistic were illustrated, especially using the *estimated standard deviation of the difference scores* ($S_{\overline{E}1-\overline{E}2}$) and the *estimated standard error of the difference* $S_{\overline{D}}$ (see dependent and independent samples t-test later in the chapter). Whether the researcher is evaluating a field of practice or conducting educational research, the results of the computational methods demonstrated here should be similar, including the use of computer programs such as the Statistical Package for the Social Sciences (SPSS; Appendix A).

THREE TYPES OF *T* TESTS

The three types of *t* test are

1. The one-sample *t* test
2. The independent samples *t* test
3. The dependent samples *t* test

VARIOUS STATISTICAL ASSUMPTIONS ABOUT THE *t* TESTS

In addition to the conditions stated, several other conditions must be met prior to using the three *t* tests. The *two conditions given plus the additional conditions that follow are statistical assumptions for the* t *tests:*

- The *t* statistic is a part of bivariate analysis, and equal variances using the sum of squares are assumed. This is known as *homogeneity of variance.* Because most research studies use homogeneity of variance, the focus here is on equal variances. Leon-Guerrero and Frankfort-Nachmias (2012) stated that when the sum of the squares of one sample is twice as large as that from another sample, then unequal variances must be assumed. Research outcomes rarely result in one project having twice the variances of another, so the focus of this chapter is on equal variances.
- The samples drawn at random from the population may or may not be equal (see the computation in this chapter for the estimated standard error when the total variances are assumed). If random selection is not possible for independent and dependent sample *t* tests, random assignment may be considered. *Random assignment* simply means dividing the participants into two groups with some sort of random draw. Sampling error should be discussed as part of the study limitations.
- The *t* tests are statistical tools used to compare either the sample mean with the population mean or two related or unrelated means $(\overline{X})$. *They are not intended to test for relationship/association or treatment effects. Even when a significant difference is detected, it shows only that one mean is significantly different from another.*
- In the case of the dependent and independent samples *t* test, the researcher must assume that the first sample mean is greater than the second mean $(\overline{X}_1 > \overline{X}_2)$, and that the sample means are greater than the population mean $(\overline{X} > \mu)$. The reason for this assumption is that the researcher must be able to recognize and clearly explain the findings about the group that did better under specific intervention. For example, the researcher must be able to explain clearly whether the experimental or control improved under certain conditions.

THE ONE-SAMPLE *T* TEST OR *T* STATISTIC

The one-sample *t* test or one-sample statistic is used for two different purposes:

1. It can be used to determine if the sample is large enough to represent the population parameter.

2.   Rather than base findings on frequency distributions and variability, the desire is to conduct an inferential test for the sampling distribution.

In the first instance, when conducting the *t* test with a sample size of 30 and a sample size of 300 participants, different results for the hypothesis test will be seen. The significantly different results are due to sample size. When sample sizes are large, the values of the *sample standard error* (S_E) *will be close to that of the population standard error, and the distribution of the* t *statistic will be very nearly normal. On the other hand, when the sample size is small, the values of* S_E *may vary considerably from the population mean* ($\mu_{\bar{x}}$) *or the hypothesized population parameter.* The *t* distribution may also depart considerably from that of the normal distribution of *z*. This is based on the validation that was completed by William S. Gosset (as cited by King et al., 2011), who published an article anonymously in 1899 using the name "Student" in Dublin, Ireland, while teaching at the University College and working for the Guinness brewery company.

For either purpose, the *one-sample* t *test* can be used to compare a sample mean or sample statistic ($\bar{X}$) to a population mean ($\mu_{\bar{x}}$). The lowercase Greek mu (μ) sign, pronounced mew, is typically used to represent the term *population parameter* and *X*-bar is used for the term *sample mean*. Therefore, when μ is used with the subscript *X*-bar, it describes the *population mean*. King et al. (2011) stated that to use the one-sample *t* test, we first must know the population parameter (μ). However, in most situations, either or both the population means ($\mu_{\bar{x}}$) or the population standard deviation (μ_{SD}) will not be known. Because μ is rarely known, the researcher must estimate the sample standard error of the difference in mean S_E using the sample standard deviation. The formula to estimate μ from the sample standard deviation is

$$S_E = \frac{SD}{\sqrt{n-1}}$$

where

S_E = Estimated standard error of the mean
SD = Sample standard deviation

Therefore, the one-sample *t* statistic is calculated by the formula

$$t = \frac{\bar{X} - \mu_{\bar{x}}}{S_E}$$

or, in simplified form, it is calculated by

$$t = \frac{\bar{X} - \mu_{\bar{x}}}{SD/\sqrt{n-1}}$$

where

t = *t* statistic (or calculated *t*)
$\bar{X}$ = Sample mean
$\mu_{\bar{x}}$ = Population mean or the hypothesized parameter for the *t* statistic

PRACTICAL SITUATION USING THE ONE-SAMPLE *t* TEST

Suppose that the department of social services in the area or region of your home residence reported that in the past 3 years there were 10,000 children temporarily or permanently removed from the custody of their parents or caretakers due to abuse and neglect. Of the children removed, your county averaged ($\overline{X}$) 1,500 children for the reporting period. The government stated that, on average ($\mu_{\overline{X}}$), 2,000 children were removed from every county in the past 3 years with a standard deviation of 800. By reviewing the numbers, it is evident that your home county's removal of the 1,500 children was below the state's overall average of 2,000 but within 1 *SD*. (The number of removals was higher than 800, but it was well within 1 *SD*.) Because of this, it is desired to examine further whether your county is statistically different from other counties based on a 95% confidence interval and a two-tailed hypothesis. The stated hypotheses are as follows:

- H_0: There is no significant difference between your home county and the overall average.
- H_a: There is a significant difference between your county and the overall average.

Based on the report,

Your home county average ($\overline{X}$) = 1,500
Overall government average ($\mu_{\overline{X}}$) = 2,000
SD = 800
n = 10,000

The t *distribution can be computed by*

$$t = \frac{1,500 - 2,000}{800 / \sqrt{10,000 - 1}} \rightarrow \text{Notice that } S_E \text{ is computed by } = SD / \sqrt{n - 1}$$

$$t = \frac{-500}{800 / \sqrt{9,999}}$$

t = −62.5 this is the t-statistic (calculated t)

Similar to chi-square (Chapter 7) and correlation (Chapter 8) statistical tests, the calculated *t* statistic of 62.5 (−62.5) still does not explain anything about the population from which the sample was drawn, particularly the null hypothesis (H_0). In the scientific community, results must be scientifically based before one can generalize findings from a sample drawn from the population. This scientific method of conclusion is done by comparing the calculated values with some types of standardized values. For this *t* test, before retaining or rejecting H_0, see Table 9.1 (which provides critical values of the *t* distribution) to determine whether the calculated *t* statistic is such that the null hypothesis is rejected. To find the critical values of the *t* distribution, two important pieces of information are required: (a) the tail of the hypothesis and (b) the degrees of freedom (*df*) involved in the research project. In computing the *t* statistic, statisticians recommend that one of the respondents/participants be allowed to vary. The reason is that in human society everyone has his or her own biases; therefore, to minimize biases it is best that one respondent's/participant's scores be allowed to vary. The degrees of freedom are computed by

$$Degrees\ of\ freedom\ (df) = (n - 1)$$
$$= 10,000 - 1$$
$$= 9,999$$

Then, check to see whether the *df* column in Table 9.1 lists the 9,999. Because the table goes only as far as 120, use the last row on the table, 95% confidence interval and two-tailed hypothesis, for the critical value of *t*. *The critical value of the* t *distribution is equal to 1.980. Notice that even though the values obtained from a standardized table are called critical values of* t *distribution, they are used interchangeably with the term* t statistic. Because the calculated *t* statistic is much larger than the critical values (ignoring the negative sign in front of *t*), the H_0 hypothesis is rejected, and H_a is supported.

In summary, findings from the one-sample *t* statistic indicate that the number of children removed by child protective services agencies was statistically different for your county compared to the overall average for all counties ($t = -62.5$, $df = 9,999$, $p < .05$). The negative calculated *t* statistic also indicates that your county had significantly fewer children removed by child protective services compared to the overall average for all counties. Because of the negative calculated *t*, the population mean ($\mu_{\overline{X}}$) is larger than the sample mean ($\overline{X}$). The statistical configurations (i.e., $t = -62.5$, $df = 9,999$, $p < .05$) are conditions required by the American Psychological Association (APA) style.

THE INDEPENDENT SAMPLES *T* TEST

INDEPENDENT SAMPLES *t* TEST AND ITS RELATION TO HEALTH AND HUMAN SERVICES

The independent samples t *test can be used to evaluate the differences in means* ($\overline{X}$) *between two unrelated, unconnected groups, or do-not-match pairs that are selected at random from the population.* For example, it can be used to study the difference between two groups of individuals given Western-style psychotherapy (i.e., cognitive behavioral modification) as an experimental group and a third given only Eastern styles of healing as the control group (i.e., Buddhist blessing) or between two randomized samples of Asian and Caucasian youth pertaining to the degrees of recidivism. The independent samples *t* test could be used to test a hypothesis concerning job satisfaction of two independent groups, such as social workers and psychologists.

HYPOTHESIZING THE DIFFERENCE BETWEEN TWO INDEPENDENT (UNRELATED) SAMPLES

Suppose that two juvenile groups were randomly drawn from the community to participate in a behavior modification program as a way to investigate whether this type of behavior modification might be a useful therapeutic tool to alleviate juvenile recidivism. One of the groups was Asian (μ_1) and the other group was Caucasian (μ_2). Assume that each group was composed of 150 youths. Without going through the long and tedious calculations, assume that the treatment helpfulness behavior modification measure was based on a scale from 1 (not helpful at all) to 10 (extremely helpful). At the end of the program, the Asian youths averaged 8.82 ($\overline{X}_1$) on the treatment helpfulness scale with the sum of the squares (SS_1^2) of 16,210, and the Caucasian youths averaged 9.65 ($\overline{X}_2$) with a sum of the squares (SS_2^2) of 17,834 (see Chapter 4 on how to calculate the sum of squares).

Table 9.1 Critical Values of *t*

df	Level of Significance for Two-Tailed Test					
	.10	.05	.025	.01	.005	.0005
	Level of Significance for Two-Tailed Test					
	.20	.10	.05	.02	.01	.001
1	3.078	6.314	12.706	31.821	63.657	36.619
2	1.886	2.920	4.303	6.965	9.925	31.598
3	1.638	2.343	3.182	4.541	5.841	12.941
4	1.533	2.132	2.776	3.747	4.604	8.610
5	1.476	2.015	2.571	3.365	4.032	6.859
6	1.440	1.943	2.447	3.143	3.707	5.959
7	1.415	1.895	2.365	2.998	3.449	5.405
8	1.397	1.860	2.306	2.896	3.355	5.041
9	1.383	1.833	2.262	2.821	3.250	4.781
10	1.372	1.812	2.228	2.764	3.169	4.587
11	1.363	1.796	2.201	2.718	3.106	4.437
12	1.356	1.782	2.179	2.681	3.055	4.318
13	1.350	1.771	2.160	2.650	3.012	4.221
14	1.345	1.761	2.145	2.624	2.977	4.140
15	1.341	1.753	2.131	2.602	2.947	4.073
16	1.337	1.746	2.120	2.583	2.921	4.015
17	1.333	1.740	2.110	2.567	2.898	3.965
18	1.330	1.734	2.101	2.552	2.878	3.922
19	1.328	1.729	2.093	2.539	2.861	3.883
20	1.325	1.725	2.086	2.528	2.845	3.850

(*continued*)

Table 9.1 Continued

df	Level of Significance for Two-Tailed Test					
	.10	.05	.025	.01	.005	.0005
	Level of Significance for Two-Tailed Test					
	.20	.10	.05	.02	.01	.001
21	1.323	1.721	2.080	2.518	2.831	3.819
22	1.321	1.717	2.074	2.508	2.819	3.792
23	1.319	1.714	2.069	2.500	2.807	3.767
24	1.318	1.711	2.064	2.492	2.797	3.745
25	1.316	1.708	2.060	2.485	2.787	3.725
26	1315	1.706	2.056	2.479	2.779	3.707
27	1.314	1.703	2.052	2.473	2.771	3.690
28	1.313	1.701	2.048	2.467	2.763	3.674
29	1.311	1.699	2.045	2.462	2.756	3.659
30	1.310	1.697	2.042	2.457	2.750	3.646
40	1.303	1.684	2.021	2.423	2.704	3.551
60	1.296	1.671	2.000	2.390	2.660	3.460
120	1.289	1.658	1.980	2.358	2.617	3.373
∞	1.282	1.645	1.960	2.326	2.576	3.291

Reprinted from J. Welkowitz, B. H. Cohen, & B. R. Lea. (2012). *Introductory statistics for the behavioral sciences* (7th ed.). Hoboken, NJ: Wiley. With permission from Wiley & Sons.

As in all inferential statistics, there are two key purposes for testing hypotheses for the independent samples *t* test.

1. Is the difference between the two sample means statistically significant? Be aware that, in statistical analyses, differences among a set of scores or some percentage changes may or may not be enough to show statistically significant differences between the variables under investigation.
2. If there is statistical significance, how will the results of the research study be generalized back to the population from which the sample was randomly drawn? Recall that in Chapter 6 the terms *generalize* and *infer* apply to the degrees of confidence in the sample being representative of the population from which it was drawn.

For these two reasons, the goal of conducting hypothesis testing on the juvenile helpfulness treatment scale is to see whether the two means are statistically different. If they are different, are the gaps between the means $(\overline{X})$ for Asian and Caucasian youth groups representative of *all* youths? The terms *youths* and *populations* are statistical concepts used to describe adolescents locally, nationally, or internationally, depending on where and how the study is conducted.

Most population parameters for the independent samples *t* test, including the one-sample *t* test, are not known $(\mu_1 - \mu_2)$. Because the population parameters are not known, the standard error is unknown. However, the sample standard error of the difference in the two means (S_{E1-E2}) can be estimated. The way to estimate the standard error for the two independent means is more complicated. The formula for estimating the *t* statistic for independent samples *t* test is

$$t = \frac{\overline{X}_1 - \overline{X}2}{S_{E1-E2}}$$

where

$\overline{X}_1$ = Sample mean for Group 1
$\overline{X}_2$ = Sample mean for Group 2
S_{E1-E2} = Estimated standard error of the difference in the two means

When equal variances (homogeneity of variance) are assumed ($N_1 = N_2$ or $\mu_1 = \mu_2$), the *estimated standard error* is computed by

$$S_{E1-E2} = \sqrt{\frac{SS_1^2 + SS_2^2}{(n_1 + n_2) - 2}\left(\frac{1}{n_1} + \frac{1}{n_2}\right)}$$

where

SS_1^2 = Sum of the square for Group 1
SS_2^2 = Sum of the square for Group 2
n_1 = Sample size for Group 1
n_2 = Sample size for Group 2

Even though the formula for calculating the *estimated standard error between two independent means* looks a bit intimidating, the calculation is not that complicated. Next, the independent *t* test calculation is shown for the situation when behavior modification regarding recidivism is based on equal variances.

CALCULATING THE CHILD RECIDIVISM TREATMENT HELPFULNESS FOR INDEPENDENT SAMPLES

Looking at the hypothetical situation concerning behavior modification for Asian and Caucasian youths, the information presented can be organized into an easily understood format, as shown in Table 9.2.

When equal variances are assumed, the *estimated standard error of the two difference means* can be calculated as follows:

$$S_{E1-E2} = \sqrt{\frac{16,210+17,834}{(150+150)-2}\left(\frac{1}{150}+\frac{1}{150}\right)}$$

$$= \sqrt{\frac{34,044}{300-2}(.0067+.0067)}$$

$$= \sqrt{\frac{34,044}{298}(.0134)}$$

$$= \sqrt{(114.24)(.0134)}$$

$$= \sqrt{1.53}$$

$$= 1.24$$

Knowing the estimated standard error of the two independent means, the *t* statistic is calculated as follows:

$$t = \frac{8.82-9.65}{1.24}$$

$$= \frac{-0.83}{1.24}$$

$$= -0.67$$

Table 9.2 *Behavior Modification for Asian and Caucasian Youth*

Concept	Race	
	Asian	Caucasian
Sample size (*n*)	150	150
Sample mean ($\overline{X}_1$) on a scale from 1 to 10	8.82	9.65
Sum of squares (SS^2) or total variances	16,210	17,834

To see whether there is a significant difference between the two independent means, the degrees of freedom for the independent samples *t* test are computed by

$$Degrees \ of \ freedom \ (df) = (n_1 + n_2 - 2)$$

$$df = 150 + 150 - 2$$

$$= 298$$

The *t* statistic is –0.67, with 298 degrees of freedom. Assume a 99% confidence interval, two-tailed hypothesis, to examine the result of this study. At 99% confidence, two-tailed hypothesis, the critical value is equal to 2.167 (see Table 9.1). The conclusion is that, at the 99% confidence interval, there is no statistically significant difference in means between Asian and Caucasian youths (*t* = –0.67, *df* = 298, *p* > .01). However, it is unknown *whether behavior modification was or was not effective in helping the two youth groups on recidivism.* To justify the effectiveness of behavior modification, other statistical results are required, such as variability (Chapter 4) or the effect size (discussed at the end of this chapter). *The independent* t *test simply indicates that there is a statistically significant difference between two means.*

THE DEPENDENT SAMPLES *T* TEST

The dependent samples t *test is an appropriate statistical procedure for comparing the means* $(\overline{X})$ *of two groups selected at random from the population that fall under one of these concepts: connected, correlated, or related to each other, matched pairs, or repeated-measure design.* Often, the two means are matched or correlated due to their similarities in *characteristics, values, and conditions* but then are split into two comparable groups. For example, address a statistical test focusing on income differential between newly hired female and male employees at a county or state agency. The term *newly hired* is a characteristic that female and male employees of a county or state agency all fall under.

First, examine hypothesized means of the population and sample means. The calculation is completed by comparing the two samples means $(\overline{D})$ with the hypothesized values of the population mean $(\mu_{\overline{D}})$ and dividing the difference by the estimated standard error of the mean of difference scores $(S_{\overline{D}})$.

$$t = \frac{\overline{D} - \mu_{\overline{D}}(hypothesized)}{S_{\overline{D}}}$$

where

$\underline{D}$ = Differences in scores between *X* and *Y* or sample of difference scores
$\overline{D}$ = Mean of the sample set of different scores
$\mu_{\overline{D}}$ (hypothesized) = Hypothesized mean of the population of difference scores
$S_{\overline{D}}$ = Estimated standard error of the mean of difference scores

Generally, the *hypothesized mean of the difference between X and Y scores* is not known $(\mu_X - \mu_Y)$. Because the hypothesized mean of the different scores is not known, the *null hypothesis* is also not known $(H_0 : \mu_D = 0)$. Therefore, the *estimated standard error of the mean of difference scores* $(S_{\bar{D}})$ *is calculated as*

$$S_{\bar{D}} = \sqrt{\frac{\sum D^2 - \dfrac{\left(\sum D\right)^2}{n}}{n-1}}$$

Thus, the t *statistic for the dependent sample* is computed by

$$t = \frac{\bar{D}}{\sqrt{\dfrac{\sum D^2 - \dfrac{\left(\sum D\right)^2}{n}}{n(n-1)}}}$$

The next section has a sample demonstration regarding how the dependent samples *t* statistic is calculated. Recall how the mean deviation, variance, and standard deviation were calculated in Chapter 4; the denominator portion of the dependent samples *t* is calculated in the same manner. The only difference between the two procedures is that measures of variability under descriptive statistics examine the values of one variable at a time, while dependent samples factor two related scores into the computation.

THE DEPENDENT SAMPLES *t* TEST AND ITS
RELATION TO HEALTH AND HUMAN SERVICES

Table 9.3 depicts scores of 15 clients receiving individual psychotherapy counseling for the past several weeks at a public mental health program. The scores were collected from the caseload of a mental health clinician and based on the Global Assessment Functioning (GAF score) scale of the *Diagnostic and Statistical Manual of Mental Disorders* (*DSM*) (APA, 2000). The GAF score was used to provide a general assessment of a client's level of functioning before receiving treatment, as well as after the client had spent several weeks with the clinician.

The dependent *t* test is calculated as follows:

$$t = \frac{-14.87 - \mu_{\bar{D}(\text{hypothesized})}}{\sqrt{\dfrac{4,199 - (-223)^2 / 15}{15(15-1)}}} \quad \left(\text{the hypothesized population mean is not known} = 0\right)$$

$$= \frac{-14.87}{\sqrt{\dfrac{4,199 - 49,729 / 15}{210}}}$$

$$= \frac{-14.87}{\sqrt{\dfrac{4,199 - 3,315.27}{210}}}$$

$$= \frac{-14.87}{2.05}$$

$t = -7.245$ (This is the calculated value for the t-statistic)

Table 9.3: GAF Score of Clients Before and After Treatment

ID	Before (*X*)	After (*Y*)	Difference (*D*) $D = X - Y$	Difference Square (*D*)^2 $D^2 = (D)(D)$
01	30	50	−20	400
02	20	55	−35	1,225
03	35	45	−10	100
04	40	65	−25	625
05	38	51	−13	169
06	27	35	−8	64
07	25	45	−20	400
08	15	30	−15	225
09	17	29	−12	144
10	28	32	−4	16
11	32	40	−8	64
12	21	30	−9	81
13	10	25	−15	225
14	25	35	−10	100
15	36	55	−19	361

$$\sum D = -223$$
$$\overline{D} = -223/15$$
$$= -14.87$$

$$\sum D^2 = 4,199$$

The degree of freedom for the dependent sample *t* test is computed by $(n - 2)$ because of two related groups:

$$Degrees\ of\ freedom\ (df) = n - 2 = 15 - 2 \rightarrow 13$$

Assume that the research study used a *p* value of .01, two-tailed hypothesis, at 13 *df*, the *t* distribution is equal to 3.012 (see Table 9.1). *Keep in mind that there are no laws of statistics requiring a specific level of confidence or tail of the hypothesis. Therefore, when testing hypotheses, the researcher specifies the confidence interval and judges whether the research project is better suited with a one- or two-tailed hypothesis.* Because the calculated *t* statistic is larger than the critical value of the *t* distribution (as discussed previously, ignore the negative symbol), H_0 is rejected. As stated in Chapter 6 concerning the various statistical assumptions about inferential statistics, it is safe to conclude that the GAF scores for the 15 individual clients receiving psychotherapy counseling also significantly improved in past weeks ($t = -7.25$, $df = 13$, $p < .01$). Again, the symbols inside the parentheses are statistical notations required by the APA. As discussed, do not confuse the negative sign. The negative signs in column 4 of Table 9.3 simply indicate that the posttest scores were higher than the pretest scores. Essentially, due to the effects of psychotherapeutic techniques, all 15 clients significantly improved their self-perceptions scores; however, in the real world that might not happen. For either situation discussed, to examine treatment effects, the effect size must be computed.

EFFECT SIZE

In addition to converting the z score into a percentile and calculating a specific score (see Chapter 5), the researcher needs to see where the z score falls under the standard normal curve. The z score can also be used to estimate the degree to which treatment effect is present in the population. For example, the researcher may want information about the means of two groups in terms of how many standard deviations one group's mean is above or below another group's mean (King et al., 2011; Weinbach & Grinnell, 2015). The difference between the size of the phenomenon in the population and the sample mean is called the *effect size*. In statistical calculation, it is better known as *Cohen's d* (Coolidge, 2013; Welkowitz et al., 2012). Most important, effect size applies the same concept as the z score (Chapter 5). The only difference between the z score and effect size is the application of the concept. While the z score is used for many different purposes, effect size is used mainly to compare mean difference between two groups, such as experimental and control group. Illustrated here is an example of the effect size for experimental group and control group means:

$$Effect\ Size\ (ES) = \frac{\text{Experimental group mean} - \text{control group mean}}{\text{Standard deviation}}$$

For example, as a mental health clinician, an intervention program for US veterans with post-traumatic stress disorder (PTSD) is established. One of the groups, assigned as the experimental group, receives several treatment modalities, including individual psychotherapy, medication, and spirituality. The other group is assigned to the control group, with the exception that both the experimental and the control group receive medication. Only the control group is encouraged to obtain spiritual help as provided by churches, temples, and mosques. After 3 months, the effectiveness of the experiment regarding psychotherapy, medication, and spirituality is measured. Contrasted with the control treatment groups, the effectiveness of medication and self-help from faith-based organizations is measured. The outcome of the study will be used to describe the mental and spiritual well-being of military personnel. Assume that the experimental group is the first mean $(\overline{X}_1)$, and the control group is the second mean $(\overline{X}_2)$. If at the end of the study the result produces a positive effect size, then the researcher can describe treatment effects.

In this scenario about veterans, suppose that an instrument with a scale ranging from 1 to 10 is used to measure the effectiveness of the two treatment programs. Calculations of effect size include

Experimental group mean $(\overline{X}_1) = 8.31$

Control group mean $(\overline{X}_2) = 4.47$

Overall (combined) standard deviation (SD) for both groups $= 1.32$

Effect Size (ES) $= ?$

This leads to solving the effect size as

$$ES = \frac{8.31 - 4.47}{1.32}$$

$$ES = +2.91 \left(\textit{This is comparable to a } z - score \textit{ of } +2.91 \textit{ as well}\right)$$

The +2.91 *ES* (use the plus sign to indicate that the result is above the mean) indicates that the experimental group achieved nearly 3 *SD* above the mean and over the control group. Because effect size is used to estimate treatment effects in population parameters in the same way as the standard score, the same rules of statistics discussed in Chapter 5 apply. By using 2.91 to find the percentile in Table 5.1, it corresponds to 49.82%. The statistics rules concerning *z* scores state that if the calculated *z* score is positive (+), add 50% to the percentile obtained from the standard normal curve table ($Z_{critical}$). Because the effect size is above the mean (positive), the final solution for this experimental project with US veterans becomes

$$+\ 50\% \ +\ 49.82\% = 99.82\%$$

The research results indicate that US veterans who received multiple treatment modalities, especially the inclusion of psychotherapy, improved their PTSD conditions over those who received only medication and encouragement from the clinicians to seek spiritual help from faith-based organizations. Although this computation is not based on a statistical test, the result of nearly 3 *SD* (*ES* = +2.91) indicates that the group of veterans who received psychotherapy along with other treatment modalities improved their levels of functioning to above 99%.

SUMMARY

In this chapter, a brief summary of how *t* tests can be applied to various situations and for evaluating one's practice outcome was provided. Overall, the one-sample *t* test can be used to examine the following possible health and human services issues:

- Any type of intervention program in which the criterion or dependent variable is interval or ratio, for example, the volume of drug and alcohol abuse based on specific criteria; the scale of personal functioning of a sample and the population; and comparing a sample mean on treatment sessions with the population mean of that group

The independent samples *t* test can be used with the following issues:

- Comparing two independently drawn samples with a health and human services component, for example, the effectiveness of an outreach program for children with attention deficit hyperactivity disorder for children's groups A and B, for which A and B are not related; school counseling methods with no more than two methods for children with learning disabilities and for which each method is independently designed; and self-rated perceptions regarding practice effectiveness of two unrelated groups, such as nurses and social workers

The dependent samples *t* test can be used in the following potential situations: comparing two related scores, for example, pretest and post-test scores of psychotherapeutic drugs; changes in cognitive behavior; behavior modification approaches; or job training compliance for two related groups.

Table 9.4 Self-Assertiveness Training Evaluation

Pair	Literature Reading	In Training Program
01	4	6
02	5	8
03	3	7
04	5	9
05	4	6
06	4	8
07	6	10
08	5	8
09	4	9
10	4	7
11	6	5
12	4	7
13	6	8
14	5	7
15	3	8

STUDY QUESTIONS

1. Suppose that the calculated t is 12.87, $df = 20$, p value $= .001$, two tailed. What should be done with H_0?
2. What are the three types of t test? List each and explain how they might be used in your field of study.
3. Table 9.4 displays scores from 15 pairs of high school students who were invited to participate in self-assertiveness training. Half of the students were enrolled in a training program conducted by a local expert in self-assertiveness, while the other half was encouraged to read the literature on self-assertiveness provided by the trainer. After 3 months, the researcher administered a research questionnaire containing variables related to self-assertiveness. Assume that the evaluative tool used a scale ranging from 1 to 10 (higher score indicates more assertive).

Complete the following tasks:

a. State the null and research hypotheses for the research study.
b. Name the type of t test for the research.
c. Complete the test of the statistic for the research study. Then, use a 99.9% confidence interval, two-tailed hypothesis, to discuss the research finding.

ANSWERS TO STUDY QUESTIONS

1. H_0 is rejected ($t = 12.87$, $df = 20$, $p < .001$).
2. One sample, independent samples, and dependent samples.

3.

    a. H_0: No significant difference between just reading the literature provided by the training and those invited to participate in self-assertiveness training. H_a: There is a significant difference between the variables under investigation.

    b.   The dependent samples *t* test

    c. H_0 is not supported. The group of high school students receiving assertiveness training performed significantly better on self-rated assertive scores than the student group provided only reading literature ($t = 7.69$, $df = 13$, $p < .001$).

INFERENTIAL STATISTICS

Simple Linear Regression

OVERVIEW

Simple linear regression is a *bivariate* (two variables) statistical application that can be used to infer or predict outcome. Regression by itself can be difficult to learn in a statistics course. The statistical computations are complex and time consuming. A course in multivariate regression is necessary to fully understand terms that are related to regression analyses, such as factors analysis, logistic regression, and causal modeling. *Multivariate* means three or more variables, a dependent and two or more independent variables.

In correlation and linear regression analysis, the *dependent* variable is better known as the *criterion* or *outcome* variable, and the *independent* variable is better known as the *predictor* variable; therefore, these two concepts are used throughout the chapter.

In this chapter, the basic predictive functions of regression are introduced. Meyers, Gamst, and Guarino (2006) stated that when we use a single variable to predict another single variable, the procedure is called *simple linear regression* (p. 127). Meyers and colleagues also stated that the Pearson correlation between two variables can be used as a basis for predicting the values for one variable given knowledge of the values of the other. As a result, linear regression amounts to an advanced version of the Pearson correlation coefficient.

In Chapter 8, the correlation coefficient (represented by an *r* and which provides an overall picture of the linear relationship between two interval/ratio variables) was discussed. The *r* also provides an understanding about the strength of the relationship. Using the laws of probability, by examining the correlation coefficient or the coefficient of determination r^2, we know that the linear relationship produced by two or more variables probably was not due to chance or sampling error. This means that the result actually represents the population from which the sample was randomly drawn. Based on the coefficient of determination alone, we know that a certain portion of the variability of the dependent variable can be explained. There is a question regarding what causes the explained portion of the variability. Another question occurs when we want to use the values of a specific independent variable to make a prediction about the effects it has on the dependent variable. Whether through correlation analyses, common sense, or other personal logic, we know that regardless of the dependent variable under investigation, many factors can affect or influence the dependent variable investigated.

In Chapter 8, we found the correlation coefficient for socialization skills of children coming from specific family sizes was equal to .8685 ($r = .8685$). *If this correlation coefficient is squared and the product multiplied by 100%, the result, 75.43%, becomes powerful.* The result of this multiplication is called the *coefficient of determination*, usually abbreviated as r squared (r^2). Notice that r and r^2 were computed and discussed in Chapter 8. To find the variation accounted for in the research study, simply recalculate the Pearson r.

While the children's socialization skills (dependent variable) can be explained by family size (independent variable), the other 24.57% ($100 - 75.43 = 24.57$) could not be accounted for. As researchers, beyond family size, it is desirable to discover what else influenced the ability of these children to socialize with their significant others. Statistically, the children's ability to socialize with other children can be explained by answering a very important question:

What other variables could be studied as predictors of children's socialization skills?

Linear regression analysis is one possible statistical tool that possibly could help answer this question. Essentially, if statistical proof exists that family size is an influential factor, then possibly the public might be encouraged to train all children to make friends at home and outside the home environment. Meyers and colleagues (2006) explained that simple linear regression is a procedure that uses a single variable to predict another single variable.

THE MEANING OF LINEAR REGRESSION

Regression analysis goes beyond correlation analysis. It is a belief among statistics teachers that if two variables are related, it is possible to make causal prediction because it provides better accuracy about the generalization of the variables under investigation. *Regression* literally means going back or returning (Weinbach & Grinnell, 2015). It is a linear function that provides either a good or a poor description of the relationships of how *Y* (the criterion variable) relates to *X* (the predictor variable) in a straight line (Agresti & Finlay, 2009). It also measures a linear relationship between two interval/ratio variables in which the observations displayed in a scatter diagram can be approximated with a straight line (Leon-Guerrero & Frankfort-Nachmias, 2012). Leon-Gurrero and Frankfort-Nachmias specifically stated that "the line itself provides a predicted value of Y for any value of X" (p. 234). In simple terms, this means that *regression results from the actions taken by the researcher* (researchers analyze outcomes by manipulating the value of *X* to predict the value of *Y*) *rather than the scores themselves.* The underlying goal in regression analysis is to organize data and explain its effects on the variables. Suppose that in a research study, a significant relationship is observed between the dependent (*Y*) and independent (*X*) variables. If nothing is done to *X*, then nothing will happen to *Y*. Take, for example, the study hours of college students. In regression analysis, the hypothesis is that knowledge gained is directly related to the time spent in study. In this case, knowledge *Y* is a direct effect of study hours *X*. We know that correlation analysis simply shows that there is a relationship between knowledge and study hours but nothing concerning other possible contributing factors. Regression takes us a step further by examining the effects of study hours. Therefore, someone who spent considerable time studying can say that X is a necessary phenomenon in understanding the empirical effects of the subject matter Y.

The amount of effects, specifically the slope of the regression line, matters most in linear regression. Why? This is because statistical analyses involving one or more forms of regression always include the correlation coefficient r and the coefficient of determination r^2 as there generally is no perfect correlation between the variables.

THE MEANING OF PREDICTION IN HEALTH
AND HUMAN SERVICES

Health and human services workers, such as social workers, nurses, physical therapists, and speech pathologists, as well as behaviorists like clinical psychologists, often are called on to make informed guesses about causes and factors that are related to certain health conditions, behavioral issues, or types of interventions. The following are several applicable statements in health and human services settings where linear regression can be helpful:

- Social workers may want to know how best to predict child maltreatment due to chemical dependency (i.e., illegal drugs and hard liquors).
- Speech pathologists may want to predict early onset intervention for children with speech impediments.
- Nurses may want to examine the causes and effects of medical noncompliance.
- Physical therapists may want to predict the effect of exercises on people who are involved in car accidents.
- Clinical psychologists may want to examine the effects of drugs prescribed by psychiatrists in treating children's attention deficit and hyperactivity disorders.

Results produced by regression will enable individuals from many professions to make educated guesses regarding certain outcome (Y) variables based on the value of a particular predictor (X) variable. Before looking at the computational formula for making predictions on these issues, let us look at the rules of statistics pertaining to linear regression.

STATISTICAL REQUIREMENTS/CONDITIONS
FOR LINEAR REGRESSION

The following conditions are important when calculating linear regression:

Similar to other forms of statistical tests, linear regression involves the use of inferential statistics. Inferential statistics is the body of statistical computations relevant to extrapolating findings based on a sample to a larger population.
- A requisite is random sampling; however, in health and human services settings, there may be situations for which random sampling is impossible, especially when

the number of clients is small. In situations like this, random *assignment* instead of random sampling may prove useful.

- The sampling distribution must be normally distributed under the areas of the normal curve.
- The dependent and independent variables must be continuous and interval or ratio level.

In addition to interval- or ratio-level data, the data must be *homoscedastic*, which means that the degree of variation in the two variables being correlated is similar and does not vary widely.

COMPUTATIONAL FORMULA
FOR LINEAR REGRESSION

Making a prediction is not as hard and complex as described. The computational formula for making a prediction is simple and can be computed by

$$Y' = a + bX$$

where

- Y' = Predicted regression coefficient (also called the *predicted Y value* from a particular X value).
- $a = Y$ *intercept*. It is the point where the regression line would intercept the y axis. It is better known as the *constant*.
- b = Slope of the regression line, where the amount of change in Y is directly related to the amount of change in X (better known as the *regression coefficient*).
- X = Selected value of the predictor variable about which researchers want to make a prediction concerning the value of the dependent variable or Y.

With all the statistical symbols used throughout the book to this point, the only one in this equation that you are familiar with is X. The symbols "a = Constant or the Y intercept" and "b = Slope of the regression line" and "Y' = Predicted regression coefficient" in the equation are new; therefore, let us see how they are calculated. The first symbol in the equation, the *constant* or a is computed by

$$a = \overline{Y} - b(\overline{X})$$

where

$\overline{Y}$ = Mean of Y (arithmetic average for the dependent variable)
$\overline{X}$ = Mean of X (arithmetic average for the independent variable)

Please note that the constant a cannot be computed without the slope b of the regression line. The computational formula for the slope of the regression is computed as

$$\textit{Slope for the regression line} \rightarrow b = \frac{N\left(\sum XY\right) - \left(\sum X\right)\left(\sum Y\right)}{N\left(\sum X^2\right) - \left(\sum XY\right)^2}$$

where

N = Total sample size for the study project

$\sum XY$ = Sum of the products between X and Y

$\sum X$ = Sum of the independent/predictor variables

$\sum Y$ = Sum of the independent/criterion variables

$\sum X^2$ = Sum of X squares

$\sum Y^2$ = Sum of Y squares

Also, note that from algebra to advanced statistics, there are different formulas to calculate the slope. What we show here is one of them. You may notice that when calculating the slope using a partial segment of the correlation formula, it is computed using the first half of the Pearson correlation coefficient (r^2) formula without the square root, the sum for Ys squared and squaring the sum of Ys (see Chapter 8, Table 8.1). To help with your recollection of the Pearson correlation coefficient, it is redisplayed next:

$$r = \frac{N\left(\sum XY\right) - \left(\sum X\right)\left(\sum Y\right)}{\sqrt{\left[N\sum X^2 - (X)^2\right]\left[N\sum Y^2 - (Y)^2\right]}}$$

Now that you understand the general statistical concepts and symbols for the meaning of linear regression, let us apply this knowledge to situations related to health and human services.

PRACTICAL EXAMPLE USING LINEAR REGRESSION

In Chapter 8 (Tables 8.2 and 8.3), we presented a human behavior–related situation where the research study focused on socialization skills of children (Y) and the size of the children's family (X). Suppose that we pick a particular child from the list and use this one child to make predictions about socialization skills of children who have a similar family size. The question is then, How do we predict it? We copied information from Table 8.5 from Chapter 8 and pasted it in this chapter as Table 10.1 to make it easier for you to see.

Suppose that we now change the original hypotheses as follows:

- H_0 = Socialization skills of children have nothing to do with family size.
- H_a = Due to ongoing interactions with other siblings at home, children who come from larger families will have an easier time interacting with teachers and other students at school.

By examining the formula for computing the predicted regression line (Y'), we must calculate the slope of the regression line b and the constant a first. *Notice that the steps occur sequentially.* Because of this, let us begin with the slope, which is computed by

$$b = \frac{10(290) - (40)(67)}{10(176) - (40)^2}$$

$$= \frac{2900 - 2680}{1760 - 1600}$$

$$= \frac{220}{160}$$

$$b = 1.375$$

Table 10.1: Socialization Skills (Y) and Family Size (X) of Children

ID	X	X²	Y	Y²	XY
01	4	16	8	64	32
02	2	4	4	16	8
03	5	25	9	81	45
04	6	36	10	100	60
05	5	25	6	36	30
06	4	16	7	49	28
07	3	9	6	36	18
08	4	16	7	49	28
09	5	25	7	49	35
10	2	4	3	9	6
	$\sum X = 40$	$\sum X^2 = 176$	$\sum Y = 67$	$\sum Y^2 = 489$	$\sum XY = 290$
	$\overline{X} = 40/10$		$\overline{Y} = 67/10$		
	$= 4$		$= 6.7$		

This slope of the regression line indicates that every unit of change in the predictor X variable will have this amount of effect on the outcome Y variable. Next, we compute the constant a for the predicted regression coefficient.

$$a = \overline{Y} - b(\overline{X})$$

The *mean for the criterion variable* ($\overline{Y}$) (Table 8.2) = 67/10 = 6.7
The *mean for the predictor variable* ($\overline{X}$) (Table 8.2) = 40/10 = 4

The constant (a) is now computed by

$$a = 6.7 - 1.375(4)$$
$$= 6.7 - 5.5$$
$$a = 1.2$$

The result indicates that the Y intercept will always start at 1.2. More important, *we can say that before children's socialization skills increase or decrease, it always begins at 1.2 on a scale from 1 to 10* (see the values for Y in Table 8.2). Once the slope and constant have been computed, prediction can be made using any of the raw scores on the data set.

Now, we can select a specific child from the list in Table 8.2 to make a prediction about socialization skills of children that come from a similar family size. Of course, the sample we used for this illustration is actually too small. However, we can conduct a large-scale study using the same research design and statistical techniques discussed here and in Chapter 8 that will allow us to generalize findings to the larger population from which the sample was drawn.

Assume that we want to make two predictions. One is based on children who come from a family of three (X column for ID number 7) and another on children who come from a family of six (X column for ID number 4). The first predicted regression coefficient is computed by

$$Y'_3 = 1.2 + 1.375(3) \text{ [the subscript 3 is used to refer to family size of 3]}$$
$$= 1.2 + 4.125$$
$$Y'_3 = 5.325$$

The result of the finding predicts that children who come from a family of three, *if the null hypothesis is false, will have socialization skills of roughly 5.33 of 10* (scale from 1 to 10, where a higher score indicates better socialization skills). In other words, we state that if H_a is true, we speculate that most of the children that come from a family of three will have average socialization skills (middle score) with their peers. As discussed in Chapter 8, many factors influence a child's socialization skills.

The second prediction based on a family size of six now can be computed by

$$Y'_6 = 1.2 + 1.375(6)$$
$$= 1.2 + 8.25$$
$$Y'_6 = 9.45$$

This result indicates that children who come from a family of six, *if the null hypothesis is false, will have socialization skills of about 9.45 of 10.* If the scores for the children were randomly drawn from the population, children who come from a family of six could be expected to have better socialization skills. Essentially, we say that children who come from a family of six should have no problem making friends or interacting with other children and teachers at school.

OTHER STATISTICAL SYMBOLS (NOTATIONS)

What we have discussed thus far has involved only *linear regression*. There are many statistical configurations regarding *regression models* and other *regression coefficients*. We stated at the beginning of the chapter that the study of regression by itself is a difficult course and involves complex statistical computations. Because this is an introductory statistics book, the computations for other regression models and coefficients are not illustrated, but we want to explain some of the common statistical configurations that appear in a regression report. Similarly, when we use computerized regression programs to analyze data, these statistical configurations always appear on the output. Even if you do not know how the symbols (notations) were calculated, you should still be able to explain these additional symbols or notations rather easily.

- *R*. *R* is the correlation coefficient between the dependent and independent variables. It is the same as *r* in Chapter 8. The Statistical Package for the Social Sciences (SPSS) as well as statistics textbooks use the capital letter *R* to help you memorize that this correlation coefficient appears on the regression computations instead of the Pearson *r*.
- R^2. Because you now know that *R* is the same as *r*, then you should know that R^2 is the same as the coefficient of determination (r^2). Therefore, R^2 represents the amount of variation in the dependent variable that can be explained by one or more independent variables.
- Adjusted *R* square. R^2 adjusted is a more conservative measure than the standard R^2. It is based on the number of factors (predictor variables) entered in the regression analysis as opposed to the sample size. In using computerized programs to compute solutions, notice that each time you enter a new predictor variable to the regression model, the adjusted R^2 *always* becomes smaller than the standard R^2.
- Unstandardized regression coefficient (*B* or *b*). The first coefficient labeled "constant" is the *Y* intercept (*a*) where *X* meets *Y* for the first time. The coefficient below the "constant" is the slope in the regression equation (*b*). Remember that the *slope* of the line refers to the

proportion of change in the criterion variable (Y) for each unit of change in the predictor variable (X).

- Standardized regression coefficient (beta, β). Lowercase beta (β) is also known as a partial correlation coefficient representing a linear correlation between the criterion and predictor variables while controlling for the effect of other predictor variables in the analysis. Please note that when writing a research report, the *standardized coefficient* (β) is more desirable than the *unstandardized coefficient* (*b*). However, the previous illustrations in this chapter were based on *b* instead of β. They are calculated nearly the same way except, when calculating β, it is treated as the standardized slope coefficient based on the *z* score.

- *Statistical Significance.* When you have only one criterion and one predictor variable, report the significant difference between the variables using the column that shows the *t* statistic (Chapter 9). When there are two criteria and two or more predictor variables, explain the statistical significance using the *F* ratio (Chapter 11).

SUMMARY

This chapter introduced the basic form of regression analyses. Normally, statistical regression can be used for several research purposes: (a) The first is to make predictions about the criterion (dependent) variable based on the value of one or more predictor (independent) variables. (b) The second is to *imply causation* on the criterion variable due to the influences of one or more predictor variables, but it does not *prove causation*. This is usually referred to as the *confounding* variable(s). *Confounding* means that the values of the predictor variable(s) influenced or contributed most to the criterion variable. (c) The researchers may want to add or subtract one or more predictor variables to/from the regression run as a way to examine the relationship that these predictor variables have on the criterion variable.

The next chapter introduces the analysis of variance and is the last chapter introducing the basic functions of inferential statistics. Once you are knowledgeable about these and all the material presented in other chapters in this book, you will be well on your way to achieving competence in handling basic data analyses and interpretations.

STUDY QUESTIONS

1. If it is given that $\overline{X}$ = 78.21, $\overline{Y}$ = 18.55, b = .23, and X = 34, calculate Y'.
2. Suppose that you conducted a study to examine the relationship between children's self-esteem and the closeness of the relationship they have with their parents/caretakers using a scale from 1 to 10 (a higher score indicates higher self-esteem and a stronger relationship); the study produced a Y' equal to 6.23. Explain the finding in relation to the field of health and human services. Essentially, explain how this finding relates to self-esteem of children (there is no right or wrong answer).
3. Suppose that you are given S_{XY} = 98.21 and (SS_x^2) = 25.21. Compute b.
4. Suppose that, in an exploratory study, a social work researcher is interested in making predictions for married couples regarding ideal family size. For this reason, the

researcher randomly recruited 20 of 4,000 high school seniors from a large unified school district to participate as respondents. As a condition for the research project, the selected students must attend several marital counseling sessions that provide them with information on social, economic, psychological, and cultural factors that married couples commonly encounter in their marriages. Similarly, after attending the marital counseling sessions, they must be willing to answer a set of questions about themselves and their future marital prospects. Among the variables collected by the researcher, boys and girls will be asked independently about the size of family they would like to have once they are married. Assuming that the researcher will use boys as the criterion and girls as the predictor variable, complete the following tasks (using Table 10.2):

a. Complete all the necessary columns to reflect a Pearson correlation coefficient for the study. You do not need to compute the Pearson correlation coefficient. You need only create the columns to facilitate computation of the slope using the correlation formula.
b. Compute the slope of the line and the Y intercept for the research project.
c. Use female ID number 17 and male ID number 08; make an independent prediction about the family size that boys and girls would like to have once they are married.

Table 10.2 Ideal Family Size That Female and Male High School Students Would Like to Have

ID	Female Students	Male Students
01	3	3
02	5	4
03	6	6
04	4	3
05	4	8
06	3	5
07	5	5
08	4	8
09	4	5
10	5	3
11	5	5
12	3	3
13	4	6
14	5	7
15	3	5
16	5	5
17	2	4
18	4	5
19	4	4
20	3	4

ANSWERS TO STUDY QUESTIONS

1. $Y' = 8.37$.
2. On a scale from 1 to 10, a predicted regression coefficient of 6.23 indicates that the self-esteem of children in this sample is above average.
3. $b = 3.9$.
4.

   a. $\sum X = 81; \sum X^2 = 317; \sum Y = 98; \sum XY = 405; \overline{X} = \dfrac{81}{20} = 4.05; \overline{Y} = \dfrac{98}{20} = 4.9$

   b. $b = \dfrac{20(405) - (81)(98)}{20(317) - (81)^2}$

   $b = -0.73$

   $a = 4.9 - (-.73)(4.05)$

   $\quad = 4.9 + 2.97$

   $a = 7.86$

   c. $Y'_{girl17} = 7.86 + (-.73)(2)$

   $Y'_{girl17} = 6.4$

   $Y'_{boy8} = 7.86 + (-.73)(8)$

   $Y'_{boy8} = 2.02$

   Due to the negative slope, it is predicted that female students who stated that they now preferred a small family size may in fact have a larger family size in the future. On the contrary, male students who now expressed interest in a larger family size may in fact have a smaller family size in the future.

CHAPTER 11

INFERENTIAL STATISTICS

One-Way Analysis of Variance

OVERVIEW

This chapter discusses the interconnectedness between the *t* test (Chapter 9) and the one-way analysis of variance (ANOVA). Chapter 9 specified that the *t* test can be used only if the independent variable has only two groups (i.e., experimental and control, female and male, rural and urban). Which statistical test can be used with *multiple nominal-level independent variables*, such as burnout rates for three groups: Asian, Mexican, and Caucasian? The one-way ANOVA (also called simple ANOVA) is an inferential statistic that can accommodate any number of groups or levels.

Computer applications consider these multilevel nominal independent variables as factors. In ANOVA, factor analysis refers to a procedure used to study the relationship of two or more independent variables to a dependent variable. A single factor includes things such as the earnings of a group of people at a particular locale or the grade point average (GPA) of college students at different levels (i.e., freshman, sophomore, junior, and senior) at a college campus. ANOVA calculates the between- and within-group variances, with the difference between the two variance estimates provided by the Fisher's *F* distribution called the *F* ratio. Meyers et al. (2006) stated that "although the terminology differs somewhat, the conceptual underpinnings of the *t* test and the ANOVA are the same. They are both computed as the ratio of the variability (or differences) of sample means to an estimate of error variance" (p. 282).

THE *T* TEST AND *F* RATIO

In Appendix A, it is noted that when computing *t* tests using the Statistical Package for the Social Sciences (SPSS), the outputs always show both the *t* and the *F*. Meyers and colleagues (2006) pointed out that when there exists just one independent variable with two correlated conditions, it is possible to use either a *t* test or the *F* ratio to compare the means. Essentially, the choice between the *t* and an *F* ratio reflects the personal preference of the researchers if the independent variable has two correlated conditions. In general, researchers use the *t* test if they have two groups and *F* ratio for three or more groups because using multiple *t* tests will increase the odds of having a Type I error. Type I error is the chance of finding significance when there is none, and conducting multiple *t* tests would increase the error rate itself. The ANOVA *F* ratio is used instead of the *t* test when examining the differences between three or more groups or when the independent variable has three or more conditions.

For example, when examining income earning at a particular location, usually there are several different groups of people. The *F* ratio measures the difference of the group means versus the grand mean of scores for all subjects and compares against the remaining error. This error is the difference between the actual scores and the means of all of the groups. Thus, the Fisher's *F* distribution is a measure of the ratio of the systematic and unsystematic variance, and higher scores are considered better than lower scores (Meyers et al., 2006).

STATISTICAL ASSUMPTIONS

The ANOVA allows researchers to examine the means among two or more independent groups (*K*) to determine whether any differences are statistically significant. The capital letter *K* is usually used to denote *group*. Because ANOVA is similar to the independent samples *t* test, the same statistical assumptions are required, mainly interval or ratio data for the dependent variable and nominal data for the independent variables. Also, because the *F* ratio reflects variations among the means of several groups, a larger sample size is required to complete the study. Some social scientists suggest that a minimum sample of 50 subjects per group is necessary.

King et al. (2011, p. 315) provided the following assumptions associated with ANOVA:

- The populations are normally distributed.
- The variances of the several populations are the same (homogeneity of variance).
- Selection of elements comprising any particular sample is independent of selection of elements of any other sample.
- Samples are drawn at random with replacement. Are the data normally distributed? Use the scatter diagram to display the obtained scores to visualize the distributions.
- Similar to the independent samples *t* test, the dependent variable must be measured at the interval/ratio level, and the independent variable must be nominal.

OVERALL MEANING OF THE *F* RATIO

King et al. (2011) stated that "the ANOVA technique allows us to simultaneously compare several means with the level of significance specified by the investigator" (p. 300). The result of the *F* ratio essentially reflects the variation *among* the means ($\overline{X}$) of several groups (K) in relation to the variation *within* a group. While revealing whether there is truly a significant difference in group means, nothing is said about the *degree* or *amount* that one sample mean differs from the other.

Before computing the F ratio, it is important to understand two sources of variability that are always involved in the computational formula. These two sources, as explained next, are variability *between group means* and variability *within group means*.

TWO SOURCES OF VARIABILITY FOR ANOVA

It is well known to statistics instructors and researchers alike that when using ANOVA there are two sources of variability: (a) between group means and (b) within group means (should be among groups, but statisticians use the term within groups). Each source of variability has a distinct meaning.

VARIABILITY BETWEEN GROUP MEANS

Variability between group means refers to the variation among the means of treatment conditions due to either treatment effect or inherent chance of variation among the individuals in a research project. It is either the treatment effects or chance because each of the groups receives a different treatment.

VARIABILITY WITHIN GROUP MEANS

Variability within groups, on the other hand, is a little more complex than variability between group means. It is the variation of individual scores around the sample mean as a direct reflection of chance rather than as caused by different types of treatment. It is the variation between the sample mean and the scores due to chance and chance alone because members of the group receive the same treatment.

Witte (1993) explained variability between groups and variability within groups as follows:

> The variability between groups is variation among scores of subjects who are in different groups receiving different experimental treatments, and who therefore must be compared using completely independent estimates of variability within groups. That is, the variation among scores of subjects who being in the same group, receive the same experimental treatment (p. 338).

PRACTICAL SITUATION

An administrator at a school district, while investigating issues pertaining to students' truancy, decides to randomly select 15 ($n = 15$) teachers each from three schools to examine whether tardiness and unexcused absences of students are significant factors affecting truancy rates. Assume that the three schools are School A, School B, and School C, and that the main variable is the combined numbers of tardiness and unexcused absences for each teacher per month. As discussed previously, once the F ratio is computed, it should reveal whether tardiness and unexcused absences are significantly different among the three schools. However, the result does

Table 11.1 *Relationship Between Tardiness and Unexcused Absences*

Teacher	School A	School B	School C
01	0	4	3
02	3	0	2
03	2	1	0
04	4	0	3
05	2	1	2
06	4	5	4
07	2	1	2
08	5	0	4
09	4	3	1
10	5	2	3
11	3	4	5
12	2	4	3
13	6	5	4
14	2	3	2
15	2	1	2
$n = 15$	$\sum A = 46$	$\sum B = 34$	$\sum C = 40$

not reveal anything about school truancy. The combined numbers of tardiness and unexcused absences are listed in Table 11.1.

Due to advancements in statistical software programs, some researchers and statistics instructors are no longer concerned about the computational formula for the F ratio. However, it is important to know how a problem is typically or scientifically solved. *It is possible, that, without knowing the detailed computational formula and understanding the meaning of the elements involved in the computations, a teacher or instructor will have trouble explaining the findings to the larger audience.*

STEPS IN CALCULATING THE *F* RATIO

Figure 11.1 illustrates how the F ratio for the simple analysis of variance is computed. The step s involved in calculating the F ratio are numbered from 1 to 4 (see Figure 11.1). As is true of regression (Chapter 10), the F-ratio calculation is another complex procedure. Therefore, to better understand ANOVA's multifunctions, it is recommended that one take a course involving both the simple and the advanced forms of analysis of variance.

Please notice that the F ratio (Step 4) is computed by dividing the *mean square between groups* ($MS_{between}$) by the *mean square within groups* (MS_{within}). Before getting to Step 4, the first three steps must be completed. First, understand how the *sum of squares total* (SS_{total}) is computed, then compute it by adding the *sums of squares (variances) between groups* ($SS_{between}$) to the *sums of squares (variances) within groups* (SS_{within}). Recall that the term *sum of squares* was introduced in Chapter 4 and repeated in other chapters. For example, in Chapter 8, we discussed how the variances in the dependent variable (DV) could be explained by a particular independent variable (IV). When the term *sum of squares* is used, either in this chapter or elsewhere, it always refers to the variability between the scores obtained from the research study and its sample mean. This variability is called the *sum of the squared deviations of the scores set and its sample mean.* However, computing the sum of squares between and within groups is much more complex than the simple variance presented in Chapter 4.

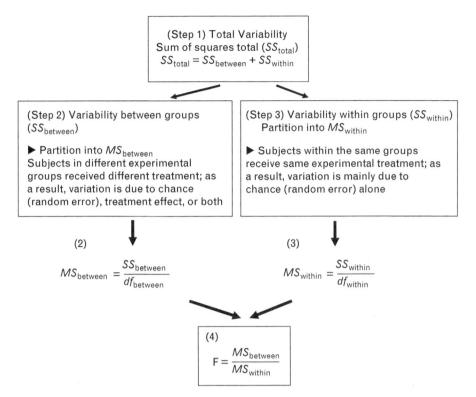

FIGURE 11.1 Visualizing total variability for the *F* ratio.

The complexity of the *F* ratio is partitioning ($SS_{between}$) and SS_{within} (see Steps 2 and 3 in Figures 11.1 and 11.2). Recall in Chapter 4 that to obtain the variability for the mean deviation and the variance, the sample mean must first be known. For simple ANOVA, it is also necessary to compute the sample mean for subjects in the study project. The only difference between measures of variability as presented in Chapter 4 and this chapter is that the meaning of the term *variance* has been changed to the *mean of the sum of squares between groups* ($MS_{between}$) and the *mean of the sum of squares within groups* (MS_{within}). The term *partition* is used to describe how to break down the sum of squares (variances) into subparts/subcomponents.

Witte (1993, p. 345) provided written illustrations (see Figure 11.2) about the computational procedures for the sum of square terms. Study the diagram in Figure 11.2 well as the *F* ratio is not difficult to compute. The tedious part of the calculation is computing the sums of the squared totals for the scores; otherwise, it is simple and straightforward.

COMPUTING THE PRACTICAL SITUATION

Table 11.2 displays again the raw scores of the school administrator's concern regarding school truancy at a hypothetical school district based on students' tardiness and unexcused absences and the respective sample means ($\overline{X}$) for all three groups. For the hypothesis test, assume that

$$H_0 = \overline{X}_{\text{School A}} = \overline{X}_{\text{School B}} = \overline{X}_{\text{School C}}$$

And that

$$H_a = \overline{X}_{\text{School A}} \neq \overline{X}_{\text{School A}} \neq \overline{X}_{\text{School C}}$$

$$SS_{between} = \text{sum of squared deviations of group means about the overall mean}$$

$$= \left[\frac{(1\text{st group total})^2}{1\text{st sampl size}} + \ldots + \frac{(\text{last group total})^2}{\text{last sampl size}} \right] - \frac{(\text{overall total})}{\text{overall sample size}}$$

$$SS_{within} = \text{sum of squared deviations of scores means about their respective group mean}$$

$$= \text{sum of all squared scores} - \frac{(1\text{st group total})^2}{1\text{st sample size}} + \ldots + \frac{(\text{last group total})^2}{\text{last sample size}}$$

$$SS_{total} = \text{sum of squared deviation of scores about the overall mean}$$

$$SS_{total} = \text{sum of all squared scores} - \frac{(\text{overall total})^2}{\text{overall sample size}}$$

FIGURE 11.2 Computation formula for SS terms.

Assume that the research project uses a p value of .05 to test the hypotheses.

With these assumptions, the sums of squares of tardiness and unexcused absences can be computed. First, compute the sample means for each of the chosen schools (see the bottom of Table 11.1). All the information needed for the F-ratio computations is displayed there. Included are the sample means for all three schools, sums of all scores, and sum of squares for the total values of the variable.

Computing the SS terms and the F ratio (see formula in Figures 11.1 and 11.2)

$$SS_{between} = \frac{(46)^2}{15} + \frac{(34)^2}{15} + \frac{(40)^2}{15} - \frac{(120)^2}{45}$$

$$= \frac{2{,}116}{15} + \frac{1{,}156}{15} + \frac{1{,}600}{15} - \frac{14{,}400}{45}$$

$$= 141.07 + 77.07 + 106.67 - 320$$

$$= 324.81 - 320$$

$$= 4.81$$

$$SS_{within} = (0)^2 + (3)^2 + (2)^2 + \cdots + (2)^2 - \left[\frac{(46)^2}{15} + \frac{(34)^2}{15} + \frac{(40)^2}{15} \right]$$

$$= 0 + 9 + 4 + \cdots + 4 - \left[141.07 + 77.07 + 106.67 \right]$$

$$= 430 - 324.81 = 105.19$$

Now that the $SS_{between}$ and SS_{within} are known, compute the SS_{total} by adding the terms together as follows:

$$SS_{total} = 4.81 + 105.19 = 110$$

Table 11.2 *Numbers of Combined Tardiness and Unexcused Absences*

Teacher	School A	Sum of Squares	School B	Sum of Squares	School C	Sum of Squares
01	0	0	4	16	3	9
02	3	9	0	0	2	4
03	2	4	1	1	0	0
04	4	16	0	0	3	9
05	2	4	1	1	2	4
06	4	16	5	25	4	16
07	2	2	1	1	2	4
08	5	25	0	0	4	16
09	4	16	3	9	1	1
10	5	25	2	4	3	9
11	3	9	4	16	5	25
12	2	4	4	16	3	9
13	6	36	5	25	4	16
14	2	4	3	9	2	4
15	2	4	1	1	2	4
$n = 15$	$\sum X_{\text{School A}} = 46$	174	$\sum X_{\text{School B}} = 34$	124	$\sum X_{\text{School C}} = 40$	130
	$\overline{X}_1 = \dfrac{46}{15} = 3.07$		$\overline{X}_2 = \dfrac{34}{15}$ $= 2.27$		$\overline{X}_3 = \dfrac{40}{15}$ $= 2.67$	

Sum of all scores $= (46 + 34 + 40 = 120)$

Sum of overall squared $= (174 + 124 + 130 = 428)$

First, notice the shortened SS_{within} computational term in the *sum of all squared scores* by starting with the first teacher who indicated no tardiness and unexcused absences and ending with the teacher who indicated a total of two tardinesses and unexcused absences per month. The mean square between groups ($MS_{between}$) and within groups (MS_{within}) can now be computed using the formula in Figure 11.1. Please note that $MS_{between}$ and MS_{within} cannot be calculated without calculating their respective degrees of freedom (df). Also, calculate the degrees of freedom between groups ($df_{between}$) by subtracting the number 1 from the number of groups ($df_{between}$ = Number of groups – 1). For simple analysis of variance, degrees of freedom are used for two major purposes: (a) to permit one group scores to vary between groups and (b) to permit two persons' scores to vary for the within groups measurement.

$$df_{between} = (3-1)$$
$$= 2$$

The mean square between ($MS_{between}$) groups is now computed by

$$MS_{between} = \frac{SS_{betwee}}{df_{between}} = 4.81/2$$
$$= 2.41$$

The degrees of freedom within groups can also computed by (df_{within} = number of scores – number of groups)

$$df_{within} = (45-3)$$
$$= 42$$

Now, compute the mean square within groups as

$$MS_{witin} = \frac{SS_{within}}{df_{within}} = 105.19/42$$
$$= 2.51$$

Finally, the *F* ratio is easily computed:

$$The\ F-ratio = \frac{MS_{between}}{MS_{within}} = \frac{2.41}{2.51}$$
$$= .960$$

As stated previously in the chapter, calculating the *F* ratio for simple analysis of variance is not difficult as long as the steps involved are remembered.

Table 11.3 shows a typical display of the ANOVA by inserting results from the previous computations. Notice that everything involved in the calculations is displayed in the table.

Table 11.3: Display Table for ANOVA

Burnout	Sum of Squares	df	Mean Square	F	Significance
	Variable Name				
Between groups	4.81	2	2.405	.960	
Within groups	105.19	42	2.505		
Total	110	44			

INTERPRETING RESULTS FROM ANOVA

The ability to read research findings and correctly report the information is important. Table 11.3 shows how to display the results from the hypothetical examinations regarding the frequencies of students' tardiness and unexcused absences per month to help the school administrators understanding of possible factors related to school truancy.

Looking at Appendix D ("Critical Values of F"), see that at the 95% confidence interval with 2 df for the numerator (going across) and 42 df for the denominator (going downward), the critical value is equal to 3.22. The same rule of statistics for all inferential statistics discussed throughout the book applies. When the calculated value is larger than the critical value, the null hypothesis (H_0) is rejected. Because the calculated F value of 0.960 is much smaller than the critical value of 3.22, the conclusion is that H_0 has been supported, which means that there is no significant difference in total tardiness and unexcused absences for the three schools where teachers were randomly selected (Schools A, B, and C) ($F = .960$, $df = 2, 42$, $p > .05$). Teachers among the three selected schools reported similar numbers of tardiness and unexcused absences.

SUMMARY

This is the last chapter formally introducing the basic tools of quantitative data analysis. Some procedures, such as calculating percentages and the sample means, are simple, while t tests and simple ANOVA are much more complex.

Chapter 11 covered the F ratio, for which there is a dependent variable with multiple nominal levels of the independent variable. The reason for doing this was to see whether one type of treatment might have had a statistical impact on different groups of the population. The next and final chapter briefly covers basic qualitative research and provides suggested guidelines for doing qualitative data analysis.

STUDY QUESTIONS

1. Suppose that a researcher conducted an experiment on three groups of people and the sums of squares were given as follows: $SS_{between} = 231.78$; $SS_{within} = 435.91$; $n = 120$. Compute the F ratio for the experimental project.

Table 11.4 *Reaction Time (Seconds)*

School 1	School 2	School 3
5	4	8
10	2	5
7	9	3
15	12	17
2	5	10
6	18	7

2. Suppose that an experiment on cognitive behavioral modification for children, especially their reaction (in seconds) to the question, "Who wants to be a people helper when you are a grownup?" is planned. Listed in Table 11.4 are the reaction times for 3 third graders from three separate schools. Compute the F ratio, and once you have completed it, use a p value of .05 to explain the finding.

ANSWERS TO STUDY QUESTIONS

1. $F = .532$, $df = 2, 117$

2. $SS_{between} = 2.78$; $SS_{within} = 399$; $df_{between} = 2$; $df_{within} = 117$

   a. $MS_{between} = 1.39$; $MS_{within} = 3.434$

   b. $F = .405$

   c. The research finding indicates that there are no significant differences in children's overall response time among the third graders from the three schools ($F = .405$, $df = 2, 117, p > .05$).

CHAPTER 12

A SNAPSHOT OF QUALITATIVE RESEARCH

OVERVIEW

Chapters 3 to 11 presented quantitative data analysis using various statistical tools and procedures. In these chapters, two important procedures were discussed. The first was how to use mathematical and nonmathematical variables in the form of *numeric forms* (numbers) to represent *attributes*, such as the characteristics of persons or things. Examples are mental illness situations, stressful life events, residents' attitudes toward social workers and nurses, and personality traits of a particular group of people. Second, by conducting hypothesis testing, we described how to understand and estimate the breadth and depth of the attributes. The result of hypothesis testing enables researchers and practitioners to explain the relationships between the data set of the sample group and the population from which the sample was drawn. This chapter takes you to a parallel way of understanding attributes; instead of using numeric forms, you will observe and describe characteristics of persons or things using *words* (English or non-English). When words are used to gather data and then are categorized or summarized, it is called *qualitative research*. Of course, qualitative research methods and qualitative data analyses are semester courses with their own detailed texts. The goal of this chapter is not to make you proficient in qualitative data analysis; rather, it is written as a reference chapter, to make you aware of possible steps in helping you organize and analyze qualitative data.

More specifically, this chapter briefly highlights statistical mechanisms that usually occur in qualitative research design. Essentially, we highlight the meaning of qualitative research and its typical data collection procedures, including data recording and analysis planning. First, let us discuss the meaning of qualitative research.

WHAT IS QUALITATIVE RESEARCH?

As human societies become more globalized every day, the traditional way of just doing quantitative research is no longer perceived as "that is it." In the past couple of decades, qualitative research methods have been combined with quantitative methods in many aspects of research. For example, when modern scientists examine the causes of lung cancer, they no longer just explore the plausible biomedical, physiological, and environmental factors that caused lung cancer; they also may want to understand the social and behavioral factors of the individuals, such as their family background and the cultural group they belong to as well. Similarly, when social workers investigate the causes of child abuse and neglect, they look for social and economic reasons as well as bruises and signs of malnourishment and behaviors of both the parents/caretakers and children. In social work, when investigating situations, such as alleged child sexual abuse, the biopsychosocial assessment must be completed. In cases like this, in addition to quantitative data, qualitative data must be gathered.

For any type of scenario, no matter how well the researchers manipulate number results produced from numerical scores it may be insufficient to fully understand the causes of lung cancer or child abuse and neglect. To better understand the causes of either situation, collecting data in the form of words (qualitative) that help to explain meaning can be insightful. In scientific terminology, even though qualitative findings are not generalizable, the methods allow researchers and practitioners the flexibility to incorporate observations and use subjectivity to generate deeper understandings of the meaning of human experiences. This is in contrast to quantitative research methods for which researchers and practitioners are not expected to insert subjectivity into the human experiences because of the generalization requirements of the findings. In addition, because researchers always caution their audience of the overgeneralization of numerical findings, supplemental qualitative data can help alleviate such concerns.

So, how does one prepare to collect qualitative data? The answer to this question is *data collection procedures*. For either quantitative or qualitative research, data collection procedures typically involve operationalizing the data collection protocols, such as types of questionnaire, when, where, and on whom to administer the questionnaire. Then, the process is followed by indicating the mechanism for data recording. To help you understand this part of the structure, let us describe a couple of concepts that commonly occur in qualitative research. These two concepts are called *fieldwork* and *field notes*.

QUALITATIVE DATA COLLECTION PROCEDURES

In contrast to quantitative data analysis, there are no scientific assumptions or statistics rules regarding data collection procedures for qualitative data analysis. Although there are no specific guidelines when it comes to the preparation and use of qualitative research methods, there are two common concepts known as *fieldwork* and *field notes*.

Fieldwork is a classical anthropological concept researchers use to operationalize the research methods (particularly design), recruitment strategies, and data collection protocols. In quantitative research methods, the researchers are actively involved in the preparation and conduct of the research project but *may or may not be directly involved with the data collection process*. However, *most qualitative researchers are not only actively involved in the preparation of the research project and the recruitment of respondents but also are engaged in the interviewing phase*. Data obtained from qualitative research is called *field notes*.

Field notes are like memos (texts) to yourself, your assistants (if any), and the recorded words/responses the respondents give during the interview. It is extremely important that *anything* the respondents say be precisely recorded. *The "text" you recorded and transcribed from the participant observations or just the observations often become "findings evidence." In quantitative research, you use numbers to understand issues confronted by people behind the scene. In qualitative research, you use words to understand the richness of human experience.* The meaning of *text* then becomes the extent to which researchers are able to reach meanings on social issues such as "how the community or people understood and interpreted it/them." Field notes can be recorded in two ways. The first is recorded word for word as precisely as possible. Why? This is because some of these notes (texts) will end up in your final report as direct quotes. The accuracy of information explained in the final report depends largely on the precision of the researcher/practitioner to narrate the field notes. Because of this, qualitative researchers always carry electronic recording devices or notepads. The second way to record field notes is a personal reaction to the interactions the researchers have with the respondents. These notes may only be used to help you as the researcher to remember what transpired during the interview. However, none of these personal summary or narrative notes should appear in your final report. Keep in mind that personal opinions and reactions do not constitute "findings" for the research study.

Despite the differences between quantitative and qualitative methods, the studies that employ them either separately or in combination follow the same research patterns. In modern days, the mixed method is actually the more popular one. A *mixed method* means that the researcher combines quantitative and qualitative research methods. For example, the researcher may structure two thirds of the questionnaires using a quantitative method and the remaining one third of the questionnaires using a qualitative design or vice versa. Just be mindful that the nature of data collection or research design does not dictate whether it is quantitative or qualitative. In the quantitative design, questionnaires are structured using mostly closed-ended questions, while the qualitative design uses mainly open-ended questions format. However, questions like "How old are you?" or "How many steps do you walk per day" will likely elicit numerical responses. Sometimes, the qualitative research design does not have formatted questions. In this case, the researcher will explore the situation more in depth with the respondent while conducting fieldwork. Just as in all forms of human inquiry, the researcher must make sure that proper human subject protection is sought and be approved accordingly. Even if a structured questionnaire is used in fieldwork, subjects involved in the study still must be fully protected from social and psychological harms. This leads us directly to various issues pertain to data recording. We use the term *data recording* to mean the structure of a database, which contains the entire data file.

QUALITATIVE DATA RECORDING

In quantitative data analysis, the reliability and validity of research findings are based on sampling, particularly probability sampling, and the accuracy of the measuring instruments. A poorly developed measurement instrument such as a questionnaire will lead not only to unreliable evidence but also to no validity, while well-developed instruments lead to stronger reliability and validity. Differing from quantitative research, qualitative research depends on the *quality and clarity of the open-ended questions. Quality* refers to the "get to the point but nonoffending, no double-barrel, no prejudicial" type of questions. *Clarity* is making the questions "clear and of easy understanding." Suppose that you ask, "What do you think about civil disobedient persons, and what should be done about them?" There are several problems with this question: (a) The question is vague. Even highly educated persons will ask, "What do you mean by civil disobedience?" (b) It is a double-barrel question. The respondent does not know what part of the question you want to be answered first. (c) The question is poorly structured. It is a confusing question. Moreover, (d) it is a prejudicial question. You are asking about the punishment that should be given to this group of people. For either quantitative or qualitative civil disobedience questions, researchers always try to obtain an in-depth understanding of the issue rather than seek punitive punishment to the individuals or group of persons. Another point about reliability and validity issues with qualitative data is the *consistency* of *note-taking* (field notes).

The more consistent your field notes are, the easier it will be to identify behavioral patterns between and among the respondents. As stated, note-taking can occur using electronics, such as recording devices, or can be handwritten notes. The philosophical roots of qualitative inquiry mandate that the respondent's answers should be recorded as fully as possible. Some qualitative scientists even suggest that note-taking occur in stages. The stages mean that at the initial interaction, the researcher only takes sketchy notes at the start of the interview or at the first interview. The researcher then writes notes in more detail in the following hour or during subsequent interviews. Then, for the question, "Do I need to do anything else before I proceed with my research questions?" Bogdan and Biklen (as cited by Monette, Sullivan, & DeJong, 2005) provided five categories for observation and recording before the interview/observation begins. The five categories are briefhly highlighted below:

I.   **The Setting.** First, describe the field setting. Field notes should contain some description of the general physical and social setting being observed. The following are sample questions about the setting:
     a.   Is the meeting place a home, an apartment, a community-based agency, a government agency?
     b.   Is it an individual interview, group interview, community forum, political forum?
II. **The People and the Geographical Setting.** Field notes should include a physical and social description of the main characters who are the focus of the observation. Examples include
     a.   Who is being observed/interviewed?
     b.   How many people?
     c.   How are they dressed?
     d.   What are their ages, genders, and socioeconomic characteristics?
     e.   What is the cultural background of the respondents?
III. **Individual Actions and Activities.** Monette and Sullivan explained that the central observations in most studies are the behaviors of the people in the setting. Possible questions in this part of the record may include
     a.   How do they relate to one another?
     b.   Who talks to whom, and in what fashion?
     c.   What sequences of behavior occur?
IV. **Group Behavior.** In some cases, the behavior of groups is important information (Monette & DeJong, 2005). Example questions include
     a.   How long does a group of people remain on the scene?
     b.   How does one group relate to another? Monette and Sullivan also stated that what we record here describes the social structure of the setting, statuses, and roles of people occupying the various relationships between or among them.

V. **Meaning and Perspectives.** Finally, field researchers are sensitive to the subjective meaning that people give to themselves and their behavior; so, field notes should contain observations about these meanings and what words or behavior are evidence of those meanings. Bogdan and Biklen (as cited by Monette, Sullivan, & DeJong, 2005) explained that *perspective* refers to the general ways of thinking that people exhibit evidence of which should appear in the field notes.

You can consider these general observations you record for yourself before and after the interviews. Similar to quantitative data analysis, these five categories will be background information about the participants/respondents, which normally is gathered first before other variables are described. Before discussing different ways of doing qualitative data analysis, let us explain the meaning of narrative data first.

NARRATIVE DATA

When someone narrates something, the person could be telling a real-life story in which the researcher records using specific structure. It can take the form of an essay, but the form can vary greatly depending on the situation or case. For example, narrative writing in college education is a form by which students try to prove a point, state an argument, or address an important issue. When combining narrative writing with narrative data analyses, it is a simplified concept that takes many shapes and forms of qualitative data analysis. *Narrative data analysis is one of many techniques that researchers can use to analyze and evaluate qualitative data.* The data sources can be clients' logs, participants' responses to a set of questions, a transcript from a community gathering, notes from an interview, diaries from a person, or text from a published source, such as books or journal articles. Therefore, the data source could come from a community, many people, several individuals, or just a single person.

The remaining sections of this chapter discuss four steps that can be utilized for qualitative data analyses. Some of the steps overlap each other, so you may want to switch back and forth between them. Before discussing the specific steps, let us discuss two of the concepts often used by researchers when reporting findings that are *research findings* and *data interpretations.*

QUALITATIVE DATA ANALYSIS

When analyzing qualitative data, similar to quantitative data analysis, you must clearly understand the differences between research findings and data interpretations. *Research findings* refer to the examination and statistical tabulations of raw scores (i.e., words or number) and displays of important results that pertain to the research purposes. Data interpretations go beyond tabulating raw scores and displaying results. *Data interpretations* are the descriptions and explanations of research findings that reflect three major components: (a) significant findings that support or do not support the research objectives; (b) significant findings that either are confirmed or not confirmed in the literature pertaining to the issue under investigation; and (c) personal reactions or personal opinions about either significant or nonsignificant research findings. Being able to understand research findings and data interpretations will help you to properly present both quantitative and qualitative data and explain findings clearly to your audience.

As a result, when analyzing qualitative data, Rubin and Babbie (2014), social worker and sociologist, provided the following linkages between research theory and analysis. You could consider the linkages as steps in completing qualitative data analysis. At the end of each step, we also provide example narratives to help you better understand the processes involved.

DISCOVERING PATTERNS

As cited by Rubin and Babbie (2014), in 1995, Lofland and Lofland suggested six different ways of looking for patterns in a particular research topic. Lofland and Lofland's six different ways are briefly summarized below:

1. *Frequencies.* These are the frequencies that the key issues under investigation mentioned by the interviewees. This process is also called *enumeration*. Enumeration is the process of quantifying data (both quantitative and qualitative). In qualitative research, you might count the number of times a word appears in a document or you might count the number of times a code is applied to the data. For example, when interviewing homeless veterans, you might count how many times are words such as "depression," "unable to sleep," and "loneliness" mentioned. In this example, you could assign "DEP" for depression, "USL" for unable to sleep, and "L" for loneliness. Suppose that you have a client log, you can count (enumerate) the number of times each code occurs by putting these codes in the log.

2. *Magnitude.* Magnitude is the degree of severity of the problem or the strength of the relationship between two concepts. For example, a homeless person may describe the relationship between loneliness (X) and self-worth (Y) or the number of times sleepless (Z) at night. By using self-worth as the main focus or title of problem, we could diagram the relationship between X and Y as in Table 12.1.

3. *Structures.* Structures are the different types of issues under the same topic and the relationship between the issues. A homeless person may talk about being a veteran, substance abuser, and rejected by his or her family.

4. *Process.* Process involves ordering categories of issues confronted by subjects under investigation/research by time and shows the characteristics or subcategories that are associated with the stages of life development. You could consider process as the "phases or stages of the occurring problem." For example, the homeless veteran may rationalize that the reason he or she becomes homeless is substance abuse. When the veteran used and abused drugs and alcohol, then a mental illness syndrome began to

Table 12.1: Example of Data Analysis Using the Magnitude Concept

The Problem (Self-Worth)	Form of Relationship
Isolation	X is a kind of Y. (Loneliness is related to self-worth. Worthlessness relates to social isolation.)
Withdrawal	X causes Y. (Client withdraws due to feeling of worthlessness.)

develop. The homeless veteran then became confrontational with family members, which is when family members began to reject him or her. It may or may not be true, but that is how the respondent/interviewee rank orders his or her reasons for becoming homeless. To put this situation into phases, you could diagram the homeless veterans' situations as follows:

a. Phase 1: Life situation before joining the military
b. Phase 2: Life situation in the military
c. Phase 3: Life situation after military service
d. Phase 4: Life situation as a homeless person
e. Phase 5: Wishing outcome for the immediate future

5. *Causes.* These are how the respondent "states" or "believes" what the causes of the problem are. Be mindful that, in qualitative research, the term *cause* does not imply causation or effect. It applies to only how the respondent believes or states it. In statistical analysis, particularly quantitative analysis, the term *cause* or *regress* usually means going back or returning. Cause is different from process. In going back, you must be able to identify the *real* factor(s) that cause the problem. Essentially, you search for the variable(s) that correlates strongest to the problem you are investigating. For example, when examining what causes veterans to become homeless, you find that chemical dependency is the primary factor. You will note that the term *chemical dependency* is too broad. You must use correlation and regression to identify the actual cause. Is it hard liquor, illegal drugs, or both? In the real world, it will be both. In this sense, qualitative study will enable researchers to explore further what veterans believe are the causes.

6. *Consequences.* Consequences refer to the magnitude or costs of the issue. Is this how the issue under investigation affects individuals, families, societies in the short and long term? The following is a sample narrative of a mentally ill client log relating to medical noncompliance[1]:

> Client rapidly shifts his moods which has been observable in the office, exhibiting odd-like behaviors (intense stares, hysterical laughing bouts, tilting head and freezing self in position) that differ from week to week, visual hallucinations (seeing 3 ghosts), distressing nightmares that biological mother has died, internal preoccupations of stimulation, poor verbal reciprocation, and thought poverty. The symptoms listed continue to affect client to a significant degree, which requires caregivers to prompt client physically and verbally to attune reality on a daily basis.

It is not necessary when analyzing qualitative data to observe evidence that is related to all six issues. For example, when studying spirituality, it will be difficult to rank order which spiritual component is more important to the individuals, families, or the community. One may argue that hiking to the mountain alone is the most spiritual, while another may argue that going to church, temple, or a mosque is the most spiritual.

---

1 Used with permission of Jenny Chang (MFT), Dignity Health, Sacramento, CA, USA.

CONTENT ANALYSIS

Content analysis is a method for summarizing any form of content, usually written words, by counting various aspects of the content. This enables a more objective evaluation than comparing content based on the understanding of the audience. The results of content analysis are numbers and percentages. Content analysis is based on the grounded theory (Glaser & Strauss, 1967) that enables a researcher to transform qualitative material into quantitative data. Rubin and Babbie (2014) stated that this method can be applied to virtually any form of communication, not just available records. It consists primarily of coding and tabulating the occurrences of certain forms of content that are being communicated: "Content analysis is essentially a coding operation. Communication whether oral, written, or other—is coded or classified according to some conceptual framework" (p. 454). Rubin and Babbie stated further that when coding content analysis, there are two choices: manifest content and latent content. *Manifest content* applies more of a quantitative approach by focusing on a specific form of communication (i.e., journal article, book, magazine, newspaper) to determine the extent to which the issue is accounted for. For example, if you want to know how much people and politicians paid attention to the needs of homeless veterans, you could select the last 12 or 60 issues of the local newspaper. You then systematically sort through the pages of the newspaper and document the number of times the selected newspaper mentioned "homeless veterans."

Latent content applies specifically to qualitative approach. You still have to select a specific form of communication but only analyze the meaning of the communication. For the situation with the homeless veterans, instead of counting the number of times the local newspaper mentioned homeless veterans, you will examine how the local reporters discussed the situation of homeless veterans. Essentially, in manifest content, you do the frequency count on the occurrences of the term *homeless veterans*. In latent content, the researchers account for the extended coverage of homeless veterans or explain the meaning of the homeless veterans as discussed or interpreted by the local reporters.

Qualitative data analysis is typically based on the inductive method. In the inductive method, the logical model is applied in which general principles are developed from observation about a whole group or class of objects from knowledge of one or a few members of that group or class. Most exploratory research studies, whether quantitative or qualitative, fall under this categorization. The reason is that researchers examine a few cases to apply their findings from this small observation to the larger population groups. Therefore, in qualitative research, we are interested in developing theoretical frameworks from the observations; in quantitative research findings, we generalize to the population in which our sample was drawn.

For example, Anders and Dinis (2009), in a latent content analysis on workplace challenges in institutions of higher education, reported one of their findings was related to ideological change. They stated that managers like "Eleanor, for instance, noted the manager has to be 'aware of the labor laws … and you have to learn to manage within a union set-up.' She thought the workplace was dealing with more rules, regulations, and laws. Marie said the workplace has become more "unionized, more litigious, more complicated" (p. 288).

SEMIOTICS

Semiotics is defined as the science of signs and has to do with symbols and meanings (Rubin & Babbie, 2014, p. 518). This is how you link words in the data set with language and cultural

Table 12.2: Example of Data Analysis Using the Semiotics Concept

Sign	Meaning
Two fingers up in a V	Victorious
Hands shake	Greetings or congratulations
Hands to mouth	Eat or ready to eat
Scream	Fear, anger, frustration

symbols of the respondents to find meanings. For example, while interviewing groups of people, you constantly notice that women do not shake hands with men. By exploring with the group, you learn that avoidance of shaking hands with a female is a sign of cultural respect. Examine Table 12.2 to help you understand semiotics.

CONVERSATIONAL ANALYSIS

Conversational analysis is almost similar to semiotics. In semiotics, you analyze signs, symbols, and cultural concepts. In conversational analysis, you analyze "terms" or "words" to uncover the inherent assumptions and structures in social life through an extreme scrutiny of the way we converse with one another. Conversational analysis usually happens when we pick up someone else's concept or theory and try to interpret its meaning. For example, one could pick up the "ecological perspective" and try to insert his or her own interpretations to the meaning of person in the environment. Not only that, but also Rubin and Babbie (2014) stated that in conversational analysis we even try to seek to uncover words like "uhs, ers, and poor grammar." Therefore, in a statistics course, when someone said, "I ain't like statistics." You will try to interpret the term *ain't* in conversational analysis. Does it mean, "I do not like statistics," "I am not like statistics," "I hate statistics," or "I can't like statistics"? You will try every possible way to understand the abbreviation ain't. Similarly, in this technological, gadget age, when someone says I want that "application," you have to try to understand whether the person is referring to a computer program or a paper application.

COMPUTER APPLICATIONS AND ONLINE RESOURCES

Even without displaying an actual example, the mechanisms discussed should give you a good idea about gathering and displaying qualitative data by hand. Next, we provide information on several computerized programs, some of which are available free online:

- *MAXQDA*: qualitative data analysis software for Windows
- *ATLAS.ti*: qualitative data analysis software
- *QDA Miner Lite*: free qualitative data analysis software
- *NVivo* 10: research software for analysis and insight
- *QDAP* (Qualitative Data Analysis Program): of the University Center for Social and Urban Research at the University of Pittsburgh, Pennsylvania

Other referenced sources that you may obtain to help with qualitative data analysis include *Analyzing Social Settings: A Guide to Qualitative Observation and Analysis* (Lofland, Anderson, & Lofland, 2006) and *Social Work Research and Evaluation: Quantitative and Qualitative Approaches* (Grinnell, 2000). In addition, the following free reference sources are available online:

- "Qualitative Data Analysis," http://www.sagepub.com/upm-data/43454_10.pdf
- "Qualitative Data Analysis," http://www.southalabama.edu/coe/bset/johnson/lectures/lec17.pdf
- *Analyzing Qualitative Data*, http://learningstore.uwex.edu/assets/pdfs/g3658-12.pdf
- *Qualitative Data Analysis*, ftp://ftp.qualisresearch.com/pub/qda.pdf
- *Steps in Qualitative Data Analysis*, http://www.slideshare.net/guest7f1ad678/qualitative-data-analysis-steps

SUMMARY

This chapter provides a briefly discussion on the meaning of qualitative research and data summary tools that beginning researchers may apply to field research. As discussed in the start of the chapter, qualitative research is as complex as quantitative research. In order to fully understand qualitative research, one must take a course specifically designed for this purpose.

STUDY QUESTIONS

Select an Observable Topic. This observation can be conducted at a public place, such as the front of a college campus, a supermarket, or a special event. Make sure to plan that your goal is to observe human behavior in the environment, for example, observe social interactions among college students. Time yourself for 30 minutes. Within that period allowance, observe how many students stopped and chatted with each other, how long each interaction lasted, and how many times they seemed to become frustrated with each other. Your task is to share your observation with the entire class.

- *On Observation Day.* Use Monette, Sullivan, and DeJong's five categories to observe and record data. Record precisely the date, time, and location of the observation. Do not tell people that they are being observed or introduce the idea that you are observing them. Take notes exactly regarding how certain behavior is observed. *Do not* take photos or record the behavior using electronic devices, such as a smartphone, without first being able to secure individual's permission through human subject review and approval. Set boundaries for yourself.
- *Data Analysis.* Use *discovering patterns* as discussed by Rubin and Babbie (2014). Write a short (half-page) paper and explain the specific behavior you observed.

APPENDIX A

Introduction to SPSS

OVERVIEW

Throughout this text, a number of statistical concepts and tools were introduced so that anyone might use them to organize and analyze data by hand. Descriptive statistics and different types of inferential statistics were introduced. Appendix A and Appendix B demonstrate how computer programs may be used to organize and compute solutions while achieving the same outcomes as completed by hand.

Specifically, Appendix A introduces a popular program called the *Statistical Package for the Social Sciences* (SPSS). In 2009, IBM purchased SPSS and renamed it *Predictive Analytics Software* (PASW), but it is still popularly known as SPSS. Appendix C introduces a program available on every personal computer: Excel ToolPak (Excel for short).

WHY COMPUTERIZED PROGRAMS?

Before the age of computers, learning statistics was similar to learning other forms of mathematics; formulas were memorized, and calculations done mostly by hand. Today, computer applications have greatly simplified statistics procedures and computing solutions. Because learning statistics has been simplified, some instructors now teach students only about concepts and guidelines for analysis and ignore almost all hand calculations. However, in this book, students and practitioners continue to be shown how to calculate statistics by hand as well as to compute solutions using computer applications. Learning how to calculate statistical solutions by hand can be not only tedious and boring but also fascinating. The two-sample *t* test, regression, and analysis of variance are examples of time-consuming calculations.

Researchers and students generally feel more assured of the accuracy of calculations when a long-accepted software application is used. For example, when using interval- or ratio-level data without outliers to compute the measures of central tendency, or for Student's *t* tests, then computer programs will ensure accurate solutions.

INTRODUCTION TO IBM SPSS/PASW

The Statistical Package for the Social Sciences, through several iterations, is a popular software package for statistical analysis and data management applications. Its graphic environment is powerful. The descriptive menus (ribbon) have simple dialog boxes useful for most facets of statistical computation. Once the data entry is complete, most other tasks are accomplished simply by pointing and clicking the mouse. Data batches or files from other applications, such as Excel, Lotus, dBase, and SAS, are easily imported. A bonus is compatibility with regular text and word-processing programs. However, certain conventions and techniques must be mastered for efficient use of the software and to obtain consistently correct answers.

In basic statistical computations, especially activities that are relevant to the contents of this book, two types of files are introduced: a data or system file and an output file. The data file is where variable names are created, the correct levels of measurement for variables are selected, and data are entered into the system. The term *data file* simply refers to the common concept of data entry. The output file is where information ready for analyses is computed and stored. In addition, the output file contains outcome information based on descriptive statistics and inferential statistics and information that is ready to be printed. Simply put, an *output file* is the result of the statistical computations.

DATA ENTRY USING SPSS

Once SPSS is started, either a blank screen or a question mark appears asking which file is to be opened. If the user is unsure, click to return to a blank screen. The blank screen is where the user can create a personal data file or open other files in the computer. Even if the user clicks **Cancel**, SPSS does not close the program. Instead, the user will be given options to search for other files or to create a new one. To create a new file, the user must create *variable names* (names for all variables in the research project, such as gender, age, etc.).

CREATING VARIABLE NAMES

SPSS is similar to other statistical software programs in that the user cannot just type scores into the system as in word processing. To compute the results of a research project using SPSS, the user must first create a *data file*, also called a *system file*. Also, the variables must be defined: the items on the questionnaire. To begin defining variables, look at the bottom left of the blank screen (see Figure A.1). Here, the user sees two items: **Data View** and **Variable View**. **Variable View** is for assigning a name, identifying a *type of value*, *label*, or *values of responses* and for selecting the correct level of measurement for each variable/item (see Figure A.2).

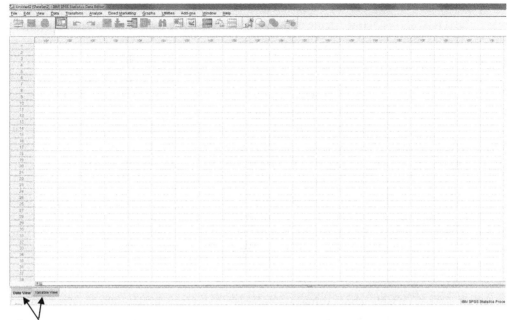

For data entry, basic
communication begins here

FIGURE A.1 SPSS blank screen.

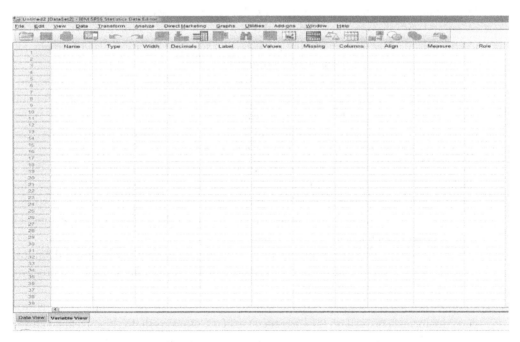

FIGURE A.2 Appearance after **Variable View** is clicked.

Specifically, once **Variable View** is selected, a new screen appears (Figure A.2). On column 1, row 1, the screen shows **Name** (name of the variable to be assigned to each of the items on the questionnaires). SPSS prefers names having no more than eight characters (e.g., "Gender" for the variable "gender of the respondent") with some restrictions. Symbols, such as the *dollar sign* ($), *exclamation mark* (!), *semicolon* (;), *forward slash* (/), *backward slash* (\), *comma* (,), *period* (.), and *space bar* are restricted and should not be used as the name of the variable because they are reserved for SPSS internal programming language use.

The next column on **Variable View** is the type of variable, labeled **Type**. SPSS automatically selects **numeric** as the preferred type of variable. If any items in the questionnaire were constructed using characters such as the dollar sign or scientific notation, the user must be sure to change the type of variable to match the questions/statements. Similarly, when importing data from Excel and dBase, some of the variables in the data set may have been structured using string and other types of mathematical notations; if so, the user must recode them. The process of *data recode* is discussed further in this appendix, "Suggested Steps in Preparing the Obtained Scores for Analysis." The following summarizes types of variables as provided by SPSS (online version 21, 2014):

- *Numeric.* A variable whose values are numbers. Values are displayed in standard numeric format. The Data Editor accepts numeric values in standard format or in scientific notation.
- *Comma.* A numeric variable whose values are displayed with commas delimiting every three places and displayed with the period as a decimal delimiter. The Data Editor accepts numeric values for comma variables with or without commas or in scientific notation. Values cannot contain commas to the right of the decimal indicator.
- *Dot.* A numeric variable whose values are displayed with periods delimiting every three places and with the comma as a decimal delimiter. The Data Editor accepts numeric values for dot variables with or without periods or in scientific notation. Values cannot contain periods to the right of the decimal indicator.
- *Scientific notation.* A numeric variable whose values are displayed with an embedded E and a signed power-of-10 exponent. The Data Editor accepts numeric values for such variables with or without an exponent. The exponent can be preceded by E or D with an optional sign or by the sign alone, for example, 123, 1.23E2, 1.23D2, 1.23E+2, and 1.23+2.
- *Date.* A numeric variable whose values are displayed in one of several calendar-date or clock-time formats. Select a format from the list. Dates may be entered with slashes, hyphens, periods, commas, or blank spaces as delimiters. The century range for two-digit year values is determined by **Options** settings (from the **Edit** menu, choose **Options**, and then click the **Data** tab).
- *Dollar.* A numeric variable displayed with a leading dollar sign ($), commas delimiting every three places, and a period as the decimal delimiter. Data values may be entered with or without the leading dollar sign.
- *Custom currency.* A numeric variable whose values are displayed in one of the custom currency formats defined on the **Currency** tab of the **Options** dialog box. Defined custom currency characters cannot be used in data entry but are displayed in the Data Editor.

- *String*. A variable whose values are not numeric and therefore are not used in calculations. The values may contain any characters up to the defined length. Uppercase and lowercase letters are considered distinct. This type is also known as an alphanumeric variable.
- *Restricted numeric*. A variable whose values are restricted to nonnegative integers. Values are displayed with leading zeros padded to the maximum width of the variable. Values can be entered in scientific notation.

The **Width** column is where the user programs SPSS to show the number of characters (symbols) for the variable name. SPSS prefers that you program every variable name using eight spaces. However, there is nothing wrong with decreasing or increasing the width. For example, the variable "gender" is good with either eight spaces or six.

The **Decimal** column is where the user changes decimal places to reflect the values of each question. For example, when asking college students for their grade point average (GPA), two decimal places are enough, while asking for gender, there should be no decimal.

Label allows the user to provide a short *title* for the variable. This is the title that will appear on top of the output table. SPSS prefers a title with no more than a single line. Keep in mind that some questions are short, while others may be several lines long. *Always paraphrase questions that are long so that the title of the variable is short.*

Values are the responses (or the answers) to questions. Be aware that some questions have precoded answers (values), while others use an open-ended format.

Missing is where the user tells SPSS whether there are any missing scores for the variable. Unless the user wants to use a specific code such as 99 or 999 for missing scores, just leave this column blank. SPSS no longer needs a precoded name for missing scores.

Measure is where the user tells SPSS about the *levels of measurement* (nominal, ordinal, interval, or ratio) for the variable. SPSS labels interval- and ratio-level data as a *scale*. Levels of measurement are important for frequency distributions, but of utmost importance for measures of central tendency and variability and for some, if not all, inferential statistics. The test statistic will compute the result based on this selection.

CONSTRUCTING VARIABLE VALUE FOR ANY VARIABLE

So that users may further understand how other variables and their corresponding values are input into SPSS, the method of entering scores from a word-processing table into an SPSS data file is illustrated next. Data from a user's own research project using questionnaires may be entered into SPSS in the same manner. Look at the questionnaire example. Table A.1 from the questionnaire was constructed for the purpose of demonstrating data entry and computing various types of statistics using SPSS. To highlight the variable, it appears in parentheses in the questionnaire. The remaining sections of Appendix A and some sections of Appendix B are based on this table. When data are imported from other programs, such as Excel and dBase, some or not all parts of the data entry demonstration example may apply. However, with even a well-constructed data file imported from Excel and dBase, it may be wise for the user to review the instructions that follow the questionnaire to double-check the data set (data cleaning) before proceeding with the computations.

RESEARCH QUESTIONNAIRE

1. (Gender) Please circle your gender.
    a. Female
    b. Male
2. (Age) How old are you? _____ / years old
3. (Statistic) How much do you like taking statistics?
    a. I do not like it at all.
    b. I somewhat dislike it.
    c. I somewhat like it.
    d. I like it very much.
4. Please rate yourself on the following items using a scale from 1 to 10. The higher the score, the better you rated yourself.
    a. _____ (Esteem) Your current level of self-worth
    b. _____ (Family) The degree of family togetherness in past 6 months
5. (Exercise) On average, how many minutes per week do you go out and exercise? _____ /minutes

Before data can be entered, the user must create names for the variables (items in the questionnaires). To start creating a variable name for Table A.1, move the cursor to column 1, row 1, in Figure A.2. Type in the variable name **Age**. After typing the name of the variable, click the rectangle immediately below the **Decimal** column, change the number **2** to **0**, and then click the column immediately below the **Label** column. Type **The student's current age** into that long rectangle. This longer sentence is the "title" (title for the output) provided when asking (first question in Table A.1) each student for current age. Leave the **Values** as **None**. Move the cursor

Table A.1: Research Data

ID	Gender	Age	Statistic	Esteem	Family	Exercise
01	2	23	4	9	10	60
02	1	19	3	7	8	40
03	2	22	1	8	9	120
04	2	20	2	5	6	0
05	1	28	4	7	4	15
06	2	31	4	5	6	30
07	1	29	3	6	7	60
08	2	26	4	4	6	30
09	2	21	1	5	7	20
10	1	24	3	6	8	0
11	2	20	4	9	8	45
12	2	34	3	8	8	100
13	2	23	4	9	7	30
14	1	26	4	7	8	15
15	2	23	4	8	9	0

to the **Measure** column and select **Scale** (select **Scale** only when SPSS has not automatically labeled it as such).

Creating a variable name for the second question is simple and straightforward. The third question is a bit more complicated because it has precoded responses, so follow these instructions:

- Move the cursor to column 1, row 2; type **Statistic**.
- Select and change **Decimals** to **0**. Then on **Label**, type, **How much students like to study statistics**.
- Click the **Values** column and a miniwindow that looks like Figure A.3 appears. *Values* are the precoded responses to the question. Notice that values in the variable were left as **None** because the question was asked using an open-ended format.
- On **Value** inside the **Values** column, type **1**, then either use the **Tab** key or move the cursor to the **Label** rectangle, type **I do not like it at all** and press **Enter** or click **Add**. Notice that the cursor jumped right back to **Value**.
- Enter **2** on **Value**, then **I somewhat dislike it**, and press **Enter** or click **Add**.
- Repeat the process until all four precoded values are entered.
- Do not click **OK** until all values are visible ("I do not like it at all" to "I like it very much") and correctly appear in the minidesktop window as in Figure A.4.
- Click **OK** and return to the original location.
- Most users do not bother with **Missing**, **Columns**, and **Align**, so move the cursor to **Measure** and select **Ordinal**. Columns are similar to **Width**, discussed previously. **Align** is where the user wants the numerical score to be displayed: left, right, or center. The last selection in **Measure** is where this question was constructed using the ordinal level of measurement.
- Repeat the same process for the remaining four variables listed in Table A.1 by assigning **Name**, **Decimals**, **Label**, **Values**, and **Measure**.

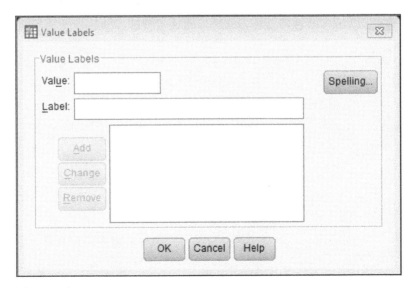

FIGURE A.3 Values column.

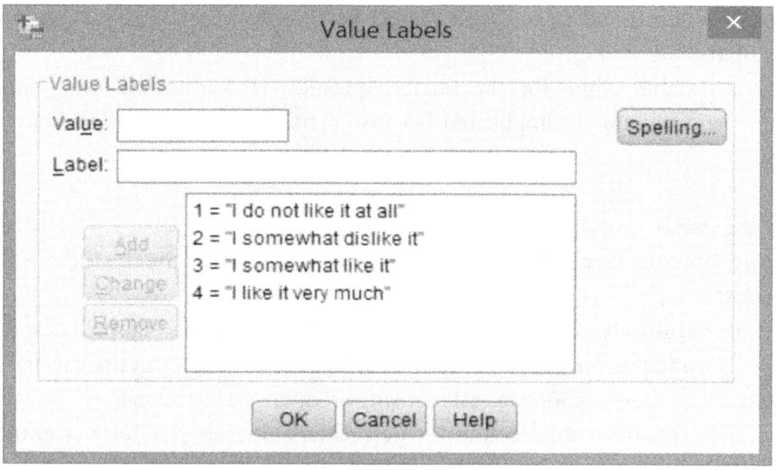

FIGURE A.4 Miniwindow for **Values** column.

- After completing the **Variable View** for all five questions, the screen will look the same as Figure A.5.
- Click **Data View** in the bottom left corner of SPSS Windows to return to the original blank screen. The completed **Variable View** screen will look like Figure A.6.
- Now input the data (scores) listed in Table A.1 into their proper variables. Once all the numerical scores in Table A.1 are entered into **Data View**, the data file or system file is complete, as shown in Figure A.7.
- At this point, the data or system file is ready to be saved.

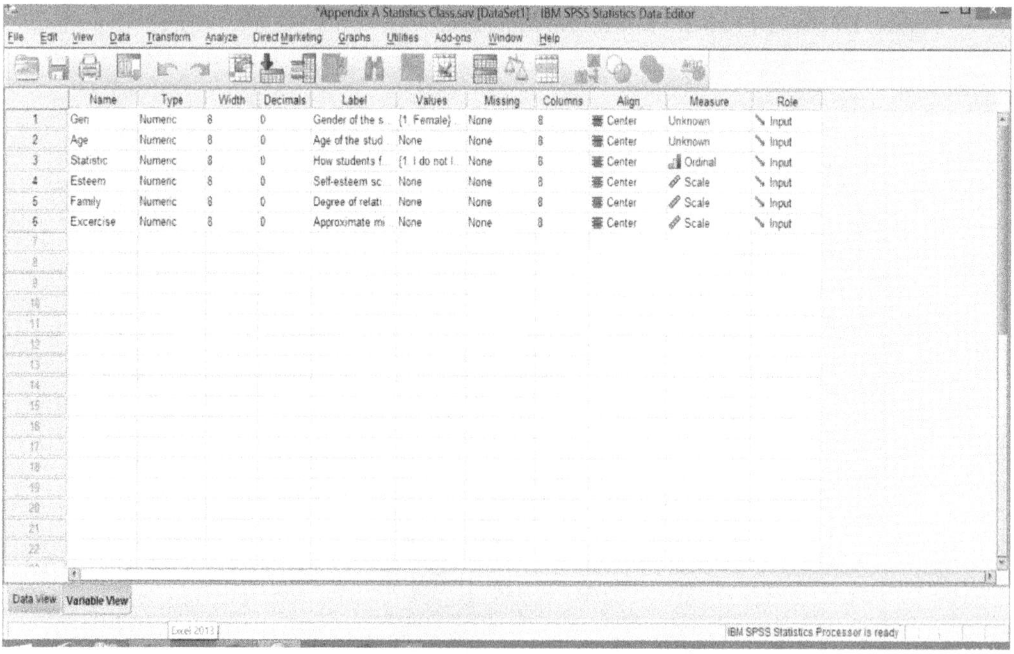

FIGURE A.5 Variable View for table.

FIGURE A.6 Data View for the completed variable.

	Gen	Age	Statistic	Esteem	Family	Excercise	var	var	var	var	var	var	var	var
1	2	23	4	9	10	60								
2	1	19	3	7	8	40								
3	2	22	1	8	9	120								
4	2	20	2	5	6	0								
5	1	28	4	7	4	15								
6	2	31	4	5	6	30								
7	1	29	3	6	7	60								
8	2	26	4	4	6	30								
9	2	21	1	5	7	20								
10	1	24	3	6	8	0								
11	2	20	4	9	8	45								
12	2	34	3	8	8	100								
13	2	23	4	9	7	30								
14	1	26	4	7	8	15								
15	2	23	4	8	9	0								

FIGURE A.7 Data View for the name of the variable.

SAVING DATA

Saving an SPSS file is no different from saving word-processing documents. In fact, there are several ways to save your files (data and output). Like most programs, SPSS automatically saves your file as a *default file* every 10 or so minutes. However, it is better to manually save your data file using a recognizable file name. Without this, SPSS will assign a random name and save in the most recent file location.

To save work, follow these brief steps: Pull down the **File Menu** from the left-hand side of the screen. Select **Save As** then **Look In** field at the top of the window. Find the location where the file is to be saved and then type a suitable file name. Also, remember whether the file is saved as **DATA**, **SYNTAX**, **OUTPUT**, or **SCRIPT**. Syntax is an alternative way of computing solutions by avoiding point-and-click operations. Script is relatively new to SPSS, so to avoid point-and-click moves, consider using Syntax.

Now that data entry using **Variable View** and **Data View** has been covered, we move to an explanation of the basics of *descriptive and inferential statistics* using SPSS/PASW. But first, frequency distributions using SPSS are introduced.

FREQUENCY DISTRIBUTIONS USING SPSS

Summarizing quantitative data into a simpler format makes it easier to explain. Look at the top of the computer screen and find the **Analyze** ribbon. To create a frequency table for the variable How much do students like statistics as displayed in Figure A.5, follow these steps:

- Pull down the **Analyze** ribbon.
- Select **Descriptive Statistics** and then move the cursor to **Frequencies**. Two square windows appear. The miniwindows (desktop windows) on the left show a list of all variables in the study project; the one on the right is currently blank. Use the mouse to highlight the variable **How students felt about statistics** and then click the arrow between the two miniwindows. Notice that the variable automatically jumps to the small desktop window on the right.
- Select options for the inclusion of descriptive statistics. For the user's own research project, *suppose that variables were constructed with interval and ratio levels of measurement without outliers*; if so, then select **Statistics** (top right screen corner) and check the descriptive statistics selected for examination. However, the variable in Figure A.5 used ordinal-level data, so click **OK**. Table A.2 will appear.

Table A.2: How Students Felt About Statistics

		Frequency	Percentage	Valid Percentage	Cumulative Percentage
Valid	I do not like it at all	2	13.3	13.3	13.3
	I somewhat dislike it	1	6.7	6.7	20.0
	I like it	4	26.7	26.7	46.7
	I like it very much	8	53.3	53.3	100.0
	Total	15	100.0	100.0	

Before going deeper into descriptive and inferential statistics, some rules of statistics and general guidelines in preparing data for analysis are reiterated.

PREPARING THE DATA FOR ANALYSES

Statisticians and researchers quickly find that, when it comes to preparing data for analyses, there is no simple way to organize, display, and analyze raw scores. Although each researcher individually makes decisions according to personal habits, styles, and objectives, those decisions must comply with the laws of statistics. Next discussed are some steps recommended for consideration when analyzing quantitative data.

SUGGESTED STEPS IN PREPARING
THE OBTAINED SCORES FOR ANALYSES

The research data. Before working on data entry, look through the research questionnaires and the raw scores obtained. Take note of areas with discrepancies or inconsistencies or areas requiring new variables. Sometimes, one or more variables emerge during the data collection process that were not part of the original questionnaire. This problem arises because participants have unexpected reactions to questions and their responses may differ from the precoded values.

1. *While doing data entry.* The information returned by the research subjects (participants) should be coded or assigned ID numbers. Use a code book/code sheet (see the variable name in parentheses before the questions in the questionnaire in this chapter). Even with the assistance of programs, a coding sheet/coding scheme is needed to help track of the variables entered. The coding sheet will make data analyses much easier.
2. *After data entry is complete.* Once data entry is complete, use frequency distributions as shown in Table A.1 to *check for typographical errors.* Incorrect data may have been mistakenly entered into the data file, perhaps an illegal character or an incorrect response. Careful researchers edit typos and correct missing data before proceeding to data analyses and interpretations.
3. *Data recoding.* For inference (i.e., generalization), the original values of one or more of the variables (both dependent and independent) may need to be recoded. For example, the researcher may need to recode several racial backgrounds into a new category such as minority and mainstream groups. Alternatively, one may need to recode ordinal data into nominal levels of measurement. *Sometimes, recoding can help make data meet specific statistical assumptions.* For example, how does a researcher recode the question about how much students like statistics (Question 3 or the fourth column in Table A.1)? Assume that now the desire is to recode the question as "Dislike" and "Like". Follow these steps:
   - Select **Variable View** (bottom left corner of the screen).
   - Put the cursor on column 1, row 4, then type **Like**.

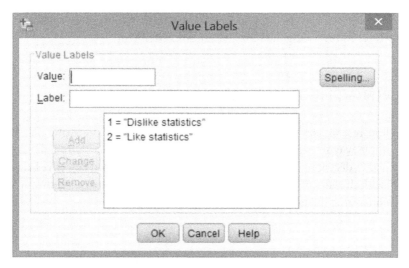

FIGURE A.8 Dislike statistics or **Like statistics**.

- Change **Decimals** to 0, then type **Students dislike or like statistics** in the **Label** column.
- In the **Values** column, type **1** on **Value** and **Dislike statistics** in the **Label** rectangle. Then, type **2** and label it **Dislike statistics**." The minidesktop appears as in Figure A.8.
- On **Measure**, select **Nominal**, then click **Data View** (bottom left corner).
- Notice that the entire column on the newly created variable name "Like" is blank with only dot, dot, dot, throughout.
- Pull down **Transform** on the main ribbon. Then, move the cursor to **Recode into different variable**. The desire is to recode the "Statistic" variable into different variables to preserve the original scores. In Recode Variable, the choices are to recode into the same or a different variable.
- Select the variable **How students felt about statistics?** then click the arrow in the middle of the two minidesktop windows. The variable should automatically move to the new miniwindow on the right as shown in Figure A.9. In **Name**, type the newly created variable Like and on **Label**, type **Students dislike or like statistics** (see top right of Figure A.9).
- Click **Old and New Values**....
- Notice that two subwindows appear. The window on the left is labeled **Old Value**, and the one on the right is labeled **New Value**. Type **1** (I do not like statistics at all) on the **Old Value**, then **1** (Dislike statistics). Click the word **Add** in the middle of the screen. Move the cursor to **Old Value**, enter **2** (I somewhat dislike statistics), then **1** (Dislike statistics). Next, type **3** (I somewhat like statistics) and **2** (Like statistics); finally, type **4** (I like statistics a lot) and **2** (Like statistics) on **Old Value** and **New Value**, respectively. The result should look like Figure A.10. The objective is to change the old values "I do not like statistics at all" and "I somewhat like statistics" into "Dislike statistics" and "I somewhat like statistics," respectively, and "I like statistics a lot" to "Like statistics."

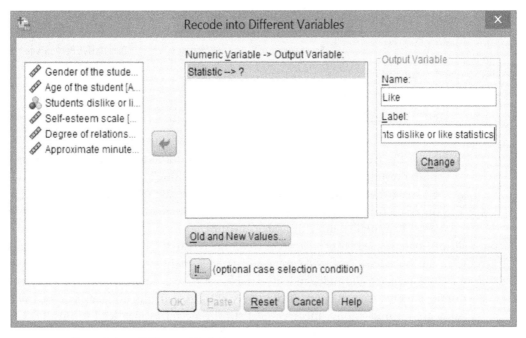

FIGURE A.9 Recode into **Different Variables**.

- Click **Change** (top right corner of the minidesktop). SPSS will ask whether this is what the user wants. Click **OK**, then click **Continue** (bottom of minidesktop).
- Notice that the Output file says that **Recode** has been executed. Close the output file and then click **Data View** to return to the data file (system file). Notice that the newly created values now appear under the variable Like (Table A.3).

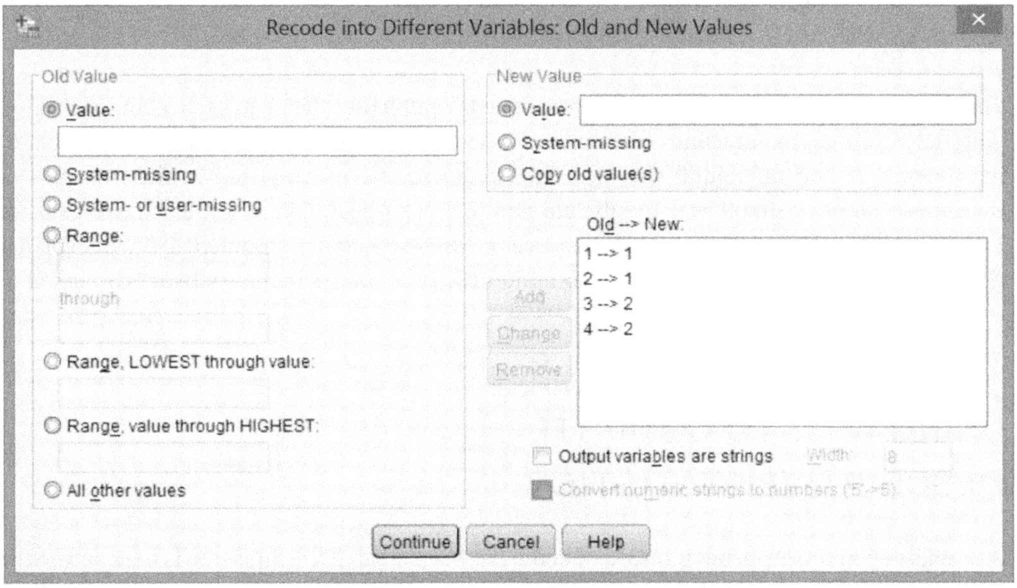

FIGURE A.10 Recode into **Different Variables: Old Value** and **New Values**.

Table A.3: Frequency Distribution for the Recode Variable "Like"

		Frequency	Percentage	Cumulative Percentage
Valid	Dislike statistics	3	20.0	20.0
	Like statistics	12	80.0	100.0
	Total	15	100.0	

- Rerun the frequency distribution as was done for Table A.2 and notice that a similar result is obtained. In Table A.1, when adding I do not like statistics at all to I somewhat dislike it, 20% of the respondents said they did not like statistics. The result from the recode remains the same. Essentially, recode reduces several values to a smaller, more desirable outcome.

4. Clearly *understand level of measurement* for the research measures. Statistics teachers often say to students that while preparing data for analyses, the level of measurement for the dependent and independent variables may be as important as the Bible, the Koran, Buddha, or a shaman. If the levels of measurements utilized for a research study are misunderstood, incorrect statistical procedures may lead to invalid data interpretations (programs will compute anything as long as a value is entered).

5. Clearly *understand measures of central tendency.* Measures of central tendency help to understand the overall distribution of the scores, find outliers, and even make educated guesses about homogeneity of variance.

6. Last but most important, *understand the tail of the hypothesis test and its statistical significance.* DO NOT rely on what is/are given by the program. For example, a correlation coefficient of .752 produced based on a sample size of 30 is not as strong as a correlation coefficient of .541 produced from a sample size of 250. Chapter 8 noted that with a large sample size, just a very small correlation coefficient is sufficient to reject H_0. Also, whenever possible, change the preset α (p value) level listed in SPSS.

The functions of SPSS have now been introduced: completing data entry, checking for typos, and statistical analysis guidelines. The remaining sections of Appendix A are devoted to explaining descriptive and inferential statistics. The frequency table completed in the first part of the chapter shows a simple way to tabulate nominal or ordinal data. If a user has interval- or ratio-level data, what other types of descriptive statistics should be computed? Last, an explanation was presented showing how SPSS computes the types of inferential statistics discussed in Chapters 7 to 11.

USING SPSS TO COMPUTE DESCRIPTIVE STATISTICS

As explained in this Appendix, once a data file has been created, the first step is to examine the frequency distributions of the variables. If the data set contains only a nominal and ordinal level of measurement and the user does not want to generalize the findings, then the display and discussion of frequency tables is sufficient (see Tables A.2 and A.3). If the user has interval- or ratio-level data, then going beyond frequency tables is important. Whenever the data set contains interval- or ratio-level data, it is crucial to compute measures of central tendency and variability. When viewing Table A.1, note that the last four variables utilized an interval scale. Accordingly, it is important to tabulate measures of central tendency and measures of variability for the table. As an illustration, select the third variable (Age) in Table A.1. To compute measures of central tendency and measures of variability for the variable Age, follow these steps:

- Pull down the **Analyze** ribbon, move the cursor to **Descriptive Statistics**, select **Frequencies**.
- Notice that two small windows appear. The window on the left lists all variables from Table A.1. The one on the right is currently blank. Use the cursor, select **Age of the students**, then click the arrow in the middle between the two windows. The variable Age of the students automatically moves into the window on the right. The selection appears as in Figure A.11.
- Click **Statistics** (top right corner of screen), then under **Central Tendency**, check **Mean**, **Median**, and **Mode**. On **Dispersion**, check **Std. deviation** and **Variance** (see Chapters 3 and 4). Selections should appear as in Figure A.12.
- Click **Continue**. Additional options available will appear at the top right of the screen. Select options that best fit the research objectives.
- Click **OK**.
- The results for the descriptive statistics (i.e., measures of central tendency and variability) for the variable Age will appear as in Table A.4.

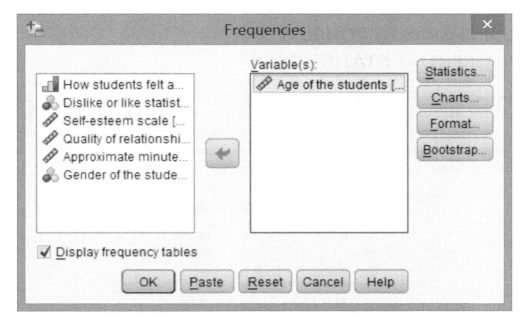

FIGURE A.11 Descriptive statistics computations.

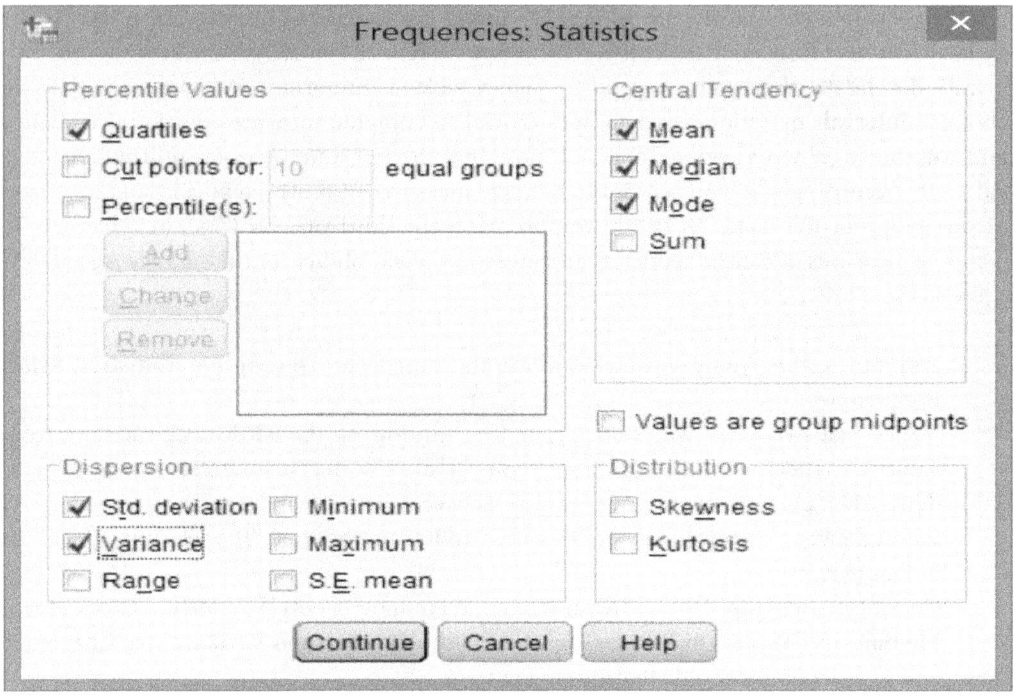

FIGURE A.12 Selecting measures of central tendency and variability.

Should the user want just the measures of central tendency (i.e., mean, median, mode, standard deviation), pull down **Analyze**, go to **Descriptive Statistics**, and then choose **Descriptive** instead of going through the steps discussed.

USING SPSS TO COMPUTE INFERENTIAL STATISTICS

This section provides several examples of how to use the SPSS program to compute inferential statistics. Step-by-step hand calculation and the proper way to report findings relating to a particular statistics test were discussed previously (see Chapter 7 through 11). As in descriptive statistics, in this appendix only the steps necessary to compute the statistical test and read solutions are shown.

Table A.4: Age of the Students

N Valid	15
Mean	24.60
Median	23.00
Mode	23
Standard deviation	4.356
Variance	18.971

THE PEARSON CORRELATION

In Table A.1, suppose that the user wants to see whether there is any relationship between student self-esteem and the quality of student relationship with family members. To complete the *Pearson correlation coefficient* (Pearson r), follow these steps:

- First, open Appendix A SPSS Data file and then pull down the **Analyze** ribbon. Move the cursor down to **Correlate**. Choose **Bivariate**.
- Select **Self-esteem score**, and **Degree of relationship with family members**. The selection will appear as in Figure A.12.
- In the middle of the screen on **Correlation Coefficient**, notice that **Pearson** was automatically checked. (*Kendall's tau b* and *Spearman* are not covered in this book.) Also, notice that on **Test significance, two-tailed** was automatically highlighted. Should the user have a personal research project, if the choice is **one-tailed**, undo the two-tailed option.
- Select other options that best fit with the research project.
- Click **OK**. The results are displayed in Table A.5.

Figure A.12. The Pearson r Correlation Computation Screen

The *Pearson correlation* matrix shows a significant relationship between student self-esteem and the relationship with family members ($r = .573$, $p < .025$). As stated in Chapter 4, when calculating solutions by computer, pay attention to the computed p value. Whenever the computed p value *falls between .000 and .05*, the user can conclude that the finding is *significant* and then substitute the word *finding* with the appropriate concept, such as relationship, association, or cause and effect. Because the p value computed is .025, the user can conclude that there is a significant relationship between the variables.

Please note that the *coefficient of determination* (r^2 or R^2) can be computed under linear regression.

THE CHI-SQUARE TEST OF INDEPENDENCE

Using the data set from Table A.1, compute the chi-square test of association (χ^2). Because chi-square requires nominal data for both dependent and independent variables, use

Table A.5: Computing the Pearson Correlation Coefficient (Pearson *r*)

		Self-Esteem Scale	Degree of Relationship the Students Have With Family Members
Self-esteem scale	Pearson correlation	1	.573[a]
	Significance (2-tailed)		.025
	N	15	15
Degree of relationship the students have with family members	Pearson correlation	.573[*]	1
	Significance (2-tailed)	.025	
	N	15	15

[a] Correlation is significant at the .05 level (two tailed).

the variables Like and Gender. To compute the chi-square test of association, do the following:

- Pull down the **Analyze** ribbon, move the cursor to **Descriptive Statistics**, and then choose **Crosstabs**.
- Some users select **Column** to display the dependent variable and **Row** for the independent variable. Others choose the opposite. The user must clearly understand which variables are to be used for the dependent and independent variables. Also, note that chi-square is a bivariate analysis, so select one variable for **Row** and one for **Column**.
- For practical purposes, select the variable **Gender** for **Column** and **Family** for **Row**.
- Click on **Statistics**, check **chi-square**, then click **Continue** to exit.
- If the user also wants to include **Expected Frequencies** and **Percentages** in the output table, click **Cells**, then select the other information desired. When selections are complete, click **Continue** to exit. The user's selections will appear as in Figure A.13.
Click **OK** and information shown in Tables A.6a and A.6b will appear.
- For an actual research report, to include the **Crosstabulation** tables, the user must include both—only in Tables A.6a and A.6b)—with the report. Without the tables, even statisticians will be at a loss to explain the findings.

As displayed in Table A.6b, the chi-square test shows no significant association between gender and whether one likes or dislikes statistics ($\chi^2 = 1.875$, $df = 1$, $p > .171$). There is no association between the variables under investigation because the p value produced by SPSS is .171—much larger than the conventional p value of .000 to .05.

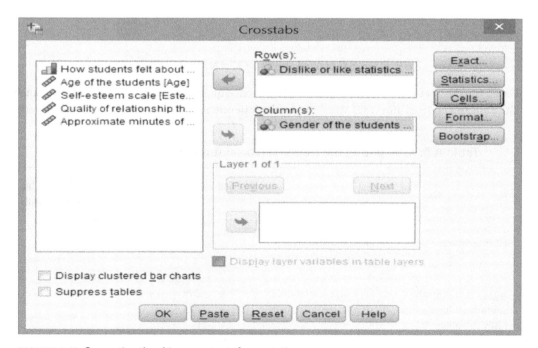

FIGURE A.13 Computing the chi-square test of association.

Table A.6a: Dislike or Like Statistics * Gender of the Students' Cross Tabulation

			Gender of the Students		Total
			Female	Male	
Dislike or like statistics	Dislike statistics	Count	0	3	3
		Expected count	1.0	2.0	3.0
		% of total	0.0%	20.0%	20.0%
	Like statistics	Count	5	7	12
		Expected count	4.0	8.0	12.0
		% of total	33.3%	46.7%	80.0%
Total		Count	5	10	15
		Expected count	5.0	10.0	15.0
		% of total	33.3%	66.7%	100.0%

Table A.6b: Chi-Square Tests

	Value	df	Asymptotic significance (2 Sided)	Exact significance (2 sided)	Exact significance (1 Sided)
Pearson chi-square	1.875[a]	1	.171		
Continuity correction	.469	1	.494		
Likelihood ratio	2.795	1	.095		
Fisher's exact test				.505	.264
Linear-by-linear association	1.750	1	.186		
N of valid cases	15				

[a] Three cells (75.0%) have expected count less than 5. The minimum expected count is 1.00.

LINEAR REGRESSION

Next presented are the steps needed to compute the linear regression (Figure A.14).

- To compute linear regression, pull down the **Analyze** ribbon. Move the cursor down to **Regression** and select **Linear**.
- Select one dependent and one or more independent variables. Keep in mind that level of measurement for the variables must be interval or higher level of measurement.
- On the top right, there are five possible selections: **Statistics, Plots**, **Save**, **Options**, and **Bootstrap**. This is where the user can change the confidence interval, remove an unwanted confidence level, plot the scatter diagram, or select another regression model.
- In the middle of the screen, see **Method**. This is another option for selecting a specific regression model. Available methods include **Stepwise**, **Remove**, **Forward**, and **Backward** models. To select the method suitable for the user's research project, click the word **Help** immediately below **Method**. SPSS/PASW provides detailed instructions for each method and gives sample illustrations.

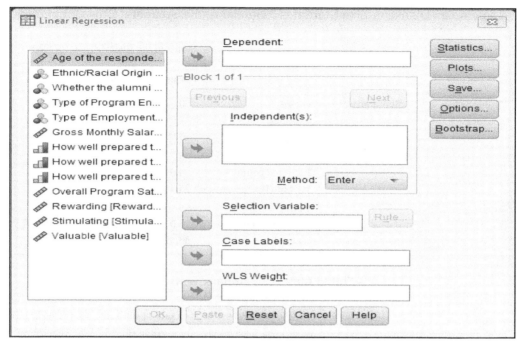

FIGURE A.14 Screen for **Linear Regression**.

- There are a few other options at the bottom of the screen. Select the option(s) that best fit the focus of the research.
- Click **OK**.

Now, assume that the linear regression is computed using Appendix A SPSS Data file, follow the steps discussed previously by putting self-esteem as the dependent variable and family relationship as the independent variable. Table A.7 shows the result of the linear regression model.

Similar to the analysis of correlation, linear regression also shows a significant relationship between self-esteem and family relationship, with a standard error of 1.396. In fact, the amount of variances in family relationship explained 32.8% (see $R = .573$ in the table) of self-esteem in this hypothetical scenario.

THE ONE-SAMPLE *T* TEST

Remember that there are three types of *t* test (one sample, independent samples, and dependent samples). Check to be certain that statistical computations comply with the rules of statistics discussed in Chapter 9. The *t* tests are one of the SPSS computations for which the laws of statistics must be obeyed or the results will be inaccurate. To compute the *t* tests, the one-sample *t* test screen is displayed in Figure A.15.

Table A.7: Linear Regression Between Self-Esteem and Family Relationship

Model	Variables Entered	Variables Removed	Method
1	Degree of relationship the students have with family members[a]	.	Enter

[a] Dependent variable: the participant's self-esteem.

Model Summary				
Model	R	R^2	Adjusted R^2	Standard Error of the Estimate
1	.573[a]	.329	.277	1.396

[a] Predictor variable: the participant's degree of family togetherness.

Analysis of Variance (ANOVA)[a]						
	Model	Sum of Squares	df	Mean Square	F	Significance
1	Regression	12.406	1	12.406	6.368	.025[a]
	Residual	25.327	13	1.948		
	Total	37.733	14			

[a] Dependent variable: the respondent's level of self-esteem.
[b] Predictors: (Constant), degree of relationship the students have with family members.

Coefficients[a]					
Model	Unstandardized Coefficients		Standardized Coefficients	t	Significance
	B	Standard Error	β		
1 (Constant)	2.230	1.872		1.191	.255
Degree of relationship the students have with family members	.627	.248	.573	2.523	.025

[a] Dependent variable: the respondent's level of self-esteem.

- Pull down the **Analyze** ribbon. Move the cursor to **Compare means** and then move the cursor over to the *CORRECT t* test.
- On **Option**, select the confidence interval that best fits with your research purposes.
- Click **Continue**.
- Click **OK**.

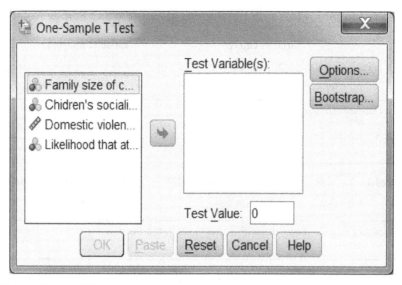

FIGURE A.15 One-Sample T Test screen.

SUMMARY

This appendix provided a quick glance at statistical analyses in general as well as the SPSS commands and functions that can be used to do statistical computations similar to those covered throughout this book. Appendix C provides illustrations for using Microsoft Excel and its Analysis ToolPak to compute basic descriptive statistics.

APPENDIX B

Nonparametric Statistics and Post Hoc Tests

OVERVIEW

When a nonnormal distribution is assumed, the chi-square (Chapter 7) is called a *nonparametric statistic*. The ordinary statistics tests discussed in Chapters 8 to 11 are called *parametric statistics*. Parametric statistics are used to do hypothesis testing that is based on the assumption of a normal distribution. A normal distribution assumes that frequency distribution of the obtained scores from the research project follow a normal curve. Most important, the values of the variables follow the interval or ratio level of measurement. Some statisticians stated that statistics that describe the entire population are called parametric as they represent a population parameter, whereas statistics that describe the sample is called nonparametric. However, this is not always the case. More specifically, nonparametric statistics are used to describe nonnormal distributions by transforming the scores to ranks. *Rank order* refers to changing a set of scores to ranks. Usually, the lowest score is ranked 1, the next higher score ranked 2, and so on.

THE LOGIC OF RANK ORDER

The rank order transforms the obtained scores from the research study into an easily understood format. Suppose that in a research project about the age of a client group at a social services agency, you obtained the following ages: 21, 27, 35, 67, 22, 31. Whether ordering them by hand or computer application, the data can be transformed into ranks 1, 2, 3, 4, 5, and 6. The 1 refers to the lowest score in the data set, which is 21, and 6 represents the highest score, which is 67. Typically, rank order is not a way of getting a normal distribution, but rather it provides researchers rectangular values, with an equal number of values for the variable(s) under investigation. Rank order enables the researchers to spread the scores evenly for the distribution set. Aron, Coups, and Aron (2011) stated that the basic logic of rank-order tests is "that researcher converts all the scores to ranks, adds up the total of the ranks in the group with the lower scores, and then compares this total to a cutoff from a special table of significance cutoffs for total ranks in this kind of situation" (p. 396). There are several types of nonparametric statistics.

TYPES OF ALTERNATIVE NONPARAMETRIC STATISTICS

When assumptions of normal distribution and interval-/ratio-level data are not met, the alternative tests are the Wilcoxon signed rank, the Wilcoxon rank sum or Mann–Whitney U, and Kruskal–Wallis H (Table B.1). Due to the complex formula involved in these tests, this appendix highlights their meanings and provides instructions in how to use the Statistical Package for the Social Sciences (SPSS) to compute solutions.

- *The Wilcoxon signed-ranks test* is a *nonparametric* test designed to evaluate the difference between two treatments or conditions for which the samples are correlated. In particular, *it is suitable for evaluating the data from a repeated-measures design if the prerequisites for a dependent samples* t *test are not met.* So, for example, it might be used to evaluate the data from an experiment that looks at the self-esteem of children before and after they undergo a period of self-assertive training.
- The *Kruskal–Wallis test* is a *nonparametric* method for one-way analysis of variance (ANOVA) used to determine if *three or more unmatched samples originate from the same distribution.* The Kruskal–Wallis test is essentially a standard one-way ANOVA, with ranks assigned to the data points replacing the data points themselves, and is similar to the Mann–Whitney U test but is applicable to more than two sample groups. Typically, a large Kruskal–Wallis statistic corresponds to a large discrepancy among rank sums. If the p value is small, you can reject the idea that the difference is due to random sampling, and you can conclude instead that the populations have different distributions. If the p value is large, the data do not give you any reason to conclude that the distributions differ. This is not the same as saying that the distributions are the same. The Kruskal–Wallis test has little power. In fact, if the total sample size is seven or less, the Kruskal–Wallis test will always give a p value greater than .05 no matter how much the groups differ.

Table B.1: Alternative Rank-Order Statistics Tests for Nonparametric Statistics

Parametric Statistic	Corresponding Nonparametric Statistic
t test for dependent means (samples)	Wilcoxon signed-rank test
t test for independent means (samples)	Wilcoxon rank sum test or Mann–Whitney U test
Analysis of variance	Kruskal–Wallis H test

SPSS FOR INFERENTIAL NONPARAMETRIC STATISTICS AND POST HOC TESTS

Brief highlights of SPSS procedures for the nonparametric statistics including the post hoc test are now presented. Recall that the goal for nonparametric statistics includes the following calculations:

- Mann–Whitney test
- Wilcoxon's matched-pairs signed-ranks test
- Kruskal–Wallis one-way ANOVA

This part of Appendix B shows how to use SPSS nonparametric statistics to compare two independent groups, two paired samples, k independent groups, and k related samples when equal variances are assumed. Note that the steps are the same. Just make sure that the correct test for the research objectives and data collection procedures for the research study is selected.

Appendix B on nonparametric SPSS data contains a hypothetical data set based nonnormal distribution, and the goal is to compare the Global Assessment Functioning (GAF) scores of 30 clients at a public mental health program who received individual psychotherapy counseling for the past several weeks. First, let us compare the GAF scores before and after treatment by gender using the *Mann–Whitney test*. To do the nonparametric statistical computation, select the computer screen on **Analyze** as in Figure B.1 and then perform the following steps:

- Pull down the **Analyze** ribbon. Move the cursor to **Nonparametric Tests**, then to **Legacy Dialogs**, and select **2 Independent Samples**. The miniwindows shown in Figure B.2 appear.

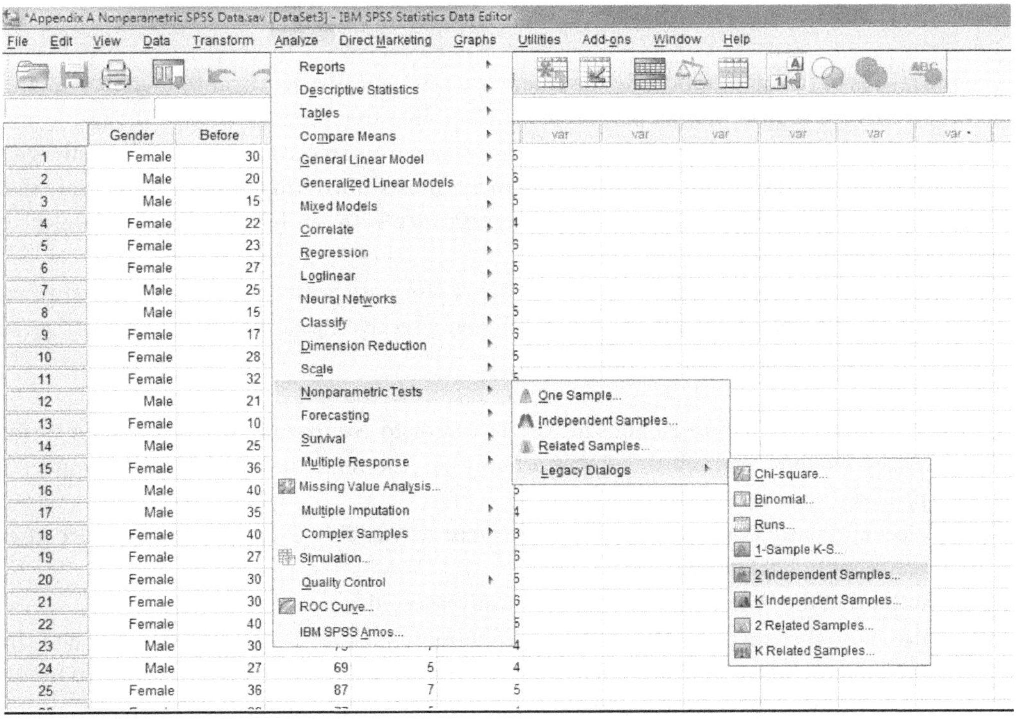

FIGURE B.1 Nonparametric statistics.

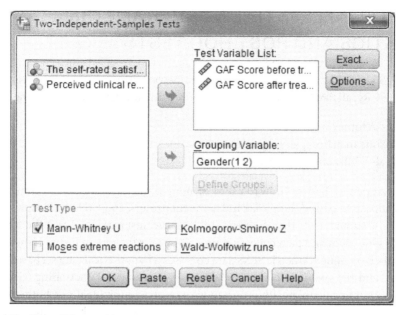

FIGURE B.2 The Mann–Whitney *U* test.

- On **Grouping Variable**, select and paste **Gender** to the small rectangle, then click **Define Groups**. Enter **1** (female) to **Group 1** and **2** (male) to **Group 2**. Notice that the Mann–Whitney *U* is automatically highlighted.
- Click **OK**. Momentarily, the nonparametric statistic for the Mann–Whitney *U* appears as in Table B.2.

The results of the output indicate that there is no statistically significant difference in GAF scores for this client group, either before ($p = .250$) or after treatment ($p = .703$). The result simply states that there were similar scores before the client group received treatment (mostly with a low GAF score) and similar scores after treatment (mostly medium to high scores). Note that the result says nothing about the statistical significance between before and after treatment (treatment effects).

Next, let us use the Wilcoxon test to compare the statistically significant difference on treatment effect before and after the group of clients received psychotherapy counseling. To obtain the Wilcoxon test, do the following:

- Pull down the **Analyze** ribbon. Move the cursor to **Nonparametric Tests**, then to the **Legacy Dialogs**, and select **2 Related Samples**. The miniwindow shown in Figure B.3 appears.
- Select and paste **GAF Score before treatment** to **Variable 1** and then **GAF Score after treatment** to **Variable 2**.
- Notice that the Wilcoxon test is automatically selected.
- Also, note that there are other statistical options, such as descriptive statistics and the **McNemar** or **Sign** test. In an actual research project, one may consider these extra options.
- Click **OK**; two tables as shown in Table B.3 appear.

Table B.2: Result of the Mann–Whitney U test

Ranks

	Gender of Respondent	N	Mean Rank	Sum of Ranks
GAF score before treatment	Female	19	16.95	322.00
	Male	11	13.00	143.00
	Total	30		
GAP score after treatment	Female	19	16.00	304.00
	Male	11	14.64	161.00
	Total	30		

	GAF Score Before Treatment	GAP Score After Treatment
Mann–Whitney U	77.000	95.000
Wilcoxon W	143.000	161.000
z	−1.187	−.410
Asymptotic significance (2 tailed)	.235	.682
Exact significance [2 * (1-tailed significance)]	.250[a]	.703[a]

* Significant difference between pretest and post-test GAF score.

Look at the row labeled z. Recall that in Chapter 5, the z score was introduced and computed. Note the lowercase letters a and b as footnotes to the first part of the table. In footnote b, it states that the GAF score after treatment was greater than the GAF score before treatment, resulting in statistical significance ($z = −4.78$, $p < .000$). This statistical significance simply

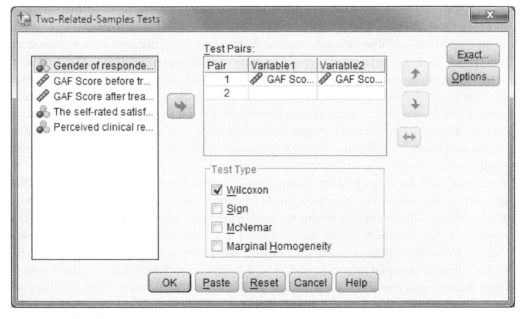

FIGURE B.3 The Wilcoxon test.

Table B.3: The Wilcoxon Test

Ranks

		N	Mean Rank	Sum of Ranks
GAP score after treatment –	Negative ranks	0[a]	.00	.00
GAF score before treatment	Positive ranks	30[b]	15.50	465.00
	Ties	0[c]		
	Total	30		

Test Statistics[a]

	GAF Score After Treatment – GAF Score Before Treatment
z	−4.783[b]
Asymptotic significance (2 tailed)	.000

[a] GAF score after treatment < GAF score before treatment.
[b] GAF score after treatment > GAF score before treatment.
[c] GAF score after treatment = GAF score before treatment

indicates that psychotherapy counseling was effective and resulted in this client group's ability to attain a much higher level of global functioning.

ONE-WAY ANOVA POST HOC TESTS

Chapter 9 (on the *t* tests), Chapter 11 (on one-way ANOVA), and the Mann–Whitney *U* and Kruskal–Wallis *H* tests, are used to statistical significant difference between the variables. They these statistics tests do not explain the place or location of the difference. The post hoc test *are used to examine where the difference exists*. Statistically significant differences obtained from these tests do not explain what specific groups are different in relation to the dependent variable. Essentially, post hoc tests compare the statistically significant differences for each pair of groups separately on the dependent variable. Most often, post hoc tests are designed for situations in which the researcher has already obtained a significant *F* test with a factor (dependent variable) that consists of three or more means. Additional exploration of the differences among means provides specific information on which means are significantly different from each other.

Because there are many post hoc tests, specific instructions from SPSS, version 22 (IBM SPSS, 2015), available on its free website. The SPSS website explains that once researchers have determined that differences exist among the means, post hoc range tests and pairwise multiple comparisons can determine which means differ. Range tests identify homogeneous subsets of means that are not different from each other. Pairwise multiple comparisons test the difference between each pair of means and yield a matrix in which asterisks indicate significantly different group means at an α level of .05. More specifically, when equal variances are assumed, SPSS states that Tukey's honestly significant difference, Hochberg's GT2, Gabriel, and Scheffé tests are multiple-comparison tests, and range tests should be considered. Other available range tests are Tukey's *b*, S-N-K (Student–Newman–Keuls), Duncan, R-E-G-W *F* (Ryan-Einot-Gabriel-Welsch *F* test), R-E-G-W *Q* (Ryan-Einot-Gabriel-Welsch range test), and Waller-Duncan tests. Available multiple-comparison tests are Bonferroni, Tukey's honestly significant difference, Sidak, Gabriel, Hochberg, Dunnett, Scheffé, and LSD (least significant difference) tests.

- *LSD*. The LSD uses *t* tests to perform all pairwise comparisons between group means. No adjustment is made to the error rate for multiple comparisons.
- *Bonferroni*. The Bonferroni test uses *t* tests to perform pairwise comparisons between group means but controls overall error rate by setting the error rate for each test to the experimentwise error rate divided by the total number of tests. Hence, the observed significance level is adjusted for the fact that multiple comparisons are being made.
- *Sidak*. This is a pairwise multiple-comparison test based on a *t* statistic. The Sidak test adjusts the significance level for multiple comparisons and provides tighter bounds than the Bonferroni test.
- *Scheffé*. Simultaneous joint pairwise comparisons are performed for all possible pairwise combinations of means and uses the *F* sampling distribution. It can be used to examine all possible linear combinations of group means, not just pairwise comparisons.
- *R-E-G-W F*. The R-E-G-W multiple-stepdown procedure is based on an *F* test.
- *R-E-G-W Q*. The R-E-G-W multiple-stepdown procedure is based on the Studentized range.
- *S-N-K*. This test makes all pairwise comparisons between means using the Studentized range distribution. With equal sample sizes, it also compares pairs of means within homogeneous subsets, using a stepwise procedure. Means are ordered from highest to lowest, and extreme differences are tested first.
- *Tukey*. The Tukey test uses the Studentized range statistic to make all of the pairwise comparisons between groups. It sets the experimentwise error rate at the error rate for the collection for all pairwise comparisons.
- *Tukey's b*. This test uses the Studentized range distribution to make pairwise comparisons between groups. The critical value is the average of the corresponding value for Tukey's honestly significant difference test and the S-N-K.
- *Duncan*. The Duncan test makes pairwise comparisons using a stepwise order of comparisons identical to the order used by the S-N-K test but sets a protection level for the error rate for the collection of tests rather than an error rate for individual tests. It uses the Studentized range statistic.
- *Hochberg's GT2*. This is a multiple-comparison and range test that uses the Studentized maximum modulus. It is similar to Tukey's honestly significant difference test.
- *Gabriel*. This is a pairwise comparison test that uses the Studentized maximum modulus and is generally more powerful than Hochberg's GT2 when the cell sizes are unequal. Gabriel's test may become liberal when the cell sizes vary greatly.
- *Waller–Duncan*. This is a multiple-comparison test based on a *t* statistic; it uses a Bayesian approach.
- *Dunnett*. The Dunnett test is a pairwise multiple-comparison *t* test that compares a set of treatments against a single control mean. The last category is the default control category. Alternatively, you can choose the first category: **2-sided** tests that the mean at any level

(except the control category) of the factor is not equal to that of the control category; < **Control** tests if the mean at any level of the factor is smaller than that of the control category; and > **Control** tests if the mean at any level of the factor is greater than that of the control category.

When selecting **Equal Variances Not Assumed**, then the following tests are offered and should be considered:

- **Tamhane's T2.** A conservative pairwise comparisons test based on a t test, this test is appropriate when the variances are unequal.
- **Dunnett's T3.** A pairwise comparison test based on the Studentized maximum modulus, this test is appropriate when the variances are unequal.
- **Games-Howell.** A pairwise comparison test that is sometimes liberal, this test is appropriate when the variances are unequal.
- **Dunnett's C.** A pairwise comparison test based on the Studentized range. This test is appropriate when the variances are unequal.

To obtain any of these tests, whether equal variances are assumed or not assumed, use the following steps:

- Pull down the **Analyze** ribbon. Move the cursor to **Compare Means**, then select **One-Way ANOVA** and then click it.
- The **One-Way ANOVA** miniwindow appears as in Figure B.4.
- In the upper right corner, four options are available: **Contrasts…**, **Post Hoc…**, **Options…**, and **Bootstrap….** Select **Post Hoc….**
- A new screen pops up as in Figure B.5.
- Enter the dependent (only one) and as many independent variables as you wish. For the dependent variable, keep in mind that the dependent variable must contain interval- or ratio-level data.

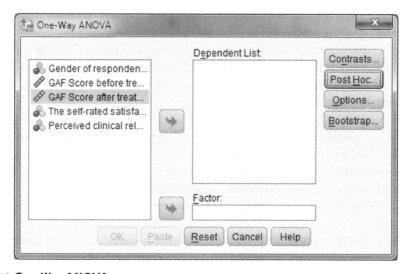

FIGURE B.4 One-Way ANOVA screen.

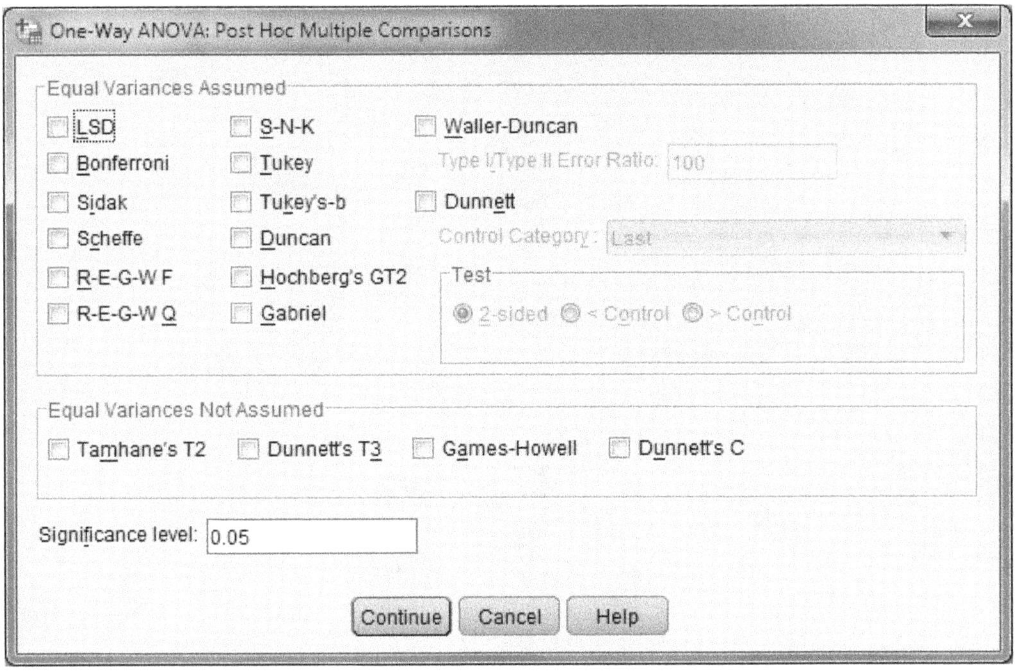

FIGURE B.5 The post hoc test screen.

- Use the statistical criteria, assumptions, and data distributions as explained by PASW/SPSS to select the correct post hoc test.
- Notice that the post hoc tests for **Equal Variances Not Assumed** are right below those for **Equal Variances Assumed**.

Explaining findings from these post hoc tests is complex. Use the instructions provided in Chapters 4, 9, and 11; numerous online instructions about choosing the correct statistics tests; as well as a free online statistics book (http://www.statsoft.com/textbook).

SUMMARY

Appendix B briefly introduces nonparametric statistics. Nonparametric statistics is one of most difficult statistics course. It involves complex statistical calculations, procedures, and assumptions. There are websites that provide excellent instructions and guidelines about the meaning, requirements, and guidelines about nonparametric statistics. We strongly recommend beginning researchers to consult those free websites before choosing a particular type of nonparametric statistical test.

APPENDIX C

How to Use Microsoft Excel Analysis ToolPak

OVERVIEW

This appendix illustrates how to use Microsoft Excel Analysis ToolPak (Excel) to perform the statistical analyses discussed in this book. Like Microsoft Word, Excel is a part of Microsoft Office, which is widely available on most personal computers. This availability is one of the biggest advantages of Excel over other software programs solely dedicated to performing statistical tasks, including SPSS: Statistical Package for the Social Sciences/Predictive Analytics Software (SPSS/PASW) Statistics, Minitab, SAS, and so on. These statistical software programs are purchased separately, and they are typically expensive. Although it does not provide advanced statistics tools like other statistics applications, Excel can perform the basic statistical tasks introduced in this book, especially those in Chapters 3 and 4. Knowing how to use Excel also helps healthcare and social workers perform tasks other than statistical analyses, such as constructing tables and charts based on numerical data.

This appendix is divided into two main sections. The first section describes the basics of Excel, such as how to enter data into the Excel program, name a certain range of data, enter the formula to calculate, and use functions that are predefined sets of formulas. In addition, this section introduces the Excel *Analysis ToolPak*. The Analysis ToolPak helps users perform various statistical tasks much more easily than by using standard Excel functions.

The final section of Appendix C describes how to produce statistical results using Excel to compute the examples introduced in the previous chapters. The use of functions to perform the statistical task is first described, followed by a description of the Analysis ToolPak performing the same task.

Note that the main purpose of this appendix is *to explain how to perform statistical tasks using Excel, not to teach the user how to use Excel.* Therefore, if the user has little or no experience with Excel, in addition to this appendix, refer to a general Excel users' guide.

GETTING STARTED WITH EXCEL

DATA ENTRY

The first step in using Excel to perform statistical tasks is to enter the data. Several ways are available. If the data are already stored in an electronic file, such as an Excel or SPSS file format, users can load the electronic file into Excel. In most cases, however, the data are not in electronic format (e.g., handwritten client records on paper), so users must enter the data manually into Excel (i.e., by typing the characters and numbers using the keyboard).

Imagine that the task is to enter the demographic data from Table C.1 ("Demographic Characteristics of Students in a Statistics Class") into Excel to present the frequency distribution. The characteristics include five variables: "ID," "Age," "Class Standing," "Anxiety Level," and

Table C.1: Demographic Characteristics of Students in a Statistics Class

ID	Age	Class Standing	Anxiety Level	Overall GPA
01	28	Freshman	Extremely high anxiety	3.89
02	18	Freshman	High anxiety	3.45
03	20	Junior	High anxiety	2.50
04	29	Sophomore	Some anxiety	4.00
05	20	Junior	High anxiety	4.00
06	24	Senior	Extremely high anxiety	3.88
07	23	Senior	Some anxiety	3.76
08	19	Sophomore	Little anxiety	4.00
09	21	Junior	Some anxiety	3.99
10	30	Senior	High anxiety	3.67
11	45	Senior	Extremely high anxiety	2.67
12	26	Freshman	Little anxiety	3.33
13	22	Junior	Some anxiety	3.26
14	20	Senior	Little anxiety	3.76
15	32	Junior	High anxiety	3.21
16	19	Freshman	High anxiety	3.00
17	22	Senior	Extremely high anxiety	2.99
18	30	Senior	High anxiety	2.89
19	26	Junior	Extremely high anxiety	2.88
20	23	Sophomore	Some anxiety	3.40
21	46	Sophomore	High anxiety	3.65
22	38	Freshman	Some anxiety	3.66
23	18	Freshman	High anxiety	3.90
24	27	Junior	Extremely high anxiety	3.20
25	25	Senior	Extremely high anxiety	3.11
26	23	Junior	Extremely high anxiety	2.28
27	20	Senior	High anxiety	2.46
28	21	Senior	High anxiety	3.06
29	30	Junior	High anxiety	2.11
30	26	Senior	Extremely high anxiety	2.77

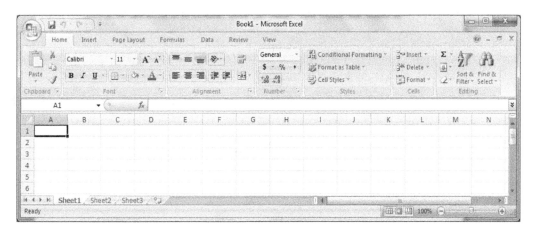

FIGURE C.1 Excel screen at startup.

"Overall GPA" (GPA is grade point average; see Chapter 2 for details about variables). When the user opens Excel, the screen will appear as in Figure C.1.

Type the variable names into the first row of the worksheet, denoted as **1** (Excel called it Name Box). Conventionally, the names of the variables are placed in the first row of the worksheet (Name Box 1). Once the names of the variables have been typed, enter the information from Table C.1 into the worksheet. Figure C.2 shows the worksheet with the data, now available for analysis.

The data in Table C.1 are easy to enter into Excel because it is structured so that each column represents the variable. In other situations, users may need to enter unstructured data (e.g., client record forms) into Excel. The data entry procedure is essentially the same as the following:

1. Identify the variable(s) in the records. The variable names were assigned to each of the items/questions as discussed in Appendix A.
2. Develop the coding scheme or the code book (see Appendix A for details about coding).
3. Similar to SPSS, once the variable names have been created, enter the data into Excel as shown previously in this section.

After these three steps are completed, statistical analyses can begin. The next topic in Excel pertains to formulas, but before discussing how to create formulas, concerning data entry, there is one major distinction between Excel and SPSS.

DIFFERENCE BETWEEN EXCEL AND SPSS IN DATA ENTRY

Note that there is a significant difference between Excel and SPSS in data entry. In Excel, first type the variables across columns and then enter the correspondence values into these columns (see Figure C.1). In SPSS/PASW, first program the names of the variables into the system under **Variable View**, then type the correspondence values into the **Data View** screen.

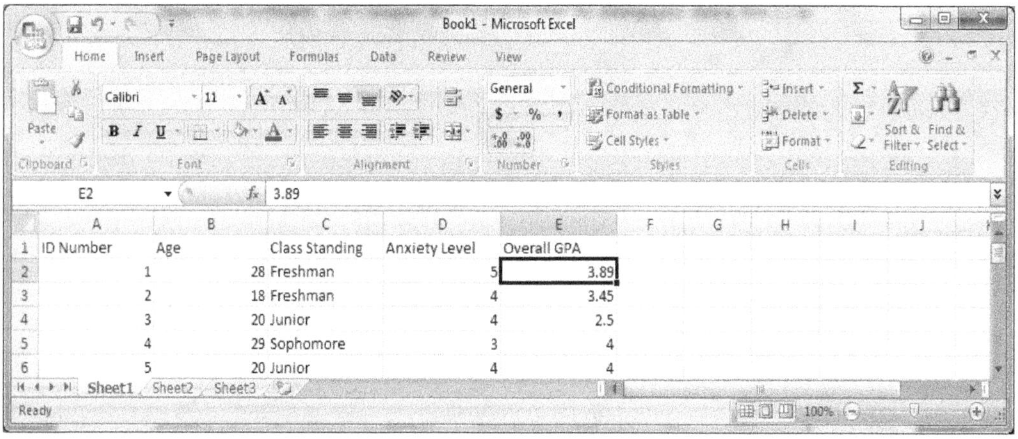

FIGURE C.2 Screen with data entry.

Formula

Excel, in some sense, is the software program that serves the oldest purpose of computerized calculation. In the early days of computer applications, researchers first literally counted the number of characters of each variable (counting spaces), then programmed the characters. This issue is no longer a problem. However, in Excel, the user must still know how to construct a formula. Calculation in Excel is done by formula. A *formula* is a set of mathematical operators used to calculate a value. For example, the simple formula to calculate the sum of the overall GPA of the first five students in Figure C.2 is

$$\text{Sum of overall GPA of first five students} = 3.89 + 3.45 + 2.5 + 4 + 4$$

Here are the four steps to make an *addition* formula in Excel to calculate the values:

1. Choose the cell in which the calculated value will be stored.
2. Enter the equals sign in the cell.
3. Type the formula after the equals sign.
4. Press **Enter** to obtain the calculated value.

Calculate the sum of overall GPA of the first five students in this example as follows:

1. First, select the cell in which the calculated value will be stored. For example, choose the cell next to the overall GPA of the first student, cell **F2** (bold rectangle in Figure C.3). Note that Excel shows the cell address, **F2** (for column F, row 2), in the name box to the left of the formula bar.
2. Next, enter the equals sign in cell F2. Note that both cell F2 and the formula bar show the equals sign (Figure C.4). Also note that the name box now shows **SUM**, the function suggested by Excel.

Now, type the formula. Do not insert any spaces into the formula while completing it.

It is important to note that the user, in typing the formula, may use either the actual values or the cell addresses. In Figure C.5, the formula includes the actual values of overall GPA. For

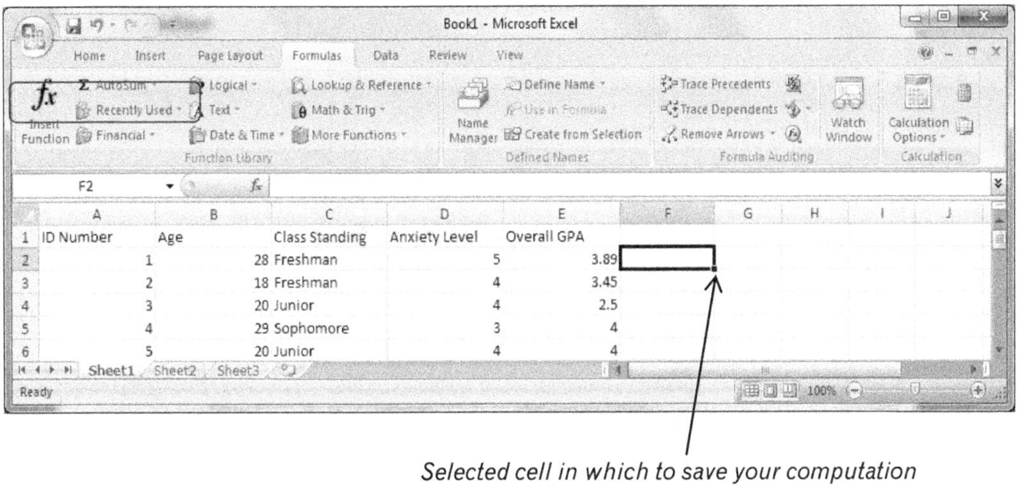

Selected cell in which to save your computation

FIGURE C.3 Using the formula, Step 1: choose the cell.

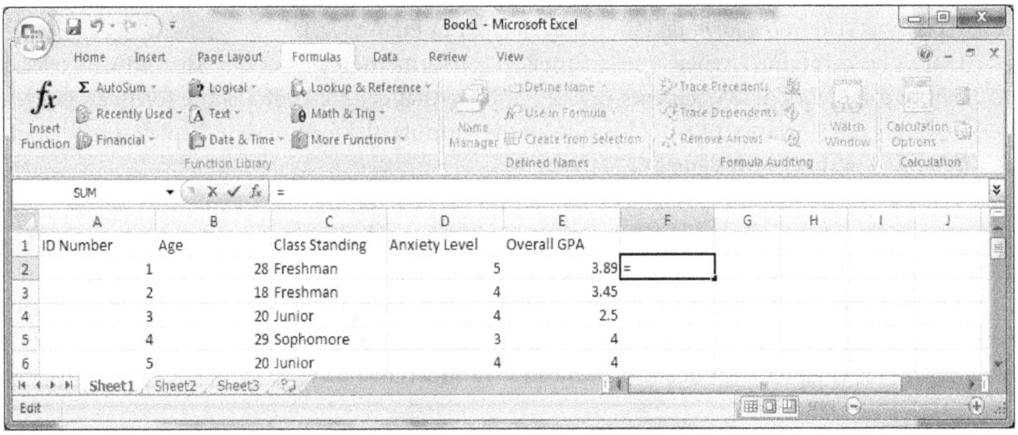

FIGURE C.4 Using the formula, Step 2: enter the equals sign.

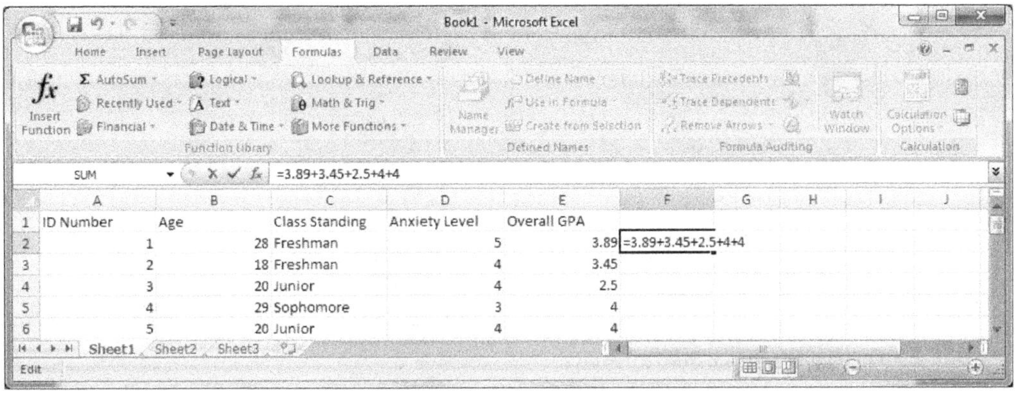

FIGURE C.5 Using the formula, Step 3: type the formula.

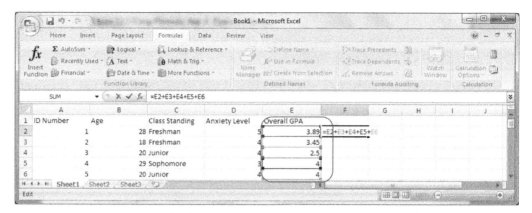

FIGURE C.6 Using the formula, Step 3: type the formula using the cell addresses.

example, 3.89 is the actual value of overall GPA of the first student. Because 3.89 is stored in cell E2, the user can substitute the actual value with the cell address. Figure C.6 shows the formula with the cell addresses. Note that, *when using the cell address, Excel automatically highlights the corresponding cells in the formula* (shown in the box in Figure C.6).

Once the formula is typed, press **Enter** to perform the calculation. The sum of overall GPA of five students, 17.84, appears in cell F2. Note that cell F2 contains the formula, not the value: While cell F2 shows 17.84, the results of the formula, the formula bar displays the formula itself (shown in the box in Figure C.7).

This example shows only one operator, addition, in Excel. *Excel can calculate five different operators:* (a) addition, (b) subtraction, (c) multiplication, (d) division, and (e) power. Table C.2 shows the operators and examples of their Excel formula.

The user can use as many operators as necessary in a single formula. For example, assume that the user wants to calculate, for the five students, the variance of overall GPA. The formula is as follows (see Chapter 4 for details; the mean is rounded to 3.57):

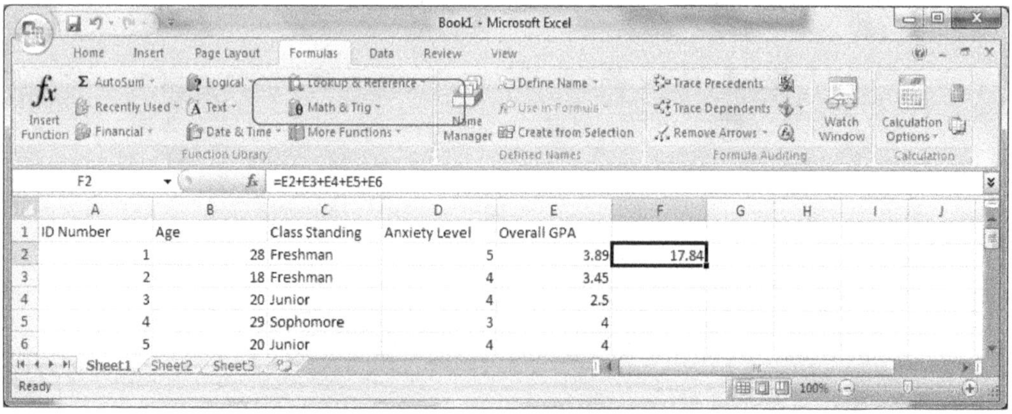

FIGURE C.7 Using the formula, Step 4: results.

Table C.2: Excel Operators, Symbols, and Formula Examples

Operator	Symbol	Excel Formula
Addition	+ (plus; **Shift-=**)	=3.89+3.45
Subtraction	– (minus sign on keyboard)	=3.89-3.45
Multiplication	* (asterisk; **Shift-8**)	=5*6
Division	/ (slash on keyboard)	=28/5
Power of	^ (caret; **Shift-6**)	=5^2 (power of 2)

$$Variance = \frac{(3.89-3.57)^2 + (3.45-3.57)^2 + (2.5-3.57)^2 + (4.0-3.57)^2 + (4.0-3.57)^2}{(5-1)}$$

$$Variance = 1.63 / 4 \rightarrow .40765$$

This formula is easily typed into Excel. All that the user needs to know is how to use parentheses. The following is the Excel formula for calculating the variance of overall GPA, shown in the formula bar in Figure C.8; press **Enter** to see it:

$0.40787 = ((3.89-3.57)^2+(3.45-3.57)^2+(2.5-3.57)^2+(4-3.57)^2+(4-3.57)^2)/(5-1)$

Now, recall that in Figure C.6 the Excel formula may have either the actual values or the cell addresses for the corresponding actual values. This means that the user can type the formula with the cell addresses instead of the actual values shown in Figure C.8. The next formula is the Excel formula to calculate the variance with the cell addresses, where the mean is denoted by "F2/5" or "7.84/5" (cell F2 stores the sum of five scores). Press **Enter**, which results in 0.40787 (the difference from 0.40765 is due to rounding of the mean to 3.57).

The complicated formula for Variance can be computed by

$$Variance = ((E2-(F2/5))^2 + (E3-(F2/5))^2 + (E4-(F2/5))^2$$
$$+ (E5-(F2/5))^2 + (E6-(F2/5))^2) / (5-1)$$

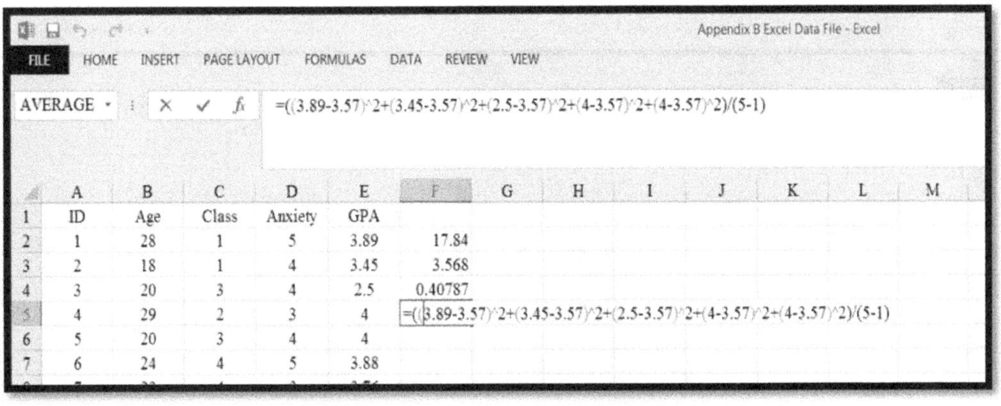

FIGURE C.8 Using the formula: complicated formula with actual values.

Function

As illustrated, many statistics are calculated by typing the corresponding formula. The formula can be useful if the calculation is simple, such as the sum of a small number of values (Figures C.4 and C.5). But, what if the calculation is complex, such as the calculation of the variance in Figure C.9? The user need not worry about typing the complicated formula by hand. Excel provides many functions to simplify the tasks. *While the user creates the formula, function is a predefined set of formulas stored in Excel. That is, the user invokes and uses the functions but does not create them.* Once the user decides on the kinds of statistics to calculate, the functions listed in the following five steps can be used:

1. Choose the cell in which the calculated value will be stored (same as for formulas).
2. Enter the equals sign in the cell.
3. Insert the appropriate function in the cell.
4. Define the range of the cells for the function to calculate.
5. Press **Enter** to obtain the calculated value.

Now, calculate the variance of five overall GPA scores in Figure C.9 using the Excel function. The first and second steps are same as for formulas, so start from the third step. There are two ways to insert the function into the cell: manually type the function and use the **Formula** ribbon. Because there are many functions available, the user needs to know in advance what kind of function will be used. For example, to calculate the *variance* (VAR) of five overall GPA scores (note that VAR in SPSS is used to stand for variable). Also, *note that in earlier Excel versions, the user simply selected VAR, but in Excel 2013, the user must choose either VAR.S (sample variance) or VAR.P (population variance).*

Step 4 of the statistical function for Excel is to define the range. In Excel, the *range* means the collection of cells containing the data. The user may want to calculate the variance of five overall GPA scores, which are stored from cell E2 through cell E6 (see Figure C.9). These five cells consist of the range of data for the user to calculate the variance. There are several ways to define the range, but it is conventional to type the first and the last cell connected by the colon mark (:). Therefore, the user types the function with range follows:

$$\text{Excel } 2007 - 2010, \text{type} = \text{VAR}(\text{E2}:\text{E6})$$

$$\text{Excel } 2013, \text{type} = \text{VAR.S}(\text{E2}:\text{E6}) \text{ or VAR.P}(\text{E2}:\text{E6})$$

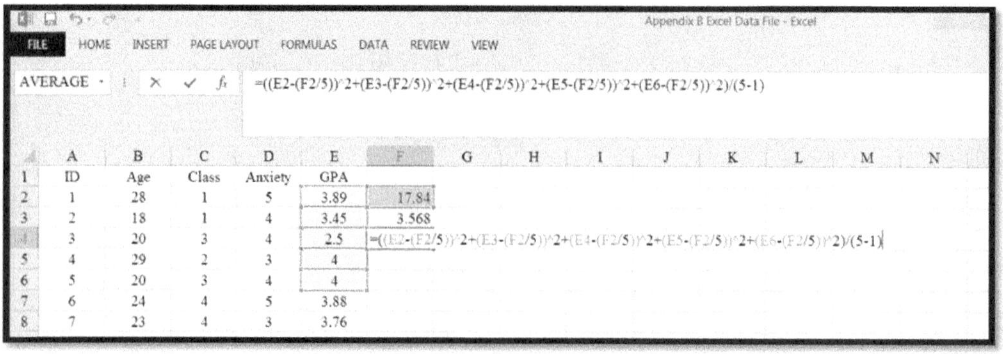

FIGURE C.9 Using the formula: complicated formula with cell addresses.

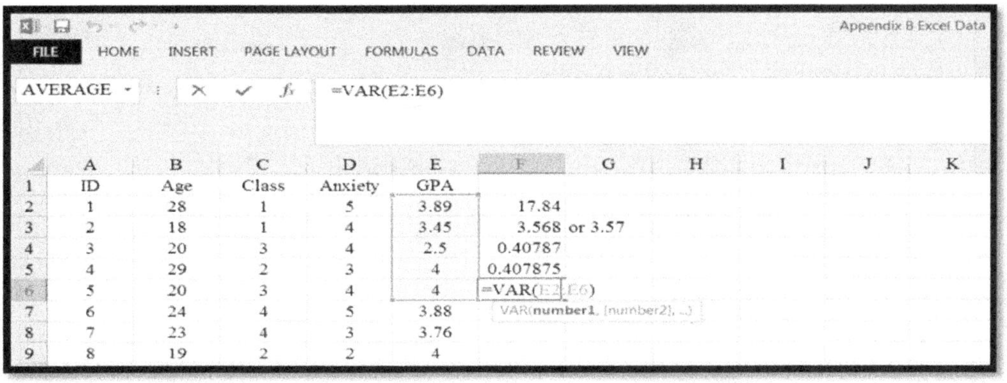

FIGURE C.10 Manually inserting the function.

Note that the function begins with the equals sign, like the formulas (no spaces between characters). Also, *the range is defined within the parentheses of the function VAR.* The function means "to calculate the variance of the values from the cell E2 through the cell E6." Figure C.10 shows how to insert the function manually. Once the function has been inserted and the range defined (*notice that in Excel 2007–2010, function was used*), press **Enter** to calculate the variance.

Manually inserting the function has some caveats. First, the user must exactly know which functions to use before inserting them. Also, be careful about incorrectly typing the function name (which returns errors). Excel does not like any single typo. Excel provides the **Formula** ribbon, which can help the user to avoid these problems. All of the statistical functions this appendix discusses can be accessed by performing the following steps:

1. Pull down the **Formulas** ribbon. Move the cursor to **More Functions**.
2. Select **Statistical**, then click the correct statistical function as shown in Figure C.11.

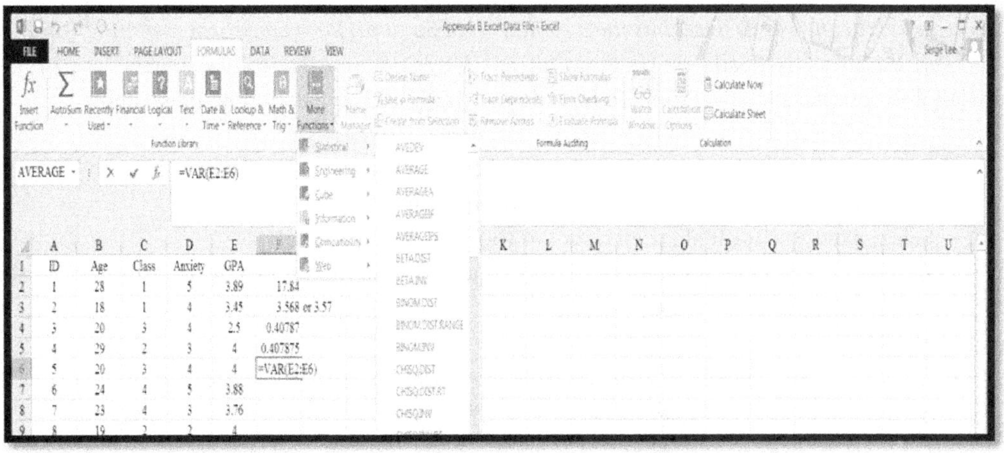

FIGURE C.11 Statistical function in Excel 2013.

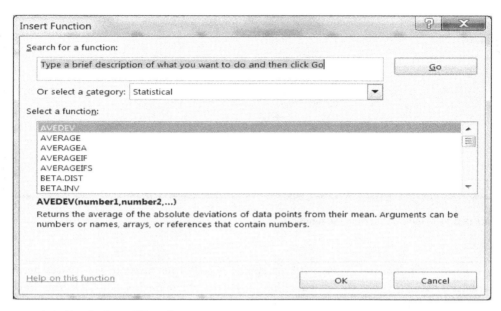

FIGURE C.12 Use the **Insert Function**.

3. If the user knows what kinds of statistics to calculate (e.g., the variance) but is not sure about which function to use, the **Insert Function** (last item on statistical function) button is the user's starting point (see Figure C.12). Click **Insert Function**, and the dialog box **Insert Function** pops up. With this dialog box, the user can either search for the functions needed or select the most recently used function. Once a particular function is selected, Excel provides a quick explanation of its meaning.

The Analysis ToolPak

To this point, the discussion has been how to enter data into Excel, how to make the formulas to calculate the values; and how to insert the functions to perform the statistical task. The user *may think that using functions for calculating values is much simpler and easier than using the formulas.* This is true; *however, Excel has tools similar to SPSS to perform statistical tasks: the Analysis ToolPak.* Because it is an add-on program for Excel, it is not automatically available. Users must install this optional statistical tool. To include the Analysis ToolPak, follow these steps:

- Pull down the **File** ribbon. Move the cursor to the last item (bottom) on **File**.
- Click **Add-Ins** in the left pane of the option window.
- Select **Analysis ToolPak**, then click **Go** (bottom of the screen).
- A small screen emerges (Figure C.13a). Check the first item (**Analysis ToolPak**) on the screen.
- Click **OK** to return to the Excel desktop window.
- Click **Data** on the main screen. The title **Data Analysis** appears at the top right corner of the screen (highlighted area of Figure C.13b). Now, the user is ready to enjoy using the Analysis ToolPak.

(a)

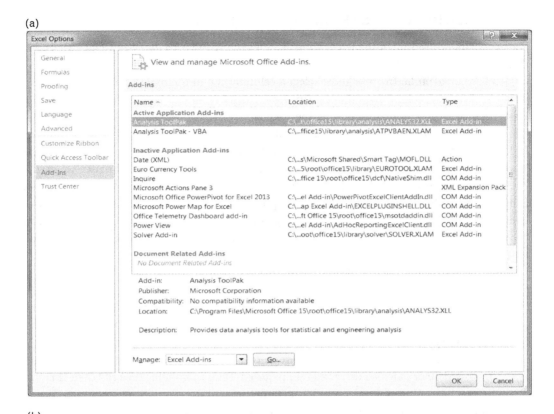

(b)

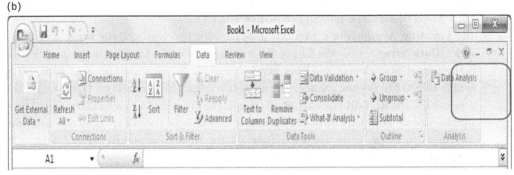

FIGURE C.13 (a) Excel with the Analysis ToolPak. (b) Highlighted area shows **Data Analysis**.

DATA ANALYSIS USING EXCEL 2007–2015

This section provides detailed examples of how to perform statistical tasks using Excel. The focus is on the Analysis ToolPak because this provides both stronger and simpler tools for performing statistical tasks. The difference between the functions and the Analysis ToolPak can be seen in the first example of frequency distribution. Each section consists of the following steps: First is data introduction. Then, the Excel functions and formulas used to calculate the statistics are briefly mentioned. Finally, a detailed explanation covers how to use the Analysis ToolPak to perform the same tasks as in the **Formula** functions.

FREQUENCY DISTRIBUTIONS: THE HISTOGRAM GRAPH

For better understanding of the Excel ToolPak, Table C.3 displays a grouped frequencies table that was computed by SPSS (see Chapter 3).

Similar to **Formula**, the user must select a cell (any cell in the main screen) to compute a result. Assume that in this hypothetical situation, the user selected cell **G1** for the histogram. First, begin with functions for creating the frequency distribution of Age. Table C.3 shows a frequency distribution table with three grouped frequencies: 18 to 20, 21 to 30, and 31 or older. In Excel, whenever the user creates a frequency distribution, the *bins and type the bins* in the worksheet are first defined. *Bins* are numbers that represent the intervals the user wants the Histogram tool to use for measuring the input data in the data analysis. Therefore, the age ranges (categories) in Table C.3 are the bins for this hypothetical situation. If the bins are grouped frequencies, or intervals, the user can type the largest value of the category. For example, "20" can be typed for the category 18 to 20, type "30" for the category "21 to 30," then leave the cell blank for the last category, "31 or older." Figure C.14 shows how to define the bins.

To create a frequency distribution table for this situation, do the following:

- Select a cell location for storage of the frequency counts; assume cell **H2** to **H4**. Once the bins are defined, the **Frequency** function can be used to create the frequency distribution table for **Age**.
- Select the cells where the frequencies are stored. There are three frequencies, 18 to 20, 21 to 30, and 30 or older, so three cells are required. Drag (highlight) the cell **H2** to **H4**.
- In the **Formulas** ribbon, click **More Functions**, select **Statistical**, and then **Insert Function** (last item on the list). Note that the **Insert Function** lists many statistical functions. Scroll down and highlight **Frequency**. Click **OK**.
- The **Function Arguments** dialog box appears with two boxes, **Data_array** and **Bins_array**. **Data_array** *defines the cells of the data the user wants to count the frequency* (that is, the ages of 30 students), and **Bins_array** *defines the bins previously created*. **Bins_array** are the cells **G2** to **G4** just created. The users check that the cursor is on **Data_array**. The user can use the **RefEdit** button, but it is simpler to move the cursor to **Data_array**, then simultaneously hold **Ctrl-Shift+down arrow** to highlight the entire **Age** column. Move the cursor to **Data_array** and then highlight the **Bins** column just created. DO NOT highlight the variable name, only the cells with scores.
- Press **Ctrl-Shift-Enter** in combination (together), not in a sequence (this is because three cells were selected as an array, not just one cell). Now, Excel returns the frequency of each category, shown in Figure C.15. Note that the brackets { } are around the function expression in the formula bar, denoting the array.

Table C.3: Grouped Frequencies for Age Category

		Frequency	Percentage	Cumulative Percentage
Valid	18–20	8	26.7	26.7
	21–30	18	60.0	86.7
	31 and older	4	13.3	100.0
	Total	30	100.0	

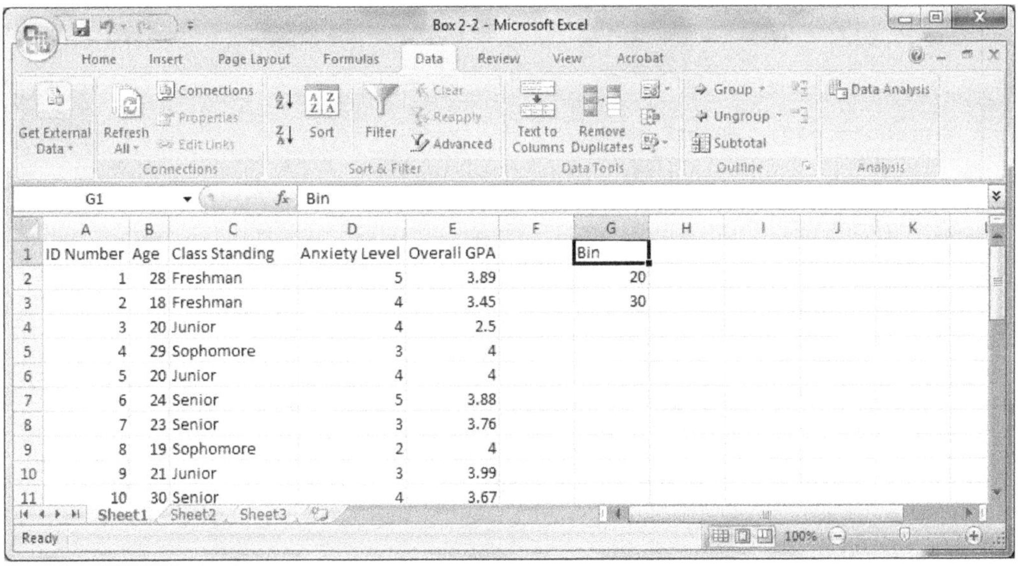

FIGURE C.14 Defining the bins.

Notice that even a simple frequency count in Excel is complicated. In SPSS, the user simply uses the **Analyze** function and highlights the needed outputs. With Analysis ToolPak, frequency distributions can be easily computed; to use the Analysis ToolPak for frequency distributions, simply follow these steps:

- Once the bins are defined, pull down **Data**, then click **Data Analysis** (upper right corner of screen) to load the Analysis ToolPak.
- In the **Data Analysis** dialog box, choose **Histogram** and click **OK** (Figure C.16).

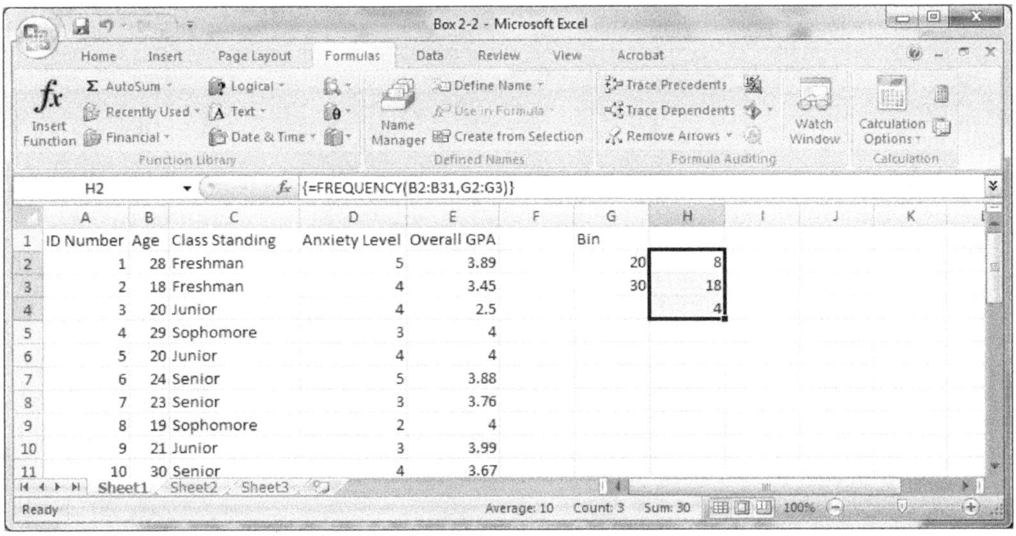

FIGURE C.15 Results of the **Frequency Function**.

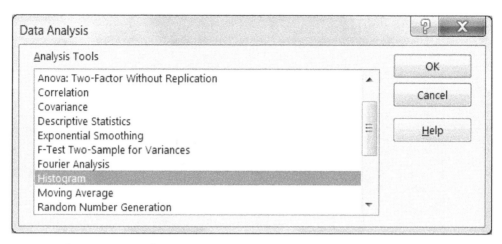

FIGURE C.16 Analysis ToolPak **Statistical Function**.

- The **Histogram** dialog box consists of two areas: **Input** and **Output options** (Figure C.17). In **Input**, define the data in **Input Range:** (the same as **Data_array** in **Frequency**) and the bin in **Bin Range:** (same as **Bins_array** in **Frequency**) using the **RefEdit** button or holding **Ctrl-Shift+down arrow**.
- In **Output options**, choose where the results will be placed. The user can select the current worksheet (**Output Range**), a different worksheet (**New Worksheet Ply:**), or even a different workbook (**New Workbook**). If the current worksheet is selected for placing results, choose the cell using the **RefEdit** button. The user may select just one cell, in the the upper left corner of the table created by Analysis ToolPak. Check **Cumulative Percentage** for the cumulative percentages in the table and **Chart Output** for the histogram. Click **OK**.
- The user will see frequency distributions as displayed in Figure C.18.

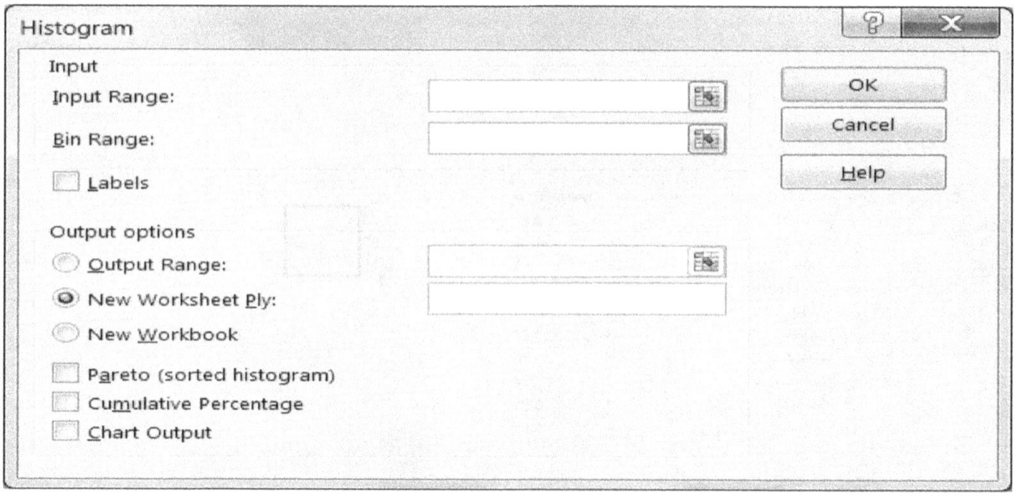

FIGURE C.17 Histogram dialog box.

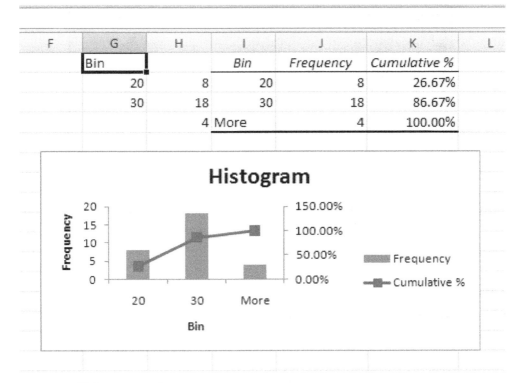

FIGURE C.18 **Histogram** result.

MEASURES OF CENTRAL TENDENCY AND VARIABILITY: DESCRIPTIVE STATISTICS

Excel provides many functions regarding central tendency and variability. For example, the Average function computes the average, the Median function calculates the median, the VAR (VAR.S and VAR.P) function shows the variance, and so on. In contrast to SPSS/PASW, each function must be used separately to obtain all central tendency and variability measures. The Analysis ToolPak offers **Descriptive Statistics** to calculate the most popular measures of central tendency and variability in a single box. Use Table C.1 data again to calculate the central tendency and variability of the variable Age. The **Descriptive Statistics** dialog box is in Figure C.19.

- Pull down the **Data** ribbon, then select **Data Analysis**.
- Select **Descriptive Statistics**; click **OK**.
- Use the **RefEdit** button or **Ctrl-Shift+down arrow** to select the data for the Age variable (**Input Range**). Because the data are stored as a column format (each column contains the variable's data in Table C.1), choose **Columns** in **Grouped By**. Note that if the variable name in the first row is selected, also check **Labels in First Row**. In the **Output options**, check the **Summary statistics** box.
- Click **OK** for the table of central tendency and variability measures (Figure C.20).

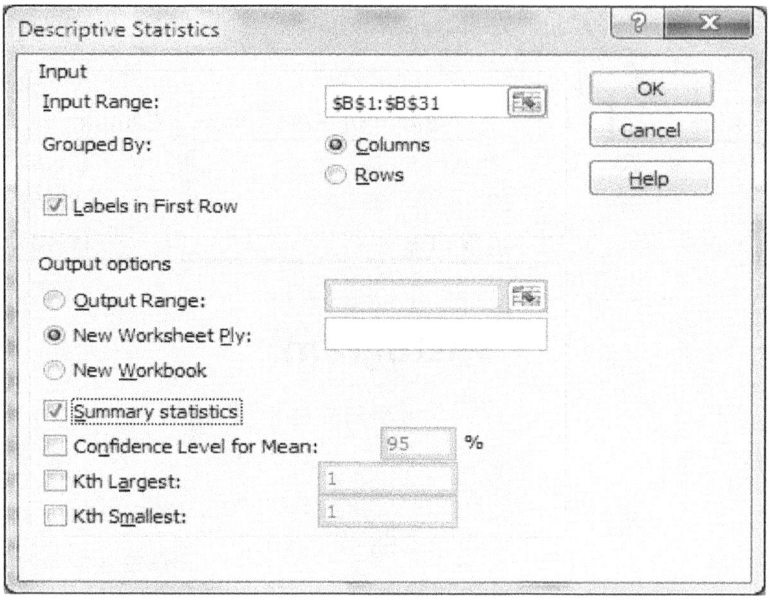

FIGURE C.19 **Descriptive Statistics** dialog box.

	A	B
1		
2		*Age*
3		
4	Mean	25.7
5	Standard Error	1.30617455
6	Median	23.5
7	Mode	20
8	Standard Deviation	7.154212649
9	Sample Variance	51.18275862
10	Kurtosis	2.346420756
11	Skewness	1.546320254
12	Range	28
13	Minimum	18
14	Maximum	46
15	Sum	771
16	Count	30
17		

FIGURE C.20 **Descriptive Statistics** result.

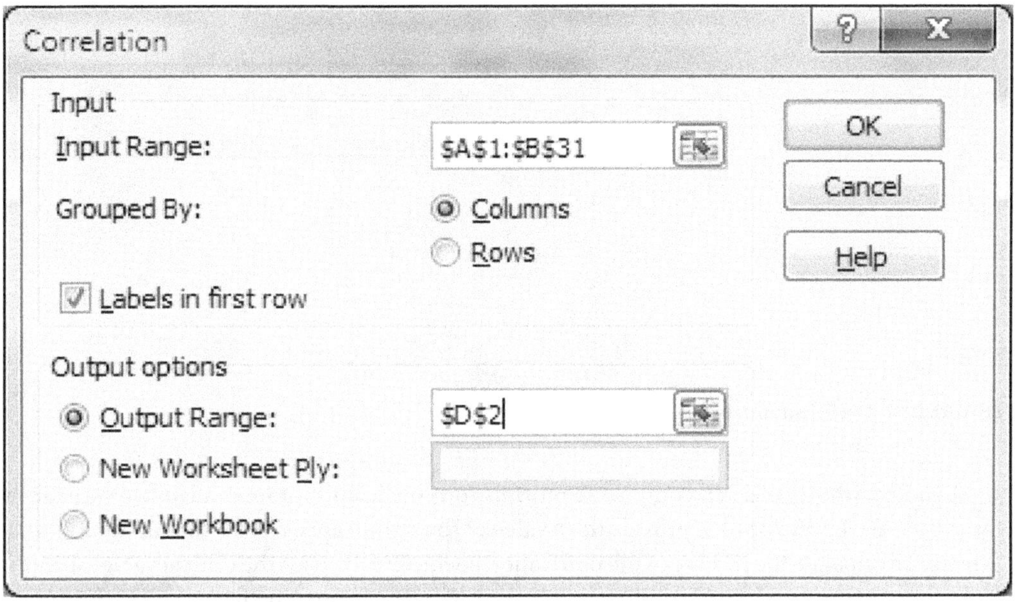

FIGURE C.21 Correlation dialog.

CORRELATION

In Chapter 8, the correlation coefficient was discussed and used to analyze the relationship between socialization and family size. Table 8.2 contains the data for two variables. Table 8.1 is used to calculate the correlation coefficient using Excel. Excel offers two functions, Correl and Pearson, to calculate the correlation coefficients. In the Analysis ToolPak, choose **Correlation**. Note that in Excel, *the variables to be correlated must be **next** to each other*. This is in contrast to SPSS, for which variables from different cells (columns) can be selected. Also, note that the Analysis ToolPak *does not compute the test of significance*. This section explains how to use the Analysis ToolPak to calculate the correlation coefficient.

- Enter the data of Table 8.2 into Excel.
- Select **Data Analysis** in the **Data** ribbon.
- Select **Correlation** and click **OK**.
- Use the **RefEdit** button or hold **Ctrl-Shift+down arrow** to highlight all values of the variables that the user wishes to correlate. In this hypothetical situation, the variables are **Family Size** and **Socialization Level**. Note that these two variables should be adjacent to each other. Because the data are stored as a column, choose **Columns** in **Grouped By:** Note that if the variable name in the first row is selected, also check **Labels in first row** (Figure C.21).
- Use the **RefEdit** button in **Output Range:** to select the cell where the correlation coefficient will be placed. Click **OK**.

Figure C.22 shows that the correlation coefficient between **Family Size** and **Socialization Skill** is .8685, as revealed in Chapter 8.

⊿	A	B	C	D	E	F
1	Family Size	Socialization Level				
2	4	8			*Family Size*	*Socialization Level*
3	2	4		Family Size	1	
4	5	9		Socialization Leve	0.868541358	1
5	6	10				
6	5	6				
7	4	7				
8	3	6				
9	4	7				
10	5	7				
11	2	3				

FIGURE C.22 Correlation result.

As noted, while Excel can compute the correlation coefficients for more than two variables at the same time, Excel does not provide the *p* value or the significance test for the correlation coefficients. To calculate the *p* value of the correlation coefficient, consult the critical value table (the Pearson *r* table from a book or online sources) for the correlation coefficient using the sample size and the desired confidence interval.

LINEAR REGRESSION

Chapter 10 introduced linear regression. For simple regression with one independent variable *X* and one dependent variable *Y*, Excel provides two functions. The **Intercept** function computes the intercept of the regression equation, and the **Slope** function computes the coefficient of the independent *X* variable. The Analysis ToolPak provides **Regression**, which can perform the regression analysis with one or more independent variables. Using the same example from Table 8.2, analyze the linear regression between family size and socialization.

- Pull down **Data**, select **Data Analysis.**
- Select **Regression** and click **OK.**
- Use the **RefEdit** button or hold **Ctrl-Shift+down arrow** in **Input** to select the data for the dependent variable, Socialization Years. Use the **RefEdit** button or **Ctrl_ Shift+down arrow** in **Input X Range:** to select the data for the independent variable, Family Size. *Unlike the correlation, these two variables do not need to be adjacent to each other.* The user may also set a different confidence level. The default confidence level is 95%. Note that if the user selects the variable name in the first row, also check **Labels** (Figure C.23).
- Use the **RefEdit** button or **Ctrl-Shift+down arrow** in **Output Range:** to select the cell where the regression analysis tables will be placed. Click **OK.**

Figure C.24 shows the results of the regression analysis. The first table shows the regression statistics, including R^2 (0.754) and number of observations (10). The next table shows the analysis of variance (ANOVA) results, and the *F* test shows that the model fits the data well.

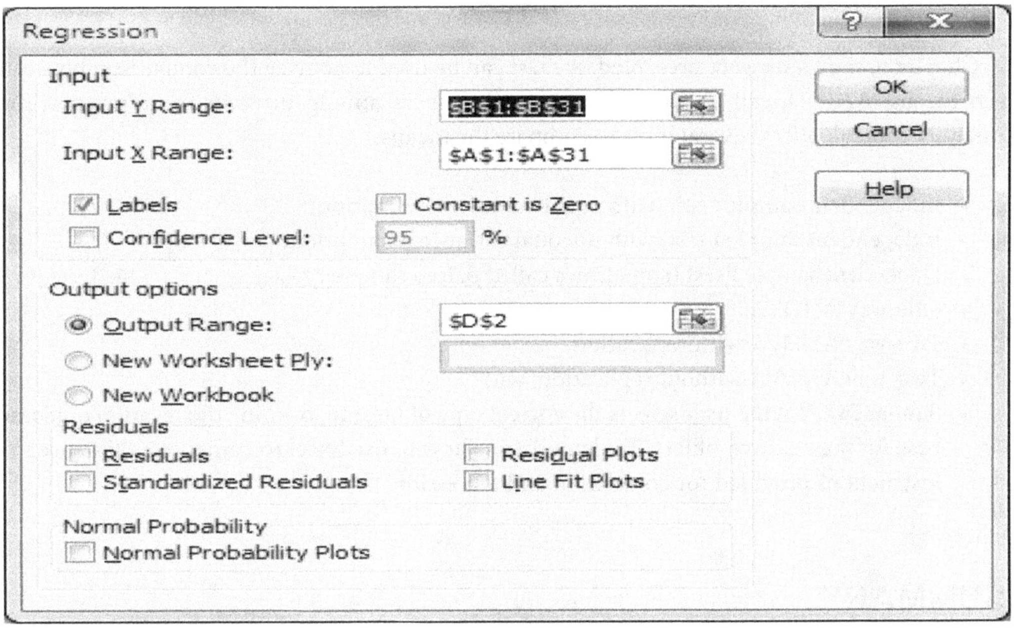

FIGURE C.23 Regression dialog box.

According to the ANOVA table, the p value of the F test (**Significance F**) is .001. The final table reports the regression coefficients. The p values of these two statistics are smaller than .05; thus, the conclusion is that the slope and intercept of this regression equation are statistically significant.

	D	E	F	G	H	I	J	K	L
SUMMARY OUTPUT									

Regression Statistics	
Multiple R	0.868541358
R Square	0.75436409
Adjusted R Squ	0.723659601
Standard Error	1.109617051
Observations	10

ANOVA

	df	SS	MS	F	Significance F
Regression	1	30.25	30.25	24.56852792	0.001111541
Residual	8	9.85	1.23125		
Total	9	40.1			

	Coefficients	Standard Error	t Stat	P-value	Lower 95%	Upper 95%	Lower 95.0%	Upper 95.0%
Intercept	1.2	1.163776181	1.031126104	0.332644405	-1.483672686	3.883672686	-1.483672686	3.883672686
Family Size	1.375	0.277404263	4.956665	0.001111541	0.735304623	2.014695377	0.735304623	2.014695377

FIGURE C.24 Regression results.

t TEST

In Chapter 9, the *t tests* were presented. A *t* test can be used to analyze the comparison between two means; ANOVA can evaluate the mean differences among three or more groups. The Analysis ToolPak offers several tools to compare the means:

- Independent sample *t* test, with equal variance assumption;
- Independent sample *t* test, with unequal variance assumption;
- Dependent sample *t* test (sometimes called paired sample *t* test);
- One-way ANOVA;
- Two-way ANOVA with replication;
- Two-way ANOVA without replication; and
- Similar to SPSS, the user selects the correct type of *t* test to examine the mean(s) outcome base for the research object. To demonstrate how to use Excel to compute a *t* test, use the instructions provided for correlation and regression.

SUMMARY

This appendix introduced Excel for statistical analysis. As a statistical software program, Excel is limited compared to other statistical package programs such as SPSS/PASW or SAS. However, the biggest advantage of Excel is that Excel is accessible to anyone who owns a computer, whether a personal computer, laptop, or tablet, compared to other statistical software programs. In addition, regarding the basic statistical tasks, Excel is robust. The Analysis ToolPak, an Excel add-in program for statistical tasks, is useful for performing most of the calculations introduced in the previous chapters. This appendix does not cover all aspects of Excel and the Analysis ToolPak, but it can be used as a starting point for utilizing Excel as a statistical software program.

APPENDIX D

*Critical Values of F (α = .05 In Standard Type, α = .01 in **Boldface**)*

| n_2 | n_1 Degrees of Freedom (For Numerator Mean Square) | | | | | | | | | | | |
	1	2	3	4	5	6	7	8	9	10	11	12
1	161	200	216	225	230	234	237	239	241	242	243	244
	4,052	**4,999**	**5,403**	**5,625**	**5,764**	**5.859**	**5,928**	**5,981**	**6,022**	**6,056**	**6,082**	**6,106**
2	18.51	19.00	19.16	19.25	19.30	19.33	19.36	19.37	19.38	19.39	19.40	19.41
	98.49	**99.00**	**99.17**	**99.25**	**99.30**	**99.33**	**99.34**	**99.36**	**99.38**	**99.40**	**99.41**	**99.42**
3	10.13	9.55	9.28	9.12	9.01	8.94	8.88	8.84	8.81	8.78	8.76	8.74
	34.12	**30.82**	**29.46**	**28.71**	**28.24**	**27.91**	**27.67**	**27.49**	**27.34**	**27.23**	**27.13**	**27.05**
4	7.71	6.94	6.59	6.39	6.26	6.16	6.09	6.04	6.00	5.96	5.93	5.91
	21.20	**18.00**	**16.69**	**15.98**	**15.52**	**15.21**	**14.98**	**14.80**	**14.66**	**14.54**	**14.45**	**14.37**
5	6.61	5.79	5.41	5.19	5.05	4.95	4.88	4.82	4.78	4.74	4.70	4.68
	16.26	**13.27**	**12.06**	**11.39**	**10.97**	**10.67**	**10.45**	**10.27**	**10.15**	**10.05**	**9.96**	**9.89**
6	5.99	5.14	4.76	4.53	4.39	4.28	4.21	4.15	**4.10**	4.06	4.03	4.00
	13.74	**10.92**	**9.78**	**9.15**	**8.75**	**8.47**	**8.26**	**8.10**	**7.98**	**7.87**	**7.79**	**7.72**
7	5.59	**4.74**	4.35	4.12	3.97	3.87	3.79	3.73	3.68	3.63	3.60	3.57
	12.25	**9.55**	**8.45**	**7.85**	7.46	**7.19**	**7.00**	**6.84**	**6.71**	**6.62**	**6.54**	**6.47**
8	5.32	4,46	4.07	3.84	3.69	3.58	3.50	3.44	3.39	3.34	3.31	3.28
	11.26	**8.65**	**7.59**	**7.01**	**6.63**	**6.37**	**6.19**	**6.03**	**5.91**	**5.82**	**5.74**	**5.67**
9	5.12	4.26	3.86	3.63	3.48	3.37	3.29	3.23	3.18	3.13	3.10	3.07
	10.56	**8.02**	**6.99**	**6.42**	**6.06**	**5.80**	**5.62**	**5.47**	**5.35**	**5.26**	**5.18**	**5.11**
10	4.96	4.10	3.71	3.48	3.33	3.22	3.14	3.07	3.02	2.97	2.94	2.91
	10.04	**7.56**	**6.55**	**5.99**	**5.64**	**5.39**	**5.21**	**5.06**	**4.95**	**4.85**	**4.78**	**4.71**
11	4.84	3.98	3.59	3.36	3.20	3.09	3.01	2.95	2.90	2.86	2.82	2.79
	9.65	**7.20**	**6.22**	**5.67**	**5.32**	**5.07**	**4.88**	**4.74**	**4.63**	**4.54**	**4.46**	**4.40**
12	4.75	3.88	3.49	3.26	3.11	3.00	2.92	2.85	2.80	2.76	2.72	2.69
	9.33	**6.93**	**5.95**	**5.41**	**5.06**	**4.82**	**4.65**	**4.50**	**4.39**	**4.30**	**4.22**	**4.16**
13	4.67	3.80	3.41	3.18	3.02	2.92	2.84	2.77	2.72	2.67	2.63	2.60
	9.07	**6.70**	**5.74**	**5.20**	**4.86**	**4.62**	**4.44**	**4.30**	**4.19**	**4.10**	**4.02**	**3.96**

n_1 Degrees of Freedom (For Numerator Mean Square)											
14	**16**	**20**	**24**	**30**	**40**	**50**	**75**	**100**	**200**	**500**	**∞**
245	246	247	248	259	251	252	253	253	254	254	254
6,142	**6,169**	**6,208**	**6,234**	**6,258**	**6,286**	**6,302**	**6,323**	**6,334**	**6,352**	**6,361**	**6,366**
19.42	19.43	19.44	19.45	19.46	19.47	19.47	19.48	19.49	19.49	19.50	19.50
99.43	**99.44**	**99.45**	**99.46**	**99.47**	**99.48**	**99.48**	**99.49**	**99.49**	**99.49**	**99.50**	**99.50**
8.71	8.69	8.66	8.64	8.62	8.60	8.58	8.57	8.56	8.54	8.54	8.53
26.92	**26.83**	**26.69**	**26.60**	**26.50**	**26.41**	**26.35**	**26.27**	**26.23**	**26.18**	**26.14**	**26.12**
5.87	5.84	5.80	5.77	5.74	5.71	5.70	5.68	5.66	5.65	5.64	5.63
14.24	**14.15**	**14.02**	**13.93**	**13.83**	**13.74**	**13.69**	**13.61**	**13.57**	**1332**	**13.48**	**13.46**
4.64	4.60	4.56	4.53	4.50	**4.46**	4.44	4.42	4.40	4.38	4.37	4.36
9.77	**9.68**	**9.55**	**9.47**	**9.38**	**9.29**	**9.24**	**9.17**	**9.13**	**9.07**	**9.04**	**9.02**
3.96	3.92	3.87	3.84	3.81	3.77	3.75	3.72	3.71	3.69	3.68	3.67
7.60	**732**	**7.39**	**7.31**	**7.23**	**7.14**	**7.09**	**7.02**	**6.99**	**6.94**	**6.90**	**6.88**
3.52	3.49	3.44	3.41	3.38	3,34	3.32	3.29	3.28	3.25	3.24	3.23
6.35	**6.27**	**6.15**	**6.07**	**5.98**	**5.90**	**5.85**	**5.78**	**5.75**	**5.70**	**5.67**	**5.65**
3.23	3.20	3.15	3.12	3.08	3.05	3.03	3.00	2.98	2.96	2.94	2.93
5.56	**5.48**	**5.36**	**5.28**	**5.20**	**5.11**	**5.06**	**5.00**	**4.96**	**4.91**	**4.88**	**4.86**
3.02	2.98	2.93	2.90	2.86	2.82	2.80	2.77	236	2.73	2.72	2.71
5.00	**4.92**	**4.80**	**4.73**	**4.64**	**4.56**	**4.51**	**4.45**	**4.41**	**4.36**	**4.33**	**4.31**
2.86	2.82	2.77	2.74	2.70	2.67	2.64	2.61	2.59	2.56	2.55	2.54
4.60	**4.52**	**4.41**	**4.33**	**4.25**	**4.17**	**4.12**	**4.05**	**4.01**	**3.96**	**3.93**	**3.91**
2.74	2.70	2.65	2.61	2.57	2.53	2.50	2.47	2.45	2.42	2.41	2.40
4.29	**4.21**	**4.10**	**4.02**	**3.94**	**3.86**	**3.80**	**3.74**	**3.70**	**3.66**	**3.62**	**3.60**
2.64	2.60	2.54	2.50	2.46	2.42	2.40	2.36	2.35	2.32	2.31	2.30
4.05	**3.98**	**3.86**	**3.78**	**3.70**	**3.61**	**3.56**	**3.49**	**3.46**	**3.41**	**3.38**	**3.36**
2.55	2.51	2.46	2.42	2.38	2.34	2.32	2.28	2.26	2.24	2.22	2.21
3.85	**3.78**	**3.67**	**3.59**	**3.51**	**3.42**	**3.37**	**3.30**	**3.27**	**3.21**	**3.18**	**3.16**

(*continued*)

n_2	n_1 Degrees of Freedom (For Numerator Mean Square)											
	1	2	3	4	5	6	7	8	9	10	11	12
14	4.60	3.74	3.34	3.11	2.96	2.85	2.77	2.70	2.65	2.6()	2.56	2.53
	8.86	**6.51**	**5.56**	**5.03**	**4.69**	**4.46**	**4.28**	**4.14**	**4.03**	**3.94**	**3.86**	**3.80**
15	4.54	3.68	3.29	3.06	2.90	2.79	2.70	2.64	2.59	2.55	2.51	2.48
	8.68	**6.36**	**5.42**	**4.89**	**4.56**	**4.32**	**4.14**	**4.00**	**3.89**	**3.80**	**3.73**	**3.67**
16	4.49	3.63	3.24	3.01	2.85	2.74	2.66	2.59	2.54	2.49	2.45	2.42
	8.53	**6.23**	**5.29**	**4.77**	**4.44**	**4.20**	**4.03**	**3.89**	**3.78**	**3.69**	**3.61**	**3.55**
17	4.45	3.59	3.20	2.96	2.81	2.70	2.62	2.55	2.50	2.45	2.41	2.38
	8.40	**6.11**	**5.18**	**4.67**	**4.34**	**4.10**	**3.93**	**3.79**	**3.68**	**3.59**	**3.52**	**3.45**
18	4.41	3.55	3.16	2.93	2.77	2.66	2.58	2.51	2.46	2.41	2.37	2.34
	8.28	**6.01**	**5.09**	**4.58**	**4.25**	**4.01**	**3.85**	**3.71**	**3.60**	**3.51**	**3.44**	**3.37**
19	4.38	3.52	3.13	2.90	2.74	2.63	2.55	2.48	2.43	2.38	2.34	2.31
	8.18	**5.93**	**5.01**	**4.50**	**4.17**	**3.94**	**3.77**	**3.63**	**3.52**	**3.43**	**3.36**	**3.30**
20	4.35	3.49	3.10	2.87	2.71	2.60	2.52	2.45	2.40	2.35	2.31	2.28
	8.10	**5.85**	**4.94**	**4.43**	**4.10**	**3.87**	**3.71**	**3.56**	**3.45**	**3.37**	**3.30**	**3.23**
21	4.32	3.47	3.07	2.84	2.68	2.57	2.49	2,42	2.37	2.32	2.28	2.25
	8.02	**5.78**	**4.87**	**4.37**	**4.04**	**3.81**	**3.65**	**3.51**	**3.40**	**3.31**	**3.24**	**3.17**
22	4.30	**3.44**	3.05	2.82	2.66	2.55	2.47	2.40	2.35	2.30	2.26	2.23
	7.9	**5.72**	**4.82**	**4.31**	**3.99**	**3.76**	**3.59**	**3.45**	**3.35**	**3.26**	**3.18**	**3.12**
23	4.28	3.42	3.03	2.80	2.64	2.53	2.45	2.38	2.32	2.28	2.24	2.20
	7.88	**5.66**	**4.76**	**4.26**	**3.94**	**3.71**	**3.54**	**3.41**	**3.30**	**3.21**	**3.14**	**3.07**
24	4.26	3.40	3.01	2.78	2.62	2.51	2.43	2.36	2.30	2.26	2.22	2.18
	7.82	**5.61**	**4.72**	**4.22**	**3.90**	**3.67**	**3.50**	**3.36**	**3.25**	**3.17**	**3.09**	**3.03**
25	4.24	3.38	2.99	2.76	2_60	2.49	2.41	2.34	2.28	2.24	2.20	2.16
	7.77	**5.57**	**4.68**	**4.18**	**3.86**	**3.63**	**3.46**	**3.32**	**3.21**	**3.13**	**3.05**	**2.99**
26	4.22	3.37	2.98	2.74	2.59	2.47	2.39	2.32	2.27	2.22	2.18	2.15
	7.72	**5.53**	**4.64**	**4.14**	**3.82**	**3.59**	**3.42**	**3.29**	**3.17**	**3.09**	**3.02**	**2.96**

n₁ Degrees of Freedom (For Numerator Mean Square)											
14	**16**	**20**	**24**	**30**	**40**	**50**	**75**	**100**	**200**	**500**	**∞**
2.48	2.44	2.39	2.35	2.31	2.27	2.24	2.21	2.19	2.16	2.14	2.13
3.70	**3.62**	**3.51**	**3.43**	**3.34**	**3.26**	**3.21**	**3.14**	**3.11**	**3.06**	**3.02**	**3.00**
2.43	2.39	2.33	2.29	2.25	2.21	2.18	2.15	2.12	2.10	2.08	2.07
3.56	**3.48**	**3.36**	**3.29**	**3.20**	3.12	**3.07**	**3.00**	**2.97**	**2.92**	**2.89**	**2.87**
2.37	2.33	2.28	2.24	2.20	2.16	2.13	2.09	2.07	2.04	2.02	2.01
3.45	**3.37**	**3.25**	**3.18**	**3.10**	**3.01**	**2.96**	**2.89**	**2.86**	**2.80**	**2.77**	**2.75**
2.33	2.29	2.23	2.19	2.15	2.11	2.08	2.04	2.02	1.99	1.97	1.96
3.35	**3.27**	**3.16**	**3.08**	**3.00**	**2.92**	**2.86**	**2.79**	**2.76**	**2.70**	**2.67**	2.65
2.29	2.25	2.19	2.15	2.11	2.07	2.04	2.00	1.98	1.95	1.93	1.92
3.27	**3.19**	**3.07**	**3.00**	**2.91**	**2.83**	**2.78**	**2.71**	**2.68**	**2.62**	**2.59**	2.57
2.26	2.21	2.15	2.11	2.07	2.02	2.00	1.96	1.94	1.91	1.90	1.88
3.19	**3.12**	**3.00**	**2.92**	**2.84**	**2.76**	**2.70**	**2.63**	**2.60**	**2.54**	**2.51**	**2.49**
2.23	2.18	2.12	2.08	2.04	1.99	1.96	1.92	1.90	1.87	1.85	1.84
3.13	**3.05**	**2.94**	**2.86**	**2.77**	**2.69**	**2.63**	**2.56**	**2.53**	**2.47**	**2.44**	**2.42**
2.20	2.15	2.09	2.05	2.00	1.96	1.93	1.89	1.87	1.84	1.82	1.81
3.07	**2.99**	**2.88**	**2.80**	**2.72**	**2.63**	**2.58**	**2.51**	**2.47**	**2.42**	**2.38**	**2.36**
2.18	2.13	2.07	2.03	1.98	1.93	1.91	1.87	1.84	1.81	1.80	1.78
3.02	**2.94**	**2.83**	2.75	2.67	2.58	2.53	2.46	2.42	2.37	2.33	2.31
2.14	2.10	2.04	2.00	1.96	1.91	1.88	1.84	1.82	1.79	1.77	1.76
2.97	2.89	2.78	2.70	2.62	2.53	2.48	2.41	2.37	2.32	2.28	2.26
2.13	2.09	2.02	1.98	1.94	1.89	1.86	1.82	1.80	1.76	1.74	1.73
2.93	2.85	2.74	2.66	2.58	2.49	2.44	2.36	2.33	2.27	2.23	2.21
2.11	2.06	2.00	1.96	1.92	1.87	1.84	1.80	1.77	1.74	1.72	1.71
2.89	**2.81**	2.70	2.62	2.54	2.45	2.40	2.32	2.29	2.23	2.19	2.17
2.10	2.05	1.99	1.95	1.90	1.85	1.82	1.78	1.76	1.72	1.70	1.69
2.86	**2.77**	**2.66**	**2.58**	**2.50**	**2.41**	**2.36**	**2.28**	**2.25**	**2.19**	**2.15**	**2.13**

(continued)

n_2	1	2	3	4	5	6	7	8	9	10	11	12
					n_1 Degrees of Freedom (For Numerator Mean Square)							
27	4.21	3.35	2.96	2.73	2.57	2.46	2.37	2.30	2.25	2.20	2.16	2.13
	7.68	5.49	4.60	4.11	3.79	3.56	3.39	3.26	3.14	3.06	2.98	2.93
28	4.20	3.34	2.95	2.71	2.56	2.44	2.36	2.29	2.24	2.19	2.15	2.12
	7.64	5.45	4.57	4.07	3.76	3.53	3.36	3.23	3.11	3.03	2.95	2.90
29	4.18	3.33	2.93	2.70	2.54	2.43	2.35	2.28	2.22	2.18	2.14	2.10
	7.60	5.42	4.54	4.04	3.73	3.50	3.33	3.20	3.08	3.00	2.92	2.87
30	4.17	3.32	2.92	2.69	2.53	2.42	2.34	2.27	2.21	2.16	2.12	2.09
	7.56	5.39	4.51	4.02	3.70	3.47	3.30	3.17	3.06	2.98	2.90	2.84
32	4.15	3.30	2.90	2.67	2.51	2,40	2.32	2.25	2.19	2.14	2.10	2.07
	7.50	5.34	4.46	3.97	3.66	3.42	3.25	3.12	3.01	2.94	2.86	2.80
34	4.13	3.28	2.88	2.65	2.49	2.38	2.30	2.23	2.17	2.12	2.08	2.05
	7.44	5.29	4.42	3.93	3.61	3.38	3.21	3.08	2.97	2.89	2.82	2.76
36	4.11	3.26	2.86	2.63	2.48	2.36	2.28	2.21	2.15	2.10	2.06	2.03
	7.39	5.25	4.38	3.89	3.58	3.35	3.18	3.04	3.04	2.86	2.78	2.72
38	4.10	3.25	2.85	2.62	2.46	2.35	2.26	2.19	2.14	2.09	2.05	2.02
	7.35	5.21	4.34	3.86	3.54	3.32	3.15	3.02	2.91	2.82	2.75	2.69
40	4.08	3.23	2.84	2.61	2.45	2.34	2.25	2.18	2.12	2.07	2.04	2.00
	7.31	5.18	4.31	3.83	3.51	3.29	3.12	2.99	2.88	2.80	2.73	2.66
42	4.07	3.22	2.83	2.59	2.44	2,32	2.24	2.17	2.11	2.06	2.02	1.99
	7.27	5.15	4.29	3.80	3.49	3.26	3.10	2.96	2.86	2.77	2.70	2.64
44	4.06	3.21	2.82	2.58	2.43	2.31	2.23	2.16	2.10	2.05	2.01	1.98
	7.24	5.12	4.26	3.78	3.46	3.24	3.07	2.94	2.84	2.75	2.68	2.62
46	4.05	3.20	2.81	2.57	2.42	2.30	2.22	2.14	2.09	2.04	2.00	1.97
	7.21	5.10	4.24	3.76	3.44	3.22	3.05	2.92	2.82	2.73	2.66	2.60
48	4.04	3.19	2.80	2.56	2.41	2.30	2.21	2.14	2.08	2.03	1.99	1.96
	7.19	5.08	4.22	3.74	3.42	3.20	3.04	2.90	2.80	2.71	2.64	2.58

	n_1 Degrees of Freedom (For Numerator Mean Square)										
14	**16**	**20**	**24**	**30**	**40**	**50**	**75**	**100**	**200**	**500**	**∞**
2.08	2.03	1.97	1.93	1.88	1.84	1.80	1.76	1.74	1.71	1.68	1.67
2.83	**2.74**	**2.63**	**2.55**	**2.47**	**2.38**	**2.33**	**2.25**	**2.21**	**2.16**	**2.12**	**2.10**
2.06	2.02	1.96	1.91	1.87	1.81	1.78	1.75	1.72	1.69	1.67	1.65
2.80	**2.71**	**2.60**	**2.52**	**2.44**	**2.35**	**2.30**	**2.22**	**2.18**	**2.13**	**2.09**	**2.06**
2.05	2.00	1.94	1.90	1.85	1.80	1.77	1.73	1.71	1.68	1.65	1.64
2.77	**2.68**	**2.57**	**2.49**	**2.41**	**2.32**	**2.27**	**2.19**	**2.15**	**2.10**	**2.06**	**2.03**
2.04	1.99	1.93	1.89	1.84	1.79	1.76	1.72	1.69	1.66	1.64	1.62
2.74	**2.66**	**2.55**	**2.47**	**2.38**	**2.29**	**2.24**	**2.16**	**2.13**	**2.07**	**2.03**	**2.01**
2.02	1.97	1.91	1.86	1.82	1.76	1.74	1.69	1.67	1.64	1.61	1.59
2.70	**2.62**	**2.51**	**2.42**	**2.34**	**2.25**	**2.20**	**2.12**	**2.08**	**2.02**	**1.98**	1.96
2.00	1.95	1.89	1.84	1.80	1.74	1.71	1.67	1.64	1.61	1.59	1,57
2.66	**2.58**	**2.47**	**2.38**	**2.30**	**2.21**	**2.15**	**2.08**	**2.04**	**1.98**	**1.94**	**1.91**
1.98	1.93	1.87	1.82	1.78	1.72	1.69	1.65	1.62	1.59	1.56	1.55
2.62	**2.54**	**2.43**	**2.35**	**2.26**	**2.17**	**2.12**	**2.04**	**2.00**	**1.94**	**1.90**	**1.87**
1.96	1.92	1.85	1.80	1.76	1.71	1.67	1.63	1.60	1.57	1.54	1.53
2.59	**2.51**	**2.40**	**2.32**	**2.22**	**2.14**	**2.08**	**2.00**	**1.97**	**1.90**	**1.86**	**1.84**
1.95	1.90	1.84	1.79	1.74	1.69	1.66	1.61	1.59	1.55	1.53	1.51
2.56	**2.49**	**2.37**	**2.29**	**2.20**	**2.11**	**2.05**	**1.97**	**1.94**	**1.88**	**1.84**	**1.81**
1.91	1.89	1.82	1.78	1.73	1.68	1.64	1.60	1.57	1.54	1,51	1.49
2.54	**2.46**	**2.35**	**2.26**	**2.17**	**2.08**	**2.02**	**1.94**	**1.91**	**1.85**	**1.80**	**1.78**
1.92	1.88	1.81	1.76	1.72	1.66	1.63	1.58	1.56	1.52	1.50	1.48
2.52	**2.44**	**2.32**	**2.24**	**2.15**	**2.06**	**2.00**	**1.92**	**1.88**	**1.82**	**1.78**	**1.75**
1.91	1.87	1.80	1.75	1.71	1.65	1.62	1.57	1.54	1.51	1.48	1.46
2.50	**2.42**	**2.30**	**2.22**	**2.13**	**2.04**	**1.98**	**1.90**	**1.86**	**1.80**	**1.76**	**1.72**
1.90	1.86	1.79	1.74	1.70	1.64	1.61	1.56	1.53	1.50	1.47	1.45
2.48	**2.40**	**2.28**	**2.20**	**2.11**	**2.02**	**1.96**	**1.88**	**1.84**	**1.78**	**1.73**	**1.70**

(continued)

	n_1 Degrees of Freedom (For Numerator Mean Square)											
n_2	1	2	3	4	5	6	7	8	9	10	11	12
50	4.03	3.18	2.79	2.56	2.40	2.29	2.20	2.13	2,07	2.02	1.98	1.95
	7.17	**5.06**	**4.20**	**3.72**	**3.41**	**3.18**	**3.02**	**2.88**	**2.78**	**2.70**	**2.62**	**2.56**
55	4.02	3.17	2.78	2.54	2.38	2.27	2.18	2.11	2.05	2.00	1.97	1.93
	7.12	**5.01**	**4.16**	**3.68**	**3.37**	**3.15**	**2.98**	**2.85**	**2.75**	**2.66**	**2.59**	**2.53**
60	4.00	3.15	2.76	2.52	2.37	2.25	2.17	2.10	2.04	1.99	1.95	1.92
	7.08	**4.98**	**4.13**	3.65	**3.34**	**3.12**	**2.95**	**2.82**	**2.72**	**2.63**	**2.56**	**2.50**
65	3.99	3.14	2.75	2.51	2.36	2.24	2.15	2.08	2.02	1.98	1.94	1.90
	7.04	**4.95**	**4.10**	**3.62**	**3.31**	**3.09**	**2.93**	**2.79**	**2.70**	**2.61**	**2.54**	**2.47**
70	3.98	3.13	2.74	2.50	2.35	2.23	2.14	2.07	2.01	1.97	1.93	1.89
	7.01	**4.92**	**4.08**	**3.60**	**3.29**	**3.07**	**2.91**	**2.77**	**2.67**	**2.59**	**2.51**	**2.45**
80	3.96	3.11	2.77	2.48	2.33	2.21	2.12	2.05	1.99	1.95	1,91	1.88
	6.96	**4.88**	**4.04**	**3.56**	**3.25**	**3.04**	**2.87**	**2.74**	**2.64**	**2.55**	**2.48**	**2.41**
100	3.94	3.09	2.70	2.46	2.30	2.19	2.10	2.03	1.97	1.92	1.88	1.85
	6.90	**4.82**	**3.98**	**3.51**	**3.20**	**2.99**	**2.82**	**2.69**	**2.59**	**2.51**	**2.43**	**2.36**
125	3.92	3.07	2.68	2.44	2.29	2.17	2.08	2.01	1.95	1.90	1.86	1.83
	6.84	**4.78**	**3.94**	**3.47**	**3.17**	**2.95**	**2.79**	**2.65**	**2.56**	**2.47**	**2.40**	**2.33**
150	3.91	3.06	2.57	2.43	2.27	2.16	2.07	2.00	1.94	1.89	1.85	1.82
	6.81	**4.75**	**3.91**	**3.44**	**3.14**	**2.92**	**2.76**	**2.62**	**2.53**	**2.44**	**2.37**	**2.30**
200	3.89	3.04	2.65	2.41	2.26	2.14	2.05	1.98	1.92	1.87	1.83	1.80
	6.76	**4.71**	**3.88**	**3.41**	**3.11**	**2.90**	**2.73**	**2.60**	**2.50**	**2.41**	**2.34**	**2.28**
400	3.86	3.02	2.62	2.39	2.23	2.12	2.03	1.96	1.90	1.85	1.81	1.78
	6.70	**4.66**	**3.83**	**3.36**	**3.06**	**2.85**	**2.69**	**2.55**	**2.46**	**2.37**	**2.29**	**2.23**
1000	3.85	3.00	2.61	2.38	2.22	2.10	2.02	1.95	1.89	1.84	1.80	1.76
	6.66	**4.62**	**3.80**	**3.34**	**3.04**	**2.82**	**2.66**	**2.53**	**2.43**	**2.34**	**2.26**	**2.20**
∞	3.84	2.99	2.60	2.37	2.21	2.09	2.01	1.94	1.88	1.83	1.79	1.75
	6.64	**4.60**	**3.78**	**3.32**	**3.02**	**2.80**	**2.64**	**2.51**	**2.41**	**2.32**	**2.24**	**2.18**

n_1 Degrees of Freedom (For Numerator Mean Square)											
14	**16**	**20**	**24**	**30**	**40**	**50**	**75**	**100**	**200**	**500**	**∞**
1.90	1.85	**1.78**	1.74	1.69	1.63	1.60	1.55	1.52	1.48	1.46	1.44
2.46	**2.39**	**2.26**	**2.18**	**2.10**	**2.00**	**1.94**	**1.86**	**1.82**	**1.76**	**1.71**	**1.68**
1.88	1.83	1.76	1.72	1.67	1.61	1.58	1.52	1.50	1.46	1.43	1.41
2.43	**2.35**	**2.23**	**2.15**	**2.06**	**1.96**	**1.90**	**1.82**	**1.78**	**1.71**	**1.66**	**1.64**
1.86	1.81	1.75	1.70	1.65	1.59	1.56	1.50	1.48	1.44	1.41	1.39
2.40	**2.32**	**2.20**	**2.12**	**2.03**	**1.93**	**1.87**	**1.79**	**1.74**	**1.68**	**1.63**	**1.60**
1.84	1.80	1.73	1.68	1.63	1.57	1.54	1.49	1.46	1.42	1.39	1.37
2.37	**2.30**	**2.18**	**2.09**	**2.00**	**1.90**	**1.84**	**1.76**	**1.71**	**1.64**	**1.60**	**1.56**
1.84	1,79	1.72	1.67	L62	1.56	1.53	1.47	1.45	1.40	1.37	1.35
2.35	**2.28**	**2.15**	**2.07**	**1.98**	**1.88**	**1.82**	**1.74**	**1.69**	**1.62**	**1.56**	**1.53**
1.82	1.77	1.70	1.65	1.60	1.54	1.51	1.45	**1.42**	1.38	1.35	1.32
2.32	**2.24**	**2.11**	**2.03**	**1.94**	**1.84**	**1.78**	**1.70**	**1.65**	**1.57**	**1.52**	**1.49**
1.79	1.75	1.68	1.63	1.57	1.51	1.48	1.42	1.39	1.34	1.30	1.28
2.26	**2.19**	**2.06**	**1.98**	**1.89**	**1.79**	**1.73**	**1.64**	**1.59**	**1.51**	**1.46**	**1.43**
1.77	1.72	1.65	1.60	**1.55**	1.49	1.45	1.39	1.36	1.31	1.27	1.25
2.23	**2.15**	**2.03**	**1.94**	**1.85**	**1.75**	**1.68**	**1.59**	**1.54**	**1.46**	**1.40**	**1.37**
1.76	1.71	1.64	1.59	1.54	1.47	1.44	1.37	1.34	1.29	1.25	1.22
2.20	**2.12**	**2.00**	**1.91**	**1.83**	**1.72**	**1.66**	**1.56**	**1.51**	**1.43**	**1.37**	**1.33**
1.74	**1.69**	1.62	1.57	1.52	1.45	1.42	1.35	1.32	1.26	1.22	1.19
2.17	**2.09**	**1.97**	**1.88**	**1.79**	**1.69**	**1.62**	**1.53**	**1.48**	**1.39**	**1.33**	**1.28**
1.72	1.67	1.60	1.54	1.49	1.42	1.38	1.32	1.28	1.22	1.16	1.13
2.12	**2.04**	**1.92**	**1.84**	**1.74**	**1.65**	**1.57**	**1.47**	**1.42**	**1.32**	**1.24**	**1.19**
1.70	1,65	1.58	1.53	1.47	1,41	1.36	1.30	1.26	1.19	1.13	1.08
2.09	**2.01**	**1.89**	**1.81**	**1.71**	**1.61**	**1.54**	**1.44**	**1.38**	**1.28**	**1.19**	**1.11**
1.69	1.64	1.57	1.52	1.46	1.40	**1.35**	**1.28**	1.24	**1.17**	**1.11**	**1.00**
2.07	**1.99**	**1.87**	**1.79**	**1.69**	**1.59**	**1.52**	**1.41**	**1.36**	**1.25**	**1.15**	**1.00**

Reprinted from J. Welkowitz, B. H. Cohen, & B. R. Lea. (2012). *Introductory statistics for the behavioral sciences* (7th ed.). Hoboken, NJ: Wiley. With permission from Wiley & Sons.

GLOSSARY

a. **The *Y* INTERCEPT** is the point where the regression line intercepts the *y* axis.

ANALYSIS OF VARIANCE (also called **Simple Analysis of Variance**). An inferential statistic is a means hypothesis test in situation where the independent has only two groups. It calculates the between and within group differences.

b. **SLOPE OF THE LINE** is where the amount of change in *Y* is directly related to the amount of change in *X*.

CHANCE is the possibility that random variation can affect the outcome of the dependent variable.

CHI-SQUARE (also called **test of association, test of independence**). A bivariate statistical test used to test hypotheses of nominal variables.

CODEBOOK/CODE SHEET. A way for researchers to assign numerical and nonnumerical symbols to each of the questions and their respective responses.

COEFFICIENT OF VARIATION The ratio of the standard deviation to the mean.

CONCEPTS are the mental images that researchers diagram. The mental images may be events, attitudes, personality traits, ideas, objects, and behaviors.

CONFIDENCE INTERVAL (The areas under the normal curve that constitute 99.74%). The proportion under the areas of the normal curve that enables researchers to calculate the standard error of a sampling distribution—and estimate with a certain degree of confidence the closeness of the true population to the sample mean.

CONTINUOUS VARIABLES (*see* Variable classification) are those whose values are at an interval or ratio level of measurement and can be arranged on a number line (scale) without breaking or being omitted (infinite), for example, age, income, numbers of calories taken in per day, and number of steps one walks per day.

CONVERSATIONAL ANALYSIS is almost similar to semiotics. In semiotics, signs, symbols, and cultural concepts are analyzed. In conversational analysis, *words* are analyzed to uncover the inherent assumptions and structures in social life by means of extreme scrutiny of modes of conversation with one another.

CORRELATION. Correlation is used to conduct hypothesis test on the significant difference of randomized interval/ratio variables.

CORRELATION COEFFICIENT. *See* Pearson correlation coefficient.

CUMULATIVE FREQUENCY (CUMULATIVE PERCENTAGE). Indicates the number of cases that have been accounted for in a value/category and cumulative percentage for representing the proportion of the sample/population of that value/category.

DATA are used interchangeably with raw scores, numbers, words, or even tables/figures collected for a research project using research methods.

DEGREES OF FREEDOM *(df)* are explained slightly differently from one statistical test to another. Normally, degrees of freedom are the attributes that are free to vary in a population size or sample.

DESCRIPTIVE STATISTICS are used to organize and summarize typical numerical values within a data set. Common statistical configurations for descriptive statistics include frequency distributions, graphs, measures of central tendency, and measures of variability.

DIRECTIONAL (ONE-TAILED) HYPOTHESIS. A method used to test hypotheses that researchers are certain of or able to predict the direction that the relationship of the variable under investigation will fall on the normal curve.

DISCRETE VARIABLES take only finite responses, such as nominal- or ordinal-scale values (e.g., gender, race, and college degree).

DISPERSION (ALSO CALLED DATA DISPERSION). The variability of a measure of difference among observations in a distribution set.

DISTRIBUTION SET (ALSO CALLED DATA SET). The scores obtained from a research project.

DV represents the dependent (also called **criterion** or **outcome**) variable that can be affected by other variables.

EXPECTED FREQUENCIES (also called **unknown frequencies**) are calculated for each of the cells in a cross-tabulation table. Also called unknown frequencies because a user must calculate using the marginal columns and marginal rows.

INFERENTIAL STATISTICS utilize use complex procedures and calculations to make generalizations and draw conclusions about a population based on a sample from that population. Common inferential statistics include chi-square, correlation, *t* tests, *F* test, and regression.

IV represents the independent variable (also called a predictor, effect, or factor). Independent variables are the variables researchers believe can cause or have an effect on the dependent variable.

EQUALS SIGN (=) is used interchangeably with the words *equal to, refers to,* or *stands for* that particular concept or attribute. For example, the variable "gender" may be coded as 1 = female and 2 = male. Here, 1 is used to stand for the word *female* and is *not* equal to "female").

EFFECT SIZE (ES) (also called **Cohen's *d***) is used in the same manner as the *z* score, but it is mainly used to examine treatment effects, for example, the difference between the experimental group mean and the control group mean.

F (*see* One-way analysis of variance). The **F ratio** is used in the same manner as the independent *t* test to examine the mean difference of a dependent variable with multiple nominal-level independent variables, such as income earnings of several groups of people.

F. Frequency count or raw score of a distribution set.

FIELD NOTES are like memos (texts) to the researcher, assistants (if any), and the recorded words/responses the respondents give during the interview. In qualitative research, words are used to understand the richness of human experience. The meaning of "text" then becomes the extent to which researchers are able to reach meaning on social issues, such as how they were understood and interpreted by the community.

FREQUENCY DISTRIBUTIONS (use is similar to **frequencies**) typically refer to the frequency count, percentage, valid percentage, and cumulative percentage for the values of the variable under investigation.

GROUNDED THEORY or **content analysis** is a way of transforming qualitative material into quantitative data. It consists primarily of coding and tabulating the occurrences of certain forms of content that are being communicated. Content analysis is essentially a coding operation.

H_a is the research hypothesis. It is a declarative sentence predicting how changes in one variable (usually the independent variable) are proposed to cause or explain changes in another variable (usually the dependent variable).

H_0 (also called the **secondary hypothesis**) is a declarative sentence stating that, despite what the same data suggest, after taking into account sampling errors or chance fluctuations, no real relationship or difference exists between the hypothesized variables.

HYPOTHESIS. A statement of an educated hunch or speculation about a presumed relationship in the real world.

INTERVAL DATA (INTERVAL VARIABLE). Used when the researchers seek to rank order the values of the variable and there are equal intervals, but no zero is specified for the values of the variable.

LATENT CONTENT is applied specifically to a qualitative approach. The researcher still must select a specific form of communication but then only analyze the meaning of the communication.

LEVEL OF MEASUREMENT. Common research terminology for all types of research. It is used by researchers for conceptualizing how the variables for the prospective research project are going to be measured. Research questionnaires are measured at the nominal, ordinal, interval, or ratio level.

LEVEL OF SIGNIFICANCE (*see also p* value). This term appears often in statistical analysis. It is used to explain the cutoff point that separates the critical region probability from the rest of the area under the normal curve (*z* score).

LINEAR REGRESSION. An analysis tool to calculate the slope of a straight line, then use the slope to make predictions concerning the variation that may occur when certain amounts of *X* change and how that affects *Y*.

MAGNITUDE is the degree of severity of the problem or the strength of the relationship between two concepts. For example, a homeless person may describe the relationship between loneliness (*X*) and self-worth (*Y*) or a count of sleepless nights (*Z*).

MANIFEST CODING is applied more to a quantitative approach by focusing on a specific form of communication (i.e., journal article, book, magazine, newspaper) to determine the extent to which form accounts for the issue at hand.

MARGINAL COLUMNS TOTAL (*C*). The summation of all columns for the nominal variable under investigation (*see* Chi-square).

MARGINAL ROWS TOTAL (*R*). The summation of all rows for the nominal variable under investigation (*see* Chi-square).

MEAN ($\overline{X}$) is better known as *sample mean* or *simple statistic* and is the arithmetic average or the numerical center of the scores in the distribution set (*see* Measures of central tendency).

MEAN DEVIATION is a measure of the dispersion, which is equal to the mean of the absolute values of the deviation scores (*see* Variability or Dispersion).

MEDIAN (MDN) is the middle score(s) (or the second quartile), which divides the scores into two equal halves or proportions (*see* Variability or Dispersion).

MEASURES OF CENTRAL TENDENCY are used to determine how values in a given distribution of scores are clustered and identify the key central locations for the distribution set. Central tendency can be explained by the mean, median, and mode.

MEASUREMENT OR SCALE refers to the measuring scale or tool the researcher uses to measure the variables under study, such as attitudes, personality traits, feelings, well-being, and events.

METHODOLOGY. Methods are steps researchers use to complete a study and safeguard their study from errors commonly made in casual human inquiries.

MIXED METHOD means that the researcher combines quantitative and qualitative research methods. For example, the researcher may structure two thirds of the questionnaires using a quantitative method and the remaining one third of the questionnaires using a qualitative design or vice versa.

MODE is the value category that appears most frequently within a data set (*see* Measures of central tendency).

NARRATIVE DATA. Narrative data analysis is one technique that researchers can use to analyze and evaluate qualitative data.

NEGATIVE CORRELATION occurs when the values of interval/ratio variables move in the opposite direction (*see* Pearson correlation coefficient). For example, when the values of one variable decrease, the values of the other variable increase.

NEGATIVELY SKEWED. Indicates scores are clustered heavily to the left-hand side of the normal distribution curve (*see* Normal distribution and *z* core).

NO CORRELATION occurs when the distribution of scores is scattered all over the scatterplot (*see* Correlation).

NOMINAL DATA (nominal variable or nominal level of measurement). Classifies the values of the variable into discrete and separate categories based on some defined characteristics or "name" of the variable (*see* Level of measurement).

NONDIRECTIONAL (TWO-TAILED) HYPOTHESIS. Used to test hypotheses for which researchers believe significant difference does exist but they are unsure or unable able to predict the direction of the relationship.

NORMAL DISTRIBUTION (NORMAL CURVE). A mathematical probability that the user can use to gain better understanding of the inferential statistics (*see z* score). This mathematical probability states that a situation may have no chance of occurring at all (0) to the possibility that it will absolutely occur (1.0).

ONE-WAY ANALYSIS OF VARIANCE (ANOVA) (*see also* Analysis of variance). A statistical test tool that tests hypotheses when there is one dependent variable and one independent variable with three or more levels, for example, income for several groups of people.

OPERATIONALIZATION is the abstract thinking process whereby vague concepts are organized into clear and precise statements around which specific research procedures can be operationalized (measured) for empirical observation of the target issue in the environment.

ORDINAL DATA (ordinal variable or ordinal level of measurement). When data are rank ordered, numbers are assigned according to the amount or quality, but no specific distance can be measured (*see* Level of measurement). A Likert scale is an example of the ordinal level of measurement.

OUTLIERS refer to the raw scores that are extraneous and out of the ordinary among the values of the variables in the distribution.

p (*see also* Level of significance). The alpha (α) coefficient, used to explain the relationship between the variables. When H_0 is retained, use $p > \#$, and when H_a is supported, use $p < \#$.

PARAMETER. A measure of a characteristic of a population. A parameter is a summary description of a given variable in a population.

PEARSON CORRELATION COEFFICIENT (Pearson r or product-moment correlation coefficient). A bivariate inferential statistical test used to examine the relationship between two continuous variables.

POPULATION (N). In most social work research, populations are composed of people and a data frame. Yet, this need not be the case. For example, populations may be case records and field notes of child abuse and neglect cases for a particular county child welfare program.

POSITIVE CORRELATION occurs when the values of interval/ratio variables move in the same direction (either increase or decrease together).

POSITIVELY SKEWED. Scores are distributed heavily to the right-hand side of the normal distribution curve.

PROBABILITY (*see also* Normal curve). A mathematical equation showing the proportion or fraction of times that particular outcome will occur. A probability can range from no chance of the event occurring at all (0 or 0%) to the event that is absolutely occurring (1.0 or 100%).

PROBLEM IDENTIFICATION is a part of the research process whereby researchers diagram the research project, particularly identifying the research topic.

PROCESS involves ordering categories (issues confronted by subjects under investigation/ research) by time and shows the characteristics (subcategories) associated with the stages of life development. Process may be considered as the phases or stages that occur in a research problem.

QUALITATIVE DATA are words or codes representing a category or a class of the sample.

QUANTITATIVE DATA or numeric variables are things, objects, characteristics, attitudes, behaviors, or personality traits collected from an observation that can be counted or represented as an amount.

R. The correlation coefficient under regression analysis.

r. The Pearson correlation coefficient; used to examine strength and direction of continuous variables.

RATIO DATA (ratio variable or ratio level of measurement). This level of measurement has all the properties of nominal, ordinal, and interval levels plus the zero point that reflects a possible absence of the characteristics measured (*see* Level of measurement).

REJECTION (ALSO CALLED EXTREME) REGION. The remaining regions (extreme left and right of the normal curve) of the areas under the normal curve that are reserved for hypothesis testing (*see* z score).

r^2. The coefficient of determination; used to examine the amount of variation in the dependent variable that can be explained or accounted for by a particular independent variable.

SAMPLE (n). A sample consists of a segment in a population. The sample is the subset of the population. It is the sample drawn from the population under study.

SAMPLING DISTRIBUTION OF THE MEAN. The probability distribution of means for all possible random samples of a given size from the same population.

SEMIOTICS. The science of signs; has to do with symbols and meanings.

SD. Standard deviation or standardized unit of measurement for the variable under investigation.

STANDARD ERROR OF THE MEAN. A theoretical sampling distribution enabling researchers to make true estimations of the sampling population; estimated by factoring the sample standard deviation over the square root of the sample size.

STATISTICAL ANALYSIS. The use of the two types of statistics: descriptive statistics and inferential statistics.

STATISTICAL SIGNIFICANCE (*see also* p or Level of significance). An inferential concept used to describe a situation where H_0 is rejected and H_a has been supported.

SS^2. Sum of squares or the variance (*see* Variance).

TRIMMED MEAN. A statistical method that eliminates a partial percentage (X%) of the greatest and smallest values before evaluating the sample mean of a given data set.

t **TESTS.** The statistical tool for bivariate analyses used to test for statistical differences between the means of two groups: either the sample mean with the population mean or two related and unrelated groups.

TYPE I ERROR. Occurs when researchers reject the wrong null hypothesis. In this case, the researchers should have retained H_0 but rejected it.

TYPE II ERROR. Occurs when the null hypothesis is false and researchers fail to reject it; that is, they falsely accepted H_0.

VARIABILITY (SEE ALSO DISPERSION). The measure of variation or difference amount observations in a distribution. The spread out of the distribution set.

VARIABLE (commonly using symbols as *X, Y,* and *Z*). Anything the researcher can quantify, measure, or categorize about the objectives of research subjects, which may contain numerical or nonnumerical meaning.

VARIABLE CLASSIFICATION. Variables can be classified as discrete or continuous based on their values (*see* Discrete variables and Continuous variables).

VALUE. In quantitative research, values are the possible scales in a measurement that may or may not be precoded. Normally, responses to continuous variables are considered values.

VALUE CATEGORY. In contrast to value, value categories are the possible responses to a question that is not scale but rather categorical.

VARIABILITY BETWEEN GROUP MEANS. Refers to the variation among the means of treatment conditions due to either treatment effect or inherent chance of variation among the individuals in a research project.

VARIABILITY WITHIN GROUP MEANS. The variation of individual scores around the sample mean as a direct reflection of chance rather than as caused by different types of treatment.

VARIANCE (also called sum of squares, SS^2). The sum of the squared deviations from the sample mean that provides an understanding of the spread of scores about the mean (*see* Measures of variability or Dispersion).

μ (mu; population mean). Used to stand for the population mean or hypothesized mean.

X, Y, Z. Symbols used to represent the name or the value of the variable. For example, X = college stress.

z **SCORE** (*see also* Normal distribution). A mathematical equation used to convert original scores to new scores to examine how many standard deviation intervals a value falls above or below the mean. The new scores then can be converted to percentiles. In most situations, the probability of occurring is ± 3 *SD* or 99.74%.

REFERENCES

Agresti, A., & Finlay, B. (2009). *Statistical methods for the social sciences* (4th ed.). Upper Saddle River, NJ: Pearson Prentice Hall.

Anders, K. L., Dinis, M. C. (2009). Workplace challenges in institutions of higher education: Perceptions of administrators. *The International Journal of Interdisciplinary Social Sciences*, 4(5), 283–294.

Aron, A., Coups, E. J., & Aron, E. N. (2011). *Statistics for the behavioral and social sciences: A brief course* (5th ed.). Boston, MA: Pearson.

Authors (Ed.). (2000). *Diagnostic and statistical manual of mental disorders* (4th ed.). American Psychological Association.

Coolidge, F. L. (2013). *Statistics: A gentle introduction* (3rd ed.). Los Angeles, CA: Sage.

Engel, R. J., & Schutt, R. K. (2013). *The practice of research in social work* (3rd ed.). Los Angeles, CA: Sage.

Field, A. (2009). *Discovering statistics using SPSS*. Thousand Oaks, CA: Sage.

Finley, R. (1999). *Survey monkey*. Palo Alto, CA: SurveyMonkey.com.

Freeman, D., Pisani, R., & Purves, R. (1978). *Statistics*. New York, NY: Norton.

Geher, G., & Hall, S. (2014). *Straightforward statistics: Understanding the tools of research*. New York, NY: Oxford University Press.

Glaser, B. G., & Strauss, A. L. (1967). *The discovery of grounded theory: Strategies for qualitative research*. Chicago, IL: Aldine.

Grinnell, R. M. (2000). *Social work research and evaluation: Quantitative and qualitative approaches* (6th ed.). Belmont, CA: Cengage Learning.

Hays, W. (1994). *Statistics* (5th ed.). Fort Worth, TX: Harcourt Brace College.

King, B. M., Rosopa, P. J., & Minium, E. J. (2011). *Statistical reasoning in the behavioral sciences*. Hoboken, NJ: Wiley.

Leon-Guerrero, A., & Frankfort-Nachmias. (2012). *Essentials of social statistics for a diverse society*. Los Angeles, CA: Sage.

Lofland, J., Anderson, L., & Lofland, L. H. (2006). *Analyzing social settings: A guide to qualitative observation and analysis* (4th ed.). Belmont, CA: Cengage Learning.

Meyers, L. S., Gamst, G., & Guarino, A. J. (2006). *Applied multivariate research: Design and interpretation*. Thousand Oaks, CA: Sage.

Mogull, R. G. (2004). *Second-semester applied statistics*. Dubuque, IA: Kendall/Hunt.

Montcalm, D., & Royse, D. (2002). *Data analysis for social workers*. Boston, MA: Pearson Education.

Monette, D. R., Sullivan, T. J., & DeJong, C. R. (2005). *Applied social research: A tool for human services.* Belmont, CA: Brooks/Cole-Thompson Learning.

Nowaczyk, R. H. (1988). **Statistics** *for Behavioral Research*. Harcourt College Publication.

Rubin, A. (2013). *Statistics for evidence-based practice and evaluation* (3rd ed.). Belmont, CA: Brooks/Cole.

Rubin, A., & Babbie, E. (2014). *Essential research methods for social workers* (3rd ed.). Belmont, CA: Brooks/Cole. *SPSS Software: Predictive analytics software and solutions.* (2015). Retrieved from SPSS Official Website: http://www-01.ibm.com/software/analytics/spss/

Weinbach, R. W., & Grinnell, R. M. (2015). *Statistics for social workers* (9th ed.). Boston, MA: Pearson.

Welkowitz, J., Cohen, B. H., & Lea, B. R. (2012). *Introductory statistics for the behavioral sciences* (7th ed.). Hoboken: Wiley.

Welkowitz, J. Cohen, B. H., & Ewen, R. B. (2006). *Introductory statistics for the behavioral sciences* (6th ed.). Hoboken: Wiley.

Witte, R. (1993). *Statistics* (4th ed.). Fort Worth, TX: Harcourt Brace Jovanovich College.

INDEX

Note: Page numbers followed by *f* and *t* indicate figures and tables, respectively.

abscissa, 35
absolute frequency, 18
absolute value, 30
alpha (α coefficient), 55
analysis of variance (ANOVA), 88, 115, 155*f*.
    See also Kruskal-Wallis *H* test; one-way
    analysis of variance
    definition of, 197
    Excel tools for, 184–185, 185*t*, 186
    practical application, 117–122
    results from, interpreting, 123
    sources of variability for, 117
    statistical assumptions associated with, 116
Analyzing Qualitative Data (free reference
    resource), 134
*Analyzing Social Settings: A Guide to Qualitative
    Observation and Analysis* (Lofland
    et al.), 134
anonymity, 15
ANOVA. *See* analysis of variance (ANOVA)
array
    in computation of median, 27–28
    definition of, 27
asymptotic, definition of, 37
ATLAS.ti, 133
attributes
    numeric forms and, 125
    words and, 125

b. See slope of the regression line
bar chart(s), 20
bar graph(s), 20, 20*f*

bivariate analysis, definition of, 61
Bonferroni test, 163

C. See marginal columns total *(C)*
cal (subscript). *See* chi-square (statistic),
    calculated value of
calculated Pearson chi-square coefficient (χ^2), 68
calculated *t. See* *t* test(s)
cause(s), in qualitative data analysis, 131
cell(s), 62, 64
cell frequencies. *See* cell(s)
central limit theorem, 49
central locations, 25
central tendency, 25. *See also* mean; measures of
    central tendency; median; mode
chance, definition of, 197
chi-square (statistic), 61–62
    calculated value of, 68
    calculation of, 67–71
    computation procedures for, 65–67, 65*f*
    critical values of, 68–70, 69*t*
    definition of, 197
    degrees of freedom for, 68–70, 69*t*
    formula for, 65, 65*f*, 66*t*
    interpretation of, 68
    for 2 × 2 study, 70–71, 71*t*
    understanding, 63–67
chi-square for goodness of fit, 63
chi-square test of association, 63
    computation using Statistical Package for
        Social Sciences (SPSS), 151–152, 152*f*, 153*t*
CI. *See* confidence interval (CI)

code book/code sheet, 145
  definition of, 197
coding sheet/coding scheme, 145
coefficient of determination (r^2), 84–85, 105–106
  computation using Statistical Package for
    Social Sciences (SPSS), 151
  definition of, 201
coefficient of variation, 32–33
  definition of, 197
  formula for, 33
Cohen's *d*, 100. *See also* effect size (ES)
column total, 64
concept(s)
  definition of, 1, 197
  in social science, 1
  statistical, 1
condition, 48
confidence interval (CI), 26, 39, 39*t*
  construction of, 54–56
  conversion to *z* score, 57–58
  decision-making using, 55–56
  definition of, 54–55, 197
  for directional hypothesis, 57–58, 59*f*
  for nondirectional hypothesis, 57–58, 59*f*
  preset values in computer applications, 55
confidentiality, 15–16
confounding variable(s), 112
consequences, in qualitative data analysis, 131
constant *(a)*, 108–110. *See also y* intercept
content
  latent, 132, 199
  manifest, 132
content analysis, 132. *See also* grounded theory
contingency (cross-tabulation) table, 61, 152,
    153*t*. *See also* cross tabulation
  columns in, 62, 64–65, 64*t*
  construction of, 62–63, 63*t*
  rows in, 62, 64–65, 64*t*
  total *(N)*, 62, 64, 64*t*, 65*f*
continuous variable(s), 9, 37–38, 63. *See also*
    variable classification
  definition of, 197
conversational analysis, 133
  definition of, 197
correlation, 106–107. *See also* no (zero)
    correlation
  vs. causation, 77
  curvilinear, 74
  definition of, 73–74, 197
  Excel calculation, 183–184, 183*f*, 184*f*
  graphical display of, 74–75
  linear, 74
  negative. *See* negative correlation

  perfect, 78
  positive. *See* positive correlation
  use of, by health and human service
    workers, 77
correlation coefficient, 77–78. *See also* Pearson
    correlation coefficient (Pearson *r*)
  calculation using Excel Analysis ToolPak,
    183–184, 183*f*, 184*f*
  range of, 84
  strength of, 148
crit (subscript). *See* chi-square (statistic), critical
    values of
criterion variable, 74, 105. *See also* dependent
    variable(s)
crosstab. *See* cross tabulation
cross tabulation, 61, 62*t*, 152, 153*t*. *See also*
    contingency (cross-tabulation) table
cumulative frequency, 19
  definition of, 198
cumulative percentage, 19
  definition of, 198
curvilinear correlation, 74
CV. *See* coefficient of variation

data
  collection of, 10, 126
  definition of, 3, 5, 10, 198
  homoscedastic, 108
  interval. *See* interval data
  narrative. *See* narrative data
  nominal. *See* nominal data
  ordinal. *See* ordinal data
  qualitative. *See* qualitative data
  quantitative. *See* quantitative data
  ratio. *See* ratio data
  statistical, 1. *See also* concept(s), statistical
data analysis. *See also specific method*
  preparation of quantitative data for, 145–148
  qualitative, 129–134
  using Excel, 177–186
data collection procedures, 10, 126
  for qualitative data analysis, 126–127
  variables that emerge during, 145
data dispersion. *See* dispersion
data interpretation(s), 129
data recoding, 138, 145–148, 146*f*, 147*f*, 148*t*
data recording, 127
  qualitative, 127–129
data reduction, 2
data set. *See* distribution set
data spread, definition of, 29
data summary, 2
definition variance, 31

degrees of freedom (df), 68–70, 69t
  definition of, 198
  for dependent sample t test, 99
  for independent samples t test, 97
  and mean square between groups (MS$_{between}$), 122, 123t
  and mean square within groups (MS$_{within}$), 122, 123t
  for one-sample t test, 91–92
de Moivre, Abraham, 36–37, 38, 39
dependent variable(s), 7, 9–10
  definition of, 198
  and null hypothesis, 52
  and research hypothesis, 51
  and t tests, 88
  variances in, 118
descriptive statistics, 2. See also frequency distribution(s); measures of central tendency; variability
  computations using Statistical Package for Social Sciences (SPSS), 148–150, 149f, 150f, 150t
  definition of, 198
  Excel tools for, 181, 182f, 183f
design flaws, 60
df. See degrees of freedom (df)
directional (one-tailed) hypothesis, 52–53, 53f
  definition of, 198
discrete variable(s), 9, 37–38, 63
  definition of, 198
dispersion
  definition of, 29, 198
  selection using Statistical Package for Social Sciences (SPSS), 149, 150f
distribution set, definition of, 198
Duncan test, 163
Dunnett's C test, 164
Dunnett's T3 test, 164
Dunnett test, 163–164
DV. See also dependent variable(s)
  definition of, 198

effect size (ES), 100–101
  definition of, 198
enumeration, 130
equals sign (=), 11
  definition of, 198
error. See also sampling error
  in hypothesis testing, 58–59, 60t
  type I. See type I error
  type II. See type II error
ES. See effect size (ES)
estimated standard deviation of the difference

scores, 88
estimated standard error between two independent means, 95–96
estimated standard error of the difference in two means, 88, 95–96
estimated standard error of the mean of difference scores, 97–99
ethical issues, 15–16
evidence-based practice, 3
Excel, 17, 167
  Analysis ToolPak, 167, 176, 177, 177f
  bins, 178, 179f
  data analysis using, 177–186
  data entry, 168–169, 169f, 170f
  descriptive statistics, 181, 182f, 183f
  formulas, 170–173, 171f, 172f, 173f, 173t, 177
  frequency distribution computations, 178–180
  functions, 174–176, 174f, 175f, 177
  getting started with, 168–169
  Histogram, 179–180, 180f, 181f
  Insert Function, 176, 176f
  Intercept function, 184
  operators, 172, 173t
  regression analysis, 184–185, 185f, 185t
  Slope function, 184
  and SPSS, differences between, in data entry, 169
  t tests, 186
expected frequency(ies) (E), 61, 65–67, 65f, 66t, 67t
  calculation of, 66–67, 66t
  definition of, 198
extreme region. See rejection region

f (frequency count), 18
  definition of, 198
F, critical values of, 123, 187–195
factor(s), 115
factor analysis, 115
field notes, 126–127
  consistency of, 128
  definition of, 198
  people in, 128
  setting in, 128
fieldwork, 126–127
figures, 20
finding(s), 127. See also research findings
  significant, 56, 68–69, 151
Fisher's F distribution. See F ratio
formula(s)
  definition of, 170
  in Excel, 170–173, 171f, 172f, 173f, 173t

F ratio, 115–117, 122, 123t. *See also* analysis of variance (ANOVA)
   calculation of, 118–119, 119f
   definition of, 198
   and t test, 115–116
frequency(ies), 17–18
   cumulative. *See* cumulative frequency
   expected. *See* expected frequency(ies) (E)
   observed. *See* observed frequencies (O)
   in qualitative data analysis, 130
   unknown. *See* expected frequency(ies) (E)
frequency count, 18, 198
frequency distribution(s), 2, 17–19
   definition of, 198
   Excel computations of, 178–180
   using Statistical Package for Social Sciences (SPSS), 144–145
frequency polygon, 21–22, 22f

Gabriel test, 163
Games-Howell test, 164
generalization, 47
Gosset, William S., 90
graph(s), 19–22
   crossover type, 20
grounded theory, 132
   definition of, 199
group, 48, 116
group behavior, in qualitative research, 128

H_0. *See* null hypothesis (H_0)
H_1. *See* research hypothesis (H_a)
H_2. *See* secondary hypothesis (H_2)
H_a. *See* research hypothesis (H_a)
histogram(s), 21, 22f
   Excel, 179–180, 180f, 181f
Hochberg's GT2, 163
homogeneity of variance, 89
homoscedastic data, 108
hypothesis. *See also* rival hypotheses
   definition of, 50, 199
   directional. *See* directional (one-tailed) hypothesis
   direction of, 52–54
   nondirectional. *See* nondirectional (two-tailed) hypothesis
   null. *See* null hypothesis (H_0)
   one-tailed. *See* directional (one-tailed) hypothesis
   research. *See* research hypothesis (H_a)
   secondary. *See* secondary hypothesis (H_2)
   two-tailed. *See* nondirectional (two-tailed) hypothesis

   types of, 51–52
hypothesis testing, 50, 148
   four possible outcomes associated with, 58–59, 60t
hypothesized mean. *See* μ

independent variable(s), 10
   definition of, 198
   and null hypothesis, 52
   and research hypothesis, 51
   and t tests, 88
individual actions/activities, in qualitative research, 128
inductive method, 132
inference, definition of, 47
inferential statistics, 2–3. *See also* analysis of variance (ANOVA); chi-square (statistic); correlation; cross tabulation; linear regression; t test(s)
   computations using Statistical Package for Social Sciences (SPSS), 150–155
   definition of, 198
   reporting, guidelines for, 56–57
information
   definition of, 5
   sensitive, 16
informed consent, 15
institutional review board (IRB), 15
interquartile range, 27
interval, definition of, 13
interval data, 13–14. *See also* correlation
   definition of, 199
   and histograms, 21, 22f
   and linear regression, 108
   and t tests, 88
interval estimate. *See* confidence interval
interval variable. *See* interval data
interview(s), in qualitative research, 128
inverse correlation coefficient, 74–76, 75f, 76f
IRB. *See* institutional review board (IRB)
IV. *See also* independent variable(s)
   definition of, 198

K (group), 116
Kruskal-Wallis H test, 158, 158t
kurtosis, 37

latent content, 132
   definition of, 199
least significant difference test, 163
level of measurement, 11–14
   definition of, 199
   importance of, 148

nominal. *See* nominal data
ordinal. *See* ordinal data
rank-ordered, 13
ratio. *See* ratio data
in Statistical Package for Social Sciences
    (SPSS), 139
and *t* tests, 88
level of significance, 55. *See also* *p* value
    definition of, 199
linear correlation, 74
linear regression
    computational formula for, 108–109
    computation using Statistical Package for
        Social Sciences (SPSS), 153–154, 154*f*, 155*t*
    definition of, 199
    Excel analysis, 184–185, 185*f*, 185*t*
    in health and human services, 107
    meaning of, 106–108
    statistical requirements/conditions for,
        107–108
    use in health and human services, 109–111
line chart(s), 21–22, 22*f*
line graph, 21–22, 22*f*
LSD (least significant difference) test, 163

magnitude
    definition of, 199
    in qualitative data analysis, 130, 130*t*
manifest coding, definition of, 199
manifest content, 132
Mann-Whitney *U* test, 158, 158*t*, 159–160,
    160*f*, 161*t*
marginal columns total *(C)*, 64, 65*f*, 66, 66*t*
    definition of, 199
marginal rows total *(R)*, 64, 65*f*, 66, 66*t*
    definition of, 199, 201
MAXQDA, 133
McNemar test, 160
MD. *See* mean deviation
mean, 25, 35–36, 36*f*. *See also* *t* test(s)
    computation of, 26, 26*t*
    definition of, 26, 199
    properties of, 29–30, 30*t*, 35
    and standard deviation, distance between,
        38–39, 39*t*
mean deviation, 29–30, 31, 32*t*
    computation of, 30, 31*t*
    definition of, 199
meaning, in qualitative research, 129
mean square between groups (MS$_{between}$),
    118–119, 119*f*, 122, 123*t*
mean square within groups (MS$_{within}$), 118–119,
    119*f*, 122, 123*t*

measurement, definition of, 11–12, 199
measures of central tendency, 2, 25–29, 35.
    See also mean; median; mode
    definition of, 199
    Excel, 181, 182*f*, 183*f*
    importance of, 148
    selection in Statistical Package for Social
        Sciences (SPSS), 149–150, 150*f*
measures of dispersion, 2
measures of variability, 2
median, 25, 35–36, 36*f*
    definition of, 27, 199
method(s), definition of, 5
methodology, 4*f*, 5
    definition of, 200
    research, 3–4
Microsoft Excel. *See* Excel
mixed method, 127
    definition of, 200
mode, 25, 35–36, 36*f*
    definition of, 28, 200
MS$_{between}$. *See* mean square between groups
    (MS$_{between}$)
MS$_{within}$. *See* mean square within groups
    (MS$_{within}$)
multiple-comparison tests, 162–164
μ, 90
    definition of, 202

N. *See* population *(N)*
n. *See* sample *(n)*
narrative data, 129
    definition of, 200
negative correlation, 74–76, 75*f*, 76*f*, 78
    definition of, 200
negatively skewed (distribution), 36, 36*f*, 50
    definition of, 36, 200
no (zero) correlation, 75–76, 76*f*, 78
    definition of, 200
nominal data, 12
    and bar graphs, 20
    and contingency table, 61
    definition of, 200
    and *t* tests, 88
nominal definition, 5
nominal level of measurement. *See* nominal data
nominal variable. *See* nominal data
nondirectional (two-tailed) hypothesis, 53–54, 54*f*
    definition of, 200
nonparametric statistics, 157
    alternative rank-order statistic tests for, 158, 158*t*
    Statistical Package for Social Sciences (SPSS)
        procedures for, 159–162

normal curve, 36, 36f
  areas under, 38–39, 38f, 39t
  asymptotic, 37–38
  continuous, 37–38
  definition of, 35, 200
  properties of, 37–38, 37f
  and standard deviation, 38, 38f
  symmetry of, 37
  unimodal, 37
normal distribution, 31, 36, 36f. See also z score
  definition of, 35, 200
  historical perspective on, 36–37
  and parametric statistics, 157
null hypothesis (H_0), 51, 52
  definition of, 199
numeric forms, 125
NVivo 10, 133

observation(s), in qualitative research, 128–129
observed frequencies (O), 64, 64t, 65f, 66, 66t, 67t
one-sided hypothesis. See directional
    (one-tailed) hypothesis
one-tailed hypothesis. See directional
    (one-tailed) hypothesis
one-way analysis of variance, 115. See also
    analysis of variance (ANOVA)
  definition of, 200
  post hoc tests, 162–165
open-ended question(s)
  clarity of, 127
  quality of, 127
operational definition, 5
operationalization, 4f, 5
  definition of, 200
ordinal data, 12–13
  definition of, 200
ordinal level of measurement. See ordinal data
ordinal variable. See ordinal data
ordinate, 35
outcome variable(s), 9. See also dependent
    variable(s)
outlier(s), 28–29, 38
  definition of, 28, 200

pairwise multiple comparisons, 162–164
parameter(s)
  definition of, 48, 200
  population, 48, 90
parametric statistics, 157
partition, 119, 119f
pattern(s), in qualitative data analysis, 130–131
Pearson chi-square, 63. See also chi-square
    (statistic)

Pearson correlation coefficient (Pearson r),
    73–74, 105, 109
  calculation of, 78–84
  computation using Statistical Package for
    Social Sciences (SPSS), 151, 151t
  critical values of, 79, 81t
  definition of, 73–74, 200
  direction of, 74–75
  formula for, 78, 78t
  negative, 74–76, 75f, 76f
  positive, 74–76, 74f, 75f
Pearson r. See Pearson correlation coefficient
    (Pearson r)
people, in field notes, 128
percentage. See also cumulative percentage;
    valid percentage
  calculation, formula for, 18, 19t
percentile calculation, 18
perspective, in qualitative research, 129
pie chart(s), 20–21, 21f
pie graph(s), 20–21, 21f
population (N), 47–48
  definition of, 47, 201
population distribution, 48
population mean, 90. See also μ
population parameter(s), 48, 90
positive correlation, 74–76, 74f, 75f, 78
  definition of, 201
positively skewed (distribution), 36, 36f, 50
  definition of, 36, 201
post hoc tests, 162–165
precoded, definition of, 8
predicted regression coefficient, 108–111
prediction, in health and human services, 107
Predictive Analytics Software (PASW).
    See Statistical Package for Social
    Sciences (SPSS)
predictor variable, 74, 105. See also independent
    variable
probability, 37, 55. See also alpha (α coefficient);
    p value
  definition of, 48, 201
probability sample, 48
problem identification, 4f, 5
  definition of, 201
process
  definition of, 201
  · in qualitative data analysis, 130–131
product-moment correlation, 74. See also
    Pearson correlation coefficient (Pearson r)
p value, 55
  for chi-square produced by SPSS, 56, 56t,
    152, 153t

for correlation produced by SPSS, 56, 57*t*,
    151, 151*t*
definition of, 200
and Kruskal-Wallis *H* test, 158

QDA Miner lite, 133
QDAP, 133
qualitative data, 11, 125
    collection procedures for, 126–127
    definition of, 201
qualitative data analysis, 129–134
    computer applications, 133–134
    online resources, 133–134
Qualitative Data Analysis (free reference
    resources), 134
qualitative research
    data collection procedures for, 126–127
    definition of, 125
    five categories for observation and recording
        in, 128–129
    and quantitative research, 125–126
quantitative data, 11. *See also* variable(s)
    definition of, 201
    preparation of, for analysis, 145–148
quartile, definition of, 27

r. See Pearson correlation coefficient (Pearson *r*)
R^2, 111
    adjusted, 111
r^2. *See* coefficient of determination (r^2)
R (correlation coefficient), 111
R (marginal rows total). *See* marginal rows
    total *(R)*
random assignment, 89, 108
random sampling, 107–108
range, definition of, 29
range tests, 162–163
rank order, 13
    definition of, 157
    logic of, 157–158
ratio data, 14. *See also* correlation
    definition of, 201
    and histograms, 21, 22*f*
    and linear regression, 108
    and *t* tests, 88
ratio level of measurement. *See* ratio data
ratio variable. *See* ratio data
recoding. *See* data recoding
regression, 105
    bivariate, 105
    definition of, 106
    multivariate, 105
    predictive functions of, 105

regression analysis, 105–106
regression coefficient, 108–109, 111
    Excel results, 184–185, 185*t*
    standardized (beta, β), 112, 155*t*
    unstandardized *(B or b)*, 111–112, 155*t*
regression models, 111
R-E-G-W *F*, 163
R-E-G-W *Q*, 163
rejection level, 55
rejection region, 39
    definition of, 201
reliability, 16, 127
    and qualitative data, 127–128
research
    methods, and statistics, 3–4
    qualitative, 11
    quantitative, 11
research cycle, 4–5, 4*f*
research findings, 129
research hypothesis (H_a), 51–52
    definition of, 199
rival hypotheses, 60
row total, 64
Ryan-Einot-Gabriel-Welsch *F* test. *See*
    R-E-G-W *F*
Ryan-Einot-Gabriel-Welsch range test. *See*
    R-E-G-W *Q*

sample *(n)*
    definition of, 48, 201
    size of, 50
sample mean. *See* mean; X-bar
sampling, method of, 50
sampling design, 50
sampling distribution of the mean, 49–50
    definition of, 201
sampling error, 50, 60
scale
    definition of, 199
    in Statistical Package for Social Sciences
        (SPSS), 139
scatterplot, 74
Scheffé test, 163
SD. *See* standard deviation (SD)
SD_E. *See* standard error of the mean
secondary hypothesis (H_2), 52. *See also* null
    hypothesis (H_0)
semiotics, 132–133, 133*t*, 197
    definition of, 201
sensitive information, 16
setting, in field notes, 128
Sidak test, 163
Sig., 56, 56*t*, 57*t*

Σ, 8
Sign test, 160
simple analysis of variance. *See* analysis of
    variance
simple linear regression, 105
    definition of, 105–106
simple random sample, 48
simple statistic. *See* mean
slope of the line, 107
    definition of, 197
slope of the regression line, 108–110
S-N-K, 163
*Social Work Research and
    Evaluation: Quantitative and Qualitative
    Approaches* (Grinnell), 134
SPSS. *See* Statistical Package for Social
    Sciences (SPSS)
spurious association, 77
SS^2, 30–31. *See also* variance
    definition of, 201
$SS_{between}$. *See* sums of squares (variances)
    between groups ($SS_{between}$)
SS_{within}. *See* sums of squares (variances) within
    groups (SS_{within})
standard deviation (SD), 26, 31–32, 85
    definition of, 201
    formula for, 32
    and normal curve, 38, 38f
    and sample mean, distance between, 38–39, 39t
standard error of the mean, 49–50
    definition of, 201
standard normal curve, producing, 41
standard score, 39–40. *See also* z score
    producing, 41
statistical analysis, 4f, 5
    definition of, 201
Statistical Package for Social Sciences (SPSS),
    17, 28, 53
    Align, 141
    alphanumeric variables in, 139
    Analyze ribbon, 144
    blank screen, 136, 137f
    Cancel, 136
    Columns, 141
    comma variables in, 138
    constructing variable values for, 139–142
    creating variable names in, 136–139
    custom currency variables in, 138
    Data (file saved as), 144
    data entry using, 136–144
    data file (system file) creation, 136
    data recode process, 138, 145–148, 146f,
        147f, 148t

Data View, 136, 142, 143f, 169
    date variables in, 138
    Decimal column, 139–141
    Descriptive Statistics, 144
    descriptive statistics computations, 148–150,
        149f, 150f, 150t
    dollar variables in, 138
    dot variables in, 138
    and Excel, differences between, in data
        entry, 169
    frequency distributions using, 144–145
    importing data to, 138
    inferential statistics computations, 150–155
    introduction to, 136
    Label column, 139–141
    Measure column, 139–141
    Missing, 139, 141
    Name, 138
    numeric variables in, 138
    one-sample *t* test computation, 154–155, 156f
    one-way ANOVA post hoc tests, 162–165,
        164f, 165f
    Output (file saved as), 144
    and Pearson *r*, 79
    procedures for nonparametric statistics,
        159–162
    p value produced from, 56, 56t, 57t, 151, 151t,
        152, 153t
    restricted numeric variables in, 139
    saving files, 144
    Scale, 141
    scientific notation in, 138
    Script (file saved as), 144
    Statistics, 144
    string variables in, 139
    symbols in, 138
    Syntax (file saved as), 144
    t test and *F* ratio outputs, 115–116
    Type, 138
    use of *R*, 111
    Values column, 139–141, 141f, 142f
    Variable View, 136–138, 137f, 142, 142f, 169
    Width column, 139, 141
statistical significance, 112. *See also p* value
    definition of, 201
statistical tests, 2–3
    results of, interpreting, 56–57, 56t, 57t
statistics
    descriptive. *See* descriptive statistics
    in evidence-based practice, 3
    inferential. *See* inferential statistics
    research methods and, 3–4
    types of, 2

statistics rules, for conversion of z score to percentile, 40, 40f, 41–43
Steps in Qualitative Data Analysis (free reference resource), 134
structure(s), in qualitative data analysis, 130
Student-Newman-Keuls. *See* S-N-K
summation, 8
sum of squares, 92, 118. *See also* SS^2; variance
and correlation, 85
sum of squares total (SS_{total}), 118–119, 119f, 123t
computational formula for, 119, 120f
sum of the squared deviations of the scores set and its sample mean, 118
sums of squares (variances) between groups ($SS_{between}$), 118–119, 119f, 123t
computational formula for, 119, 120f
sums of squares (variances) within groups (SS_{within}), 118–119, 119f, 123t
computational formula for, 119, 120f
Survey Monkey, 16

Tamhane's T2 test, 164
test of association. *See* chi-square
test of independence. *See* chi-square
tests of mean difference, 50–51
text(s), 126–127
trimmed mean, 27
computation of, 27
definition of, 201
t statistic. *See also* t test(s)
critical value of, 92, 93t–94t
t test(s), 87
calculation of, 88
computational formulas for, 88
definition of, 202
dependent samples, 89, 97–99, 101
Excel tools for, 186
and F ratio, 115–116
independent samples, 89, 92–97, 101
meaning of, 88
one-sample, 89–90, 91–92, 101, 154–155, 156f
statistical assumptions about, 89
types of, 89
Tukey's b, 163
Tukey test, 163
two-sided hypothesis. *See* nondirectional (two-tailed) hypothesis
two-tailed hypothesis. *See* nondirectional (two-tailed) hypothesis
type I error, 59, 60t, 116
definition of, 202
type II error, 59, 60t
definition of, 202

typographical errors, checking for, 145

unknown frequency(ies). *See* expected frequency(ies)

validity, 16, 127
and qualitative data, 127–128
valid percentage, calculation, formula for, 18, 19t
value(s)
definition of, 8, 202
numerical vs. nonnumerical, 8–9, 9t
of variable, 8
value category, 8
definition of, 202
variability, 25. *See also* dispersion
definition of, 29, 202
Excel measures, 181, 182f, 183f
variability between group means, 117
definition of, 117, 202
variability within group means, 117
definition of, 117, 202
variable(s), 7–10
continuous. *See* continuous variable(s)
definition of, 7–8, 202
dependent. *See* dependent variable(s)
discrete. *See* discrete variable(s)
independent. *See* independent variable(s)
of interest, 9
interval. *See* interval data
level of measurement of, 50
numeric, 11
ordinal. *See* ordinal data
ratio. *See* ratio data
types of, 9
variable classification, 9. *See also* continuous variable(s); discrete variable(s)
definition of, 202
variance, 30–31, 32t, 119
and correlation, 85
definition of, 202
Excel formula for, 173, 173f
formula for, 31
homogeneity of, 89
selection using Statistical Package for Social Sciences (SPSS), 149, 150f
variation, measures of, 29–33

Waller-Duncan test, 163
Wilcoxon rank sum test, 158, 158t. *See also* Mann-Whitney U test
Wilcoxon (signed-rank) test, 158, 158t, 160–162, 161f, 162t

x. *See* mean
x axis, 35
X-bar, 90

Y′. *See* predicted regression coefficient
y axis, 35
y intercept, 108
    definition of, 197

zero correlation. *See* no (zero) correlation
z score, 39–41. *See also* normal distribution
    calculation of, 40–41, 40f
    constructing confidence interval using, 57–58
    conversion of proportion into, 57–58
    conversion to percentile rank, 40–43, 40f
    definition of, 39, 202
    and effect size, 100
    uses of, 43–44